NOT MY KID

Not My Kid

What Parents Believe about
the Sex Lives of Their Teenagers

Sinikka Elliott

NEW YORK UNIVERSITY PRESS
New York and London

NEW YORK UNIVERSITY PRESS
New York and London
www.nyupress.org

Library of Congress Cataloging-in-Publication Data
Elliott, Sinikka.
Not my kid : what parents believe about the sex lives of their teenagers / Sinikka Elliott.
p. cm.
Includes bibliographical references and index.
ISBN 978-0-8147-2258-9 (cl : alk. paper)
ISBN 978-0-8147-2259-6 (pb : alk. paper)
ISBN 978-0-8147-7169-3 (ebook)
ISBN 978-0-8147-7134-1 (ebook)
1. Teenagers—Sexual ethics. 2. Teenagers—Sexual behavior. 3. Parent and child. 4. Parenting.
5. Sex instruction for teenagers. I. Title.
HQ35.E45   2012
306.70835—dc23   2012008070

References to Internet Websites (URLs) were accurate at the time of writing.
Neither the author nor New York University Press is responsible for URLs that
may have expired or changed since the manuscript was prepared.

New York University Press books are printed on acid-free paper,
and their binding materials are chosen for strength and durability.
We strive to use environmentally responsible suppliers and materials
to the greatest extent possible in publishing our books.

Manufactured in the United States of America
c 10 9 8 7 6 5 4 3 2 1
p 10 9 8 7 6 5 4 3 2 1

CONTENTS

Acknowledgments   *vii*

Introduction   *1*

1. Sex Panics: Debates over Sex Education
   and the Construction of Teen Sexuality   9

2. The Asexual Teen: Naïveté, Dependence, and Sexual Danger   20

3. Negotiating the Erotic: When Parents and Teens Talk about Sex   47

4. The Hypersexual Teen: Sexy Bodies, Raging Hormones,
   and Irresponsibility   63

5. Other Teens: How Race, Class, and Gender Matter   83

6. Anxious Monitoring: Strategies of Protection and Surveillance   99

7. Uncertainty in Parents' Sexual Lessons   118

8. Conclusion: Reconstructing Teen Sexuality   144

Methods Appendix   *157*

Notes   *165*

References   *183*

Index   *203*

About the Author   *216*

ACKNOWLEDGMENTS

I am profoundly grateful to the parents in this book who shared their rich stories with me; many also opened their homes to me, introduced me to their children, and encouraged me to write about their lives. I am also indebted to the public school sex educators who allowed me into their classrooms to observe their lessons and helped me reach out to their students' parents. In addition to the parents and sex educators whose generous gifts of time and insight helped make this book possible, I thank my mentor and adviser, Christine Williams, who taught me how to ask questions, infused me with an abiding curiosity, and challenged me every step of the way to be better. I owe a great debt to Debra Umberson as well for being a wonderful mentor and collaborator. An academic book is never the product of a single individual or even a handful of individuals, and I am thankful for all those whose thinking, research, and writing have helped shape my own. I have been fortunate to learn from and work with Gloria Gonzalez-Lopez, Sharmila Rudrappa, Douglas Foley, Michael Schwalbe, Catherine Connell, Corinne Reczek, Gretchen Webber, Julie Reid, Elyshia Aseltine, and many others. I am also grateful for the anonymous reviewers, who provided generous and helpful feedback on the book when it was in manuscript form, and for my editor at New York University Press, Ilene Kalish, whose unwavering enthusiasm and great direction made the book a reality. My colleagues at North Carolina State University created a supportive environment that helped nurture this project through its completion. Some material in the book appeared previously in *Symbolic Interaction* 33, no. 2 (spring 2010): 191–212; *Sex Education: Sexuality, Society, and Learning* 10, no. 3 (summer 2010): 239–250; and *Sexuality Research and Social Policy* 7, no. 4 (December 2010): 310–322. I thank these journals for allowing me to use that material here. And finally, I am deeply thankful to my family and friends for all their love and support.

When Rose described her 14-year-old son, who is just going through the physical changes of puberty, her face lit up. He is "very intelligent," "very responsible," and "loves outdoor activities." She thinks her son revels in the pubertal
changes: he proudly shows off his armpit hair and is anxiously awaiting his
"happy trail" (a slender path of pubic hair running from the belly button to the
pubic area), uses his deeper voice to be heard over his younger siblings, and,
when he began to shave a year ago, displayed his shaving kit like "a status sym-
bol." But Rose is also worried. Two years ago she and her husband sat their son
down for "the talk": "We told him the basics of what happens. You know, what
sex is." Since then, they have taken him aside regularly to talk about sex and
dating: "He got to the point where he was like, 'Uh oh, oh no!' and he would
like get scared every time we said we need to talk." Rose has persisted, however,
because "I want to make sure he knows all the risks that are out there."

Rose does not think her son is interested in sex yet, but she is concerned
that girls might make advances toward him. The first time she and her
husband talked with him about sex, "We just sat him down and said, 'You

need to watch out for girls.'" As far as Rose is concerned, "girls are more aggressive than boys . . . both in pursuing the boy and in having sex." She has heard that some middle school girls now wear different colored hair bands as bracelets; each color represents what a girl will do sexually: kiss, let a boy feel her up, have oral sex, and so on. Rose also relayed experiences that have solidified her belief that girls really are more forward than boys. A few months ago Rose's husband stumbled upon a topless picture of one of her son's female classmates in the son's e-mail inbox. Rose immediately "forwarded the picture to her mom, so her mom would know what her daughter was up to" and talked extensively with her son about the type of girl who would send such a picture: "I told him she was probably trying to get him to be her boyfriend, but boys really lose respect for girls who act like that. Boys don't respect girls who are showy."

Rose has many concerns about teenagers having sex. She worries about sexually transmitted infections and teen pregnancy, and she thinks young people are too cavalier in their approach to sex. Popular teen movies and TV shows contribute to this attitude, she said, by portraying teen sex "as if it's perfectly normal. It's like brushing your teeth. It *shouldn't* be that way. They just *should not* be that intense at that age." For Rose, teenagers are not yet mature enough to understand the significance of sex. In describing her 16-year-old niece and her niece's boyfriend, she passionately declared: "They're just *babies*. They're just too young, too immature. It would be a huge mistake for them [to have sex]. I've told my niece that, too." Rose hopes to instill these beliefs in her son as well, so that, if the opportunity arises, he will think twice before having sex. She tells her son that sex is "something special between a husband and a wife—that's how you have children" and prefers that he remain a virgin until his wedding day.

Yet, even though Rose is committed to the idea that sex is restricted to marriage, she doubts that her son will wait until he's married: "I know, in reality, that's probably not going to be the case. But I hope it won't be until he's in his twenties." Although Rose expressed strong opinions on a number of topics, on this issue she is torn between what she ideally prefers and what she thinks is realistic. She worries that if she argues too forcefully that sex should only happen within marriage, her son will feel guilt ridden if he ever does have sex outside marriage: "I don't want him to have, like, a big guilty complex about it. But I don't want him to have sex when he's 14 either." Thus, in talking with her son, she emphasizes his youth and vulnerability in a highly sexualized culture surrounded by sexually driven girls. She hopes this will sufficiently scare him into waiting without producing too much guilt if and when he does have sex.

Countless other parents echo Rose's fears for her son, the scrutiny she and her husband employ in their efforts to keep him safe, her lessons about sexuality, and her conflicted feelings about these lessons. Whether rich or poor; black, white, or Latino/a; liberal or conservative—virtually all parents seem flummoxed when dealing with their teens' sexuality. Although Rose is a 43-year-old affluent white woman who is a stay-at-home mother of three boys, her feelings of concern and uncertainty resonate with those of Corina, a 39-year-old working-class black mother of three daughters. Corina so desperately wants her daughters to abstain from sex until marriage that she has had them sign a contract promising to do so, but at the same time she has taken them to Planned Parenthood and has spoken with them about contraception.[1]

Like Corina and Rose, the parents in this book expressed both liberal and conservative sentiments, often seamlessly blending polar opposite beliefs. Ideally they want their teens to abstain from sex until marriage, but they do not want them to marry too young. Many expect their children to wait to have sex until they are adults but talk to them about contraception "just in case." Some want their children to be well informed about sex but worry that too much knowledge robs sex of its mystery. And almost all insist that their children are not sexual. Other teenagers may be sexual, even hypersexual, engaging in risky and promiscuous sexual behavior, but their own children, regardless of their age or actual behavior, are "not that kind of kid."

Not My Kid tries to understand this disconnect. In the pages that follow I situate the parents' narratives in the context of intense conflicts over sexuality, the framing of teen sexual activity in terms of danger and risk, and an ever widening income gap between American households. I argue that, within this context, constructing their own children as asexual allows parents to cope with their anxieties about sexuality, parenting, and their teenagers' (and their own) present and future opportunities in life. In particular, given the "danger discourse" surrounding teen sexuality—the widespread belief that teen sexual activity has dire physical, psychological, and financial consequences—parents have a great incentive to desexualize their teenagers. I will show, however, that the process of desexualization is accomplished largely through the "othering" of their children's peers. Parents frequently explained that their concerns about their children's sexual safety and well-being are prompted by the dangers posed by their children's more sexual peers. These concerns are influenced by sexual stereotypes associated with race, class, and gender. Thus, although complex dynamics shape how parents talk to their children about sexuality, I argue that these conversations often sustain and legitimate sexual hierarchies and inequalities.

The focus of this book is on how parents interpret and attempt to guide teen sexuality amid intense local and nationwide conflicts over sexuality, including sex education, gay rights, and censorship. Throughout the book I ask parents how they understand the sexual changes of adolescence and how they deal with the sexuality of their teenage children. The broad strands running through the parents' narratives, as presented in the following pages, reflect the dominant understandings of teen sexuality in today's world. But their narratives are also more complicated. When these parents spoke about teen sexuality, they did not simply refer to some nebulous "adolescent"; they were thinking about how their own children conduct their lives and about their own hopes and dreams for their teenagers' futures. As such, their stories are important counterpoints to the abstract, ideologically driven debates over teen sexuality.

Foundation of the Book

As debates over sex education continue throughout America and government policy has scaled back sex education in public schools and given parents greater governance of their children's sexual lives, parents are pressured to properly guide their children through the difficult and often controversial issues of sexuality. Based on interviews with nearly fifty parents of teenagers, *Not My Kid* provides a window into this demanding process. It explores the narratives and strategies of a diverse group of parents of teenagers in order to better understand how parents view teen sexuality and how these views connect to dominant discourses and social inequalities and influence parents' strategies for controlling teen sexuality.

The parents interviewed in this book were mostly recruited through their children's health classes at four public schools—three high schools and one middle school. They live in a liberal city in a conservative state, hold diverse religious and political beliefs, and are from varied socioeconomic backgrounds. About one-fifth are upper-middle class, half are lower-middle class, and almost one-third are working class or poor. One-third identify as Latino/a, one-eighth as black, and the remainder identify as white. Most parents indicated a religious affiliation, with more than half identifying as either Catholic or Christian. All the parents have at least one teenage child, and many have more than one. They are mostly mothers, no doubt reflecting that mothers are more likely than fathers to talk to their children about sexuality.[2] Thus, although I use the term "parents" throughout the book, it should be emphasized that my data came primarily from mothers and that mothers are doing the bulk of the work of talking to children about sex.[3] The voluntary nature of the interviewing process enabled me to select parents who had reflected upon and in many cases talked with their children about issues related to sexuality. These parents were able to guide me through the problems related to adolescence, sex education, and family life, as well as sexuality. I am profoundly grateful for their openness and try to honor it by paying close attention to the intricacies of their experiences.

The goal of this book is not to generalize about all parents: readers may or may not recognize their own and others' beliefs, actions, and experiences on the following pages. My aim is, instead, to demonstrate the complex processes by which this particular group of parents understood the sexuality of their own teen children as well as teenagers in general—and to situate these understandings amid individual, family, local, state, and national contexts.[4] The parents I interviewed live in what has been dubbed a "red" state, one that has historically voted Republican and where residents tend to hold conservative family and sexual values, such as abstinence from sex until marriage and the belief that abortion should be illegal; in contrast, "blue," or Democratic, states lean toward more liberal views.[5] These differences between states, however, mask profound diversity within a state, reflected in family values and patterns shaped by religion, immigration, income, education, urbanization, and life experiences. Undoubtedly the perceptions of the parents in the study are influenced by their residence in a "red" state (albeit, in a very liberal part of that state), but myriad other factors have shaped their worldviews. In the book I try to tease out these complex dynamics.

In addition to interviewing parents, I attended forums where sex education was discussed or debated, observed school-based sex education classes, followed various sex education debates in local and national media, and was broadly attuned to media reports pertaining to adolescence and sexuality. Between 2006 and 2007 I also attended Parent-Teacher Association (PTA) meetings and a parent-information night at one of the schools where I recruited parents for interviews. Although I draw only sparingly on this fieldwork in the following chapters, the views I recorded helped me understand the dominant and institutional discourses around adolescence and teen sexuality. By connecting parental interviews to a larger cultural and sociopolitical context, I was able to avoid an overly individualistic analysis. A more detailed account of the study sample and methodology is provided in the appendix.

Organization of the Book

In talking with their teenagers about sexuality, parents negotiate a fraught, often contradictory, terrain. Chapter 1 situates this terrain within local and national debates over sex education and provides the historical background necessary to make sense of America's complex relationship to sexuality. Chapter 2 traces how a pervasive culture of sexual fear (especially around teen sexuality), coupled with teenagers' financial dependence, make it difficult for parents to view their children as sexual beings. By this I mean that parents did not think of their teenage children as sexually agentic, desiring subjects. Instead they described their teen children as immature, naïve, and sexually vulnerable. In chapter 3 I explore the tone, dynamics, and content of parent-teen conversations about sexuality; namely, family talk about what sexual activity means and what it encompasses, including pleasure, shame, and risk. Whereas previous research implies that parents either teach their children about sexuality or neglect to provide their children with sexual information, the parents I interviewed perceive that their children are active participants in these conversations, including actively resisting them. Teenage resistance to family sex talks in turn reinforces parents' perceptions of their teen children as asexual.

The next few chapters delve deeper into parents' understandings of, and strategies of control over, their children's sexuality. These chapters show how social inequality shapes, and is reproduced through, parents' lessons to their children about sexuality. In chapter 4 I show that parents resist the discourse of the sexually driven and hypersexual teen when it comes to their own teenage children, but they perceive most other teenagers as sex-crazed to a greater or lesser degree. In the course of constructing their children's peers as hypersexual Others, parents rely on and reproduce race, class, and gender stereotypes and inequalities, as discussed in chapter 5. Reflecting parents' sense that their children are surrounded by highly sexualized teenagers and that teen sexual activity is inherently risky, parents fear a host of sexual perils confronting their teenagers. To keep their children safe, they engage in strategies of protection and surveillance, yet, as chapter 6 reveals, have different resources with which to do so.

Chapter 7 looks at parents' uncertainty around their lessons to their teen children about sexuality. Much of the research on teen sexuality suggests that Americans hold strong and polarized views on this issue. The parents in this book, in contrast, expressed deep conflict and ambiguity about how best to guide their children's sexuality. Parents are especially unsure about promoting abstinence: many want their teen children to abstain from sex until adulthood or, ideally, marriage, yet simultaneously wonder whether this is probable. This chapter also shows how parental conflict and ambivalence is magnified by gender and sexual inequalities. I explore the story of one mother, in particular, who wants her teenage daughters to feel empowered sexually but worries about how they will achieve this in a society that sexually objectifies girls and women while debasing those who seek sexual pleasure.

In the concluding chapter I consider the social and cultural conditions that might make it easier for parents to recognize their children as sexual subjects and to talk with their teens about sexuality. As I emphasize throughout the book, the difficulties that parents encounter in this regard are not matters of any individual parent's faulty understanding. In fact, as chapter 2 describes, a couple of parents I interviewed who tried to be open and frank with their children about human sexual anatomy and reproduction found themselves under investigation by Child Protective Services. Thus although I critically analyze parents' strategies of control over their children's sexuality in the book, I also emphasize that these strategies are tied to how U.S. society currently frames and deals with childhood and teen sexuality and the social inequalities underlying these framings. American parents today have few avenues to think about their children's sexuality that do not involve risk, compulsion, vulnerability, and unhappiness. Instead of suggesting how to "fix" parents then, I propose that public policy designed to address the culture of sexual fear and dominant constructions of adolescence—as well as policies that tackle social inequality in the United States—will help create an environment in which parents are better able to embrace and acknowledge their children as sexual subjects.

1

Sex Panics

Debates over Sex Education
and the Construction of Teen Sexuality

In the summer and fall of 2004, like many states around the nation, Texas was mired in a debate over sex education. One side thought that youth should learn about contraception in public schools (typically called comprehensive sex education), whereas the opposite side felt that schools should teach youth to abstain from sex until marriage and should not provide contraceptive information (known as abstinence-only sex education). I attended three public State Board of Education meetings where this debate unfolded, allowing Texans to voice their opinions about sex education. Curious to learn how teen sexuality would be discussed in this public venue, I found that, in keeping with dominant discourses around teen sexuality in the United States, speakers on both sides justified their stance by invoking images of diseased, pregnant, vulnerable, at-risk teenagers. Similarly proposed textbooks, regardless of their discussions of contraceptives, warned of the grave social, physical, and psychological consequences of teen sexual activity, and, indeed, all sex outside marriage.

I also attended the meetings as a parent of two children (at the time my son was 11 and my daughter was 8). Listening to speaker after speaker, I grew increasingly aware of the extent to which "parents" were being mobilized on one side of the debate or the other. Many who spoke before the board introduced themselves and justified their standpoint "as a parent" or, in some cases, "as a grandparent." I also frequently heard the phrases "no parent would want" and "any parent can see." Most speakers assumed that parents have strong convictions about sex education, differing only in whether they endorse an abstinence-only or comprehensive curriculum. Speakers also generally implied that parents want greater control over what, when, how, and, for some, whether their children learn about sex in school. These assumptions about parents and teen sexuality have governed policy decisions over the past three decades. The "Chastity Act" passed early in Reagan's administration, for example, identified parents as the rightful dispatchers of sex education. In a speech, President Reagan expressed the prevailing view: "The rights of parents and the rights of family take precedence over those of Washington-based bureaucrats and social engineers."[1] In line with Reagan's vision, shifts in sex education over the past few decades have increasingly designated parents as the "guardians of their children's sexual lives."[2]

Yet, the portrait of parents that was painted in the Texas debate—as polarized and firmly convinced of the rightness of *their* view—did not fit easily with my own sense as a parent. Nor did it match positions I had heard parents express privately. It was not clear to me, then, what parents really thought, and I left these Texas meetings full of questions: What do parents who are not involved in the battle over sex education say to their kids about sex and sexuality? I also wanted to understand *why* parents say what they say and how they feel about talking (or not) to their children about sex. What do parents think about teenage sexuality, their own children's as well as their children's peers'? In particular, I wondered how parents were making sense of teen sexuality at a time when sex education was regularly in the spotlight, offering divergent views on how best to teach teens about sex but portraying teen sexuality generally as a menace to teenagers and society. *Not My Kid* takes up these questions.

Shifting Understandings of Sex Education and Teen Sexuality

To understand why Texans were debating sex education in the first place, it is worth looking back at the events leading up to 2004. Teenage sexual activity in the United States is frequently framed as a social problem, leading to unintended pregnancies and teen motherhood, disease, heartache, low self-esteem, lower socioeconomic status, and even death. Yet social policy about how best to deal with teen sexuality has been radically reframed over the past few decades.

In the 1970s, fears of an "epidemic" of teen pregnancies, especially among African Americans, and the belief that teenage motherhood contributes to rising poverty in America, led to increased support for comprehensive sex education programs that instruct students in contraceptives' proper uses.[3] Owing largely to the decentralization of education at the time, sex education was not implemented nationally or uniformly in public schools, but the programs that did exist in the 1970s and early 1980s were largely comprehensive in nature.[4] They were also widely considered as successful in view of declining teen pregnancy rates. Studies found that even though teenagers were more likely to have sex in the 1970s and 1980s compared to the 1960s, the overall birthrate among teens decreased over the course of the 1970s.[5] Youthful sexual intercourse was, if not endorsed, at least grudgingly accepted as inevitable by government, sex educators, and other professionals. The 1970s also saw changes in policies and practices around abortion with the Supreme Court's ruling in 1973 establishing abortion as a constitutional right.

A shift occurred in the early 1980s. In 1981, President Reagan signed the Adolescent Family Life Act (AFLA), Title XX of the Public Health Service Act, also known as the "Chastity Act," which denied federal funds to most programs or projects that provided abortions or abortion counseling. In addition, the AFLA mandated abstinence education and, in the sex education programs it funded, stipulated the inclusion of units promoting "self-discipline and responsibility in human sexuality."[6] The passage of the AFLA represented a concerted "attempt to shift the discourse on the prevention of teenage pregnancy away from contraception and instead to 'chastity' or 'morality.'"[7] As such, it had a profound effect on sex education, shifting the debates away from the question of *whether* sex education should be offered in public schools to the issue of *which* sex education curriculum should be taught. Conservative groups designed new sex education curricula "to convey an unambiguous condemnation of sexual activity outside of marriage."[8] These programs became broadly known as abstinence-only sex education. By the early 1990s, amid mounting concerns about HIV/AIDS, a growing number of schools had implemented this type of sex education.

In 1996 under the auspices of the Personal Responsibility and Work Reconciliation Act (also known as welfare reform), President Bill Clinton signed into law a new entitlement program for abstinence-only education. The new law defined abstinence education as any sex education program that teaches, among other things, "that a mutually faithful monogamous relationship in the context of marriage is the expected standard of human sexual activity, . . . that sexual activity outside the context of marriage is likely to have harmful psychological and physical effects, and . . . the importance of attaining self-sufficiency before engaging in sexual activity."[9] Hence this legislation discursively bound sexual activity to marriage, personal responsibility, and financial self-sufficiency, thus overwhelmingly stressing the antisocial repercussions of nonmarital (i.e., teen) sexuality. This law, part of sweeping welfare reforms imposing stringent work requirements and time limits for welfare recipients,[10] coincided with increasing economic deindustrialization, a rapid rise in (low-paying) service-sector jobs, and an ever widening gap between the rich and the poor. In this context, such legislation bolstered the notion that Americans must be responsible for their own well-being, and that sexual behavior can either help secure a promising future (e.g., through abstinence) or hinder future prospects (e.g., through nonmarital/teen sexual intercourse).

This legislation also helped support and build a thriving abstinence-only sex education industry. With renewed funding under the Bush administration, and expansion under a new federal program established in 2001— Community Based Abstinence Education—abstinence-only sex education programs grew in popularity. In 1988, only 2 percent of public school teachers taught abstinence as the only way to prevent pregnancy and sexually transmitted diseases. By 2003, 30 percent of the nation's instructors reported teaching abstinence only, providing no information about condoms or other contraceptives other than their failure rates.[11] Midway through the first decade of the twenty-first century, an increasing number of American youth were receiving instruction in school on how to "just say no" to sex without learning what to do if they decide to say yes.[12]

These shifts in sex education did not occur without controversy. The debate in Texas I observed was not an isolated event, as similar debates have occurred in communities across the nation in recent years. Although national polls indicate that most Americans support sex education, and despite the fact that expressions of sexuality in popular culture have become far more open and explicit since the 1960s, battles over sex education have increased in intensity over the past four decades—a period marked by "sex panics," explosive political and local clashes over issues of sexuality such as gay rights, censorship, and sex education.[13] Despite the controversy and despite a recent backlash against abstinence-only sex education,[14] by the mid-2000s, when I started interviewing parents, abstinence-only sex education was beginning "to assert a kind of natural cultural authority, in schools and out."[15] In other words, abstinence-only-until-marriage had emerged as the dominant discourse around teen sexuality, promoted as the only surefire way to prevent disease, pregnancy, and the heartache and financial ruin regularly associated with nonmarital sexual intercourse. How does this discourse shape parents' understandings of teen sexuality?

Parents and the Discourses of Teen Sexuality

Sexuality is commonly thought of as a purely biological drive,[16] but, as the cultural historian Michel Foucault reminds us, sexual mores and expressions change over time and are closely linked to power relations, values, and culture. In this sense, sexuality is not so much about what people *do* as it is about the beliefs we associate with sexual beings—the discourses around sexuality. By discourses I mean powerful, taken-for-granted assumptions that shape how people think, talk, and act. For example, the discourse of teen sexuality as risky and hormonally fueled shapes how adults respond to teen sexual activity and teach youth about sexuality.

Discourses are neither accidental nor neutral but reflect dominant interests. "Experts" and moral entrepreneurs in scientific, medical, political, and religious communities play prominent roles in crafting and promulgating popular discourses of sexuality.[17] Although unquestioned assumptions about sexuality may be internalized and become powerful motivators directing action, as entrenched as any other personal truths, individuals may also resist or adapt dominant discourses in their everyday lives and practices.

Discourses are not monolithic or omnipotent: competing discourses often vie for prominence, contest and contradict one another.[18] The dominant discourse of sexuality in recent U.S. history has been a negative one, picturing sexuality as a potentially dangerous and immoral pursuit, particularly for the young, the unmarried, and those marked as Other.[19] Parallel to this discourse, however, is the belief that sexuality is central to individual identity and personal fulfillment. Stemming in large part from a complex blend of free-market economics and restrictive sexual morality, U.S. society is characterized by a "paradoxical mix of sexual obsessions and sexual shames."[20] In what follows, I briefly establish the historical context necessary to understand these and other discourses of sexuality and to locate, in time and space, the narratives of the parents interviewed within these pages. Seeing what has come before can also help us imagine new ways of thinking about teen sexuality. We turn to that issue in the concluding chapter.

Sexuality and Sexual Regulation: A Brief History

American sexual practices over the past 300 years have been closely linked to larger social processes, such as America's urbanization and industrialization, and to social inequalities based on gender, race, and social class. During this time, moreover, our ideas about and efforts to control sexuality have changed considerably. For example, whereas many assume that sexuality in the United States was highly regulated during the colonial period, and that sexual freedoms gradually evolved, historical evidence suggests otherwise. A comprehensive investigation into the history of sexuality in America from the 1600s to the contemporary era, by historians John D'Emilio and Estelle Freedman, argues that sexual activity among the young and unmarried during colonial times was widespread and generally accepted, as long as it was covert and preceded marriage. In examining marriage certificates and birth records, D'Emilio and Freedman discovered that children were often born only a few months after a wedding, indicating that premarital sexual intercourse was relatively commonplace among the early colonists.[21]

Despite efforts on behalf of churches, families, local communities, and, increasingly, the judicial system to prevent premarital sex, premarital pregnancy rates increased in the late 1600s and throughout the 1700s, as young couples increasingly used a pregnancy to gain their families' permission to marry.[22] Premarital pregnancies plummeted in the first few decades of the Victorian era, however—a period generally attributed by scholars to a distinct shift in American sexual culture and regulation.[23] During the Victorian era, from 1830 to 1890, talk about sex increased dramatically. As sociologist Steven Seidman observes, "Victorians made sex into a topic of urgent public and personal concern."[24] Through the proliferation of discourses about sexuality, the regulation of sexuality shifted inward to complex forms of self-regulation and self-surveillance.[25] Consider women's sexuality. In the Victorian period, women—particularly middle-class, white women—were increasingly described as asexual, pure, and passionless beings, at least outside marriage.[26] As this discourse mushroomed outside "expert" circles to everyday people, women felt encouraged to police and restrict their own sexuality.

The 1800s heralded new ideas not simply of female sexuality but also of children and childhood sexuality. As the United States grew increasingly urbanized in the late 1800s, young people were gradually removed from their role in the labor force and were conceptualized as innocent and vulnerable. The statutes governing the minimum age under which sex cannot be legally consensual, and laws concerning marriage and workers' rights, were modified to reflect these changing discourses around childhood. Age of sexual consent, for example, rose from 7 during colonial times to 10, 12, and eventually as high as 14 during the eighteenth and nineteenth centuries. By the late 1800s, the average age of consent in the United States was 14. Across the nation, however, the age of consent was raised slowly, unevenly, and with great reluctance. Legislators' opposition to changing age of consent laws reveals important pre-nineteenth century understandings of childhood and child sexuality, as well as female sexuality. Many were opposed because they feared girls would use these statutes to blackmail their older male lovers, revealing a perception of preadolescent girls as "not only competent enough to decide to have sexual intercourse, but also sufficiently clever to use that competence to compromise men."[27] Reflecting a major shift in ideas about childhood sexuality and children's competence, today the most common age at which teenagers can legally consent to sexual activity in the United States is 16 (thirty states plus the District of Columbia). Eight states, including Texas, set the age of consent at 17, and youth in twelve states must be 18 before they can legally consent to sexual activity.[28]

The first significant calls for sex education emerged at the beginning of the twentieth century, in tandem with the belief that sex is dangerous for the young and the unmarried and the recognition of a newly discovered developmental stage in the life course—"adolescence," a term coined in 1904.[29] School-based sex education was historically predicated on the assumption that knowledge about the dangers of sex would prevent youthful sexual activity and that parents, mothers especially, were ill-equipped to impart this information to their children.[30] School-based sex education, however, was not widely implemented until fairly late in the twentieth century, and parents were, and continue to be, held accountable for their children's sexual safety and well-being.

In fact, the newfound idea of childhood innocence and vulnerability that took hold in the late 1800s and early 1900s not only transformed notions about childhood and sexuality, it radically reframed the parent-child relationship. Good parents were increasingly defined as those who protect their children from adult responsibilities and worries, including sexual activity. Within this ideology of parenting, children's innocence reflected parents' ability to shelter them.[31] The innocent child was thus constructed in parallel with ideas of parental accountability, meaning that parents were responsible not just for raising children but for protecting, nurturing, and, increasingly, cultivating them.[32] This new cult of parenting, however, ignored the social conditions surrounding families and established a middle-class standard that was largely unattainable for the majority of Americans. The specter of parental failure continues to loom large in contemporary Western culture: according to the common wisdom, "bad" kids are a product of "bad" parenting and parents are blamed, or at least suspected, when bad things happen to their children.[33]

The past few decades have witnessed an expansion of the dangers from which parents are held accountable for protecting their children.[34] Much of the concern about children and their well-being in relation to sexuality is tied to child sexual abuse. Despite its long history, child sexual abuse was defined as a widespread social problem in the United States only in the late 1970s, urged on by an uneasy alliance of feminists, physicians, social workers, and social conservatives who joined "in nationwide campaigns to protect children against a variety of abuses and abusers."[35] This was not the first time child sexual abuse was brought to the public's attention, but previous efforts, most notably those spearheaded by feminists in the late 1800s, had largely slipped from public consciousness by the turn of the twentieth century.[36]

The anti-sexual abuse movement of the 1970s and 1980s defined and recognized child sexual abuse and achieved significant and salutary changes in policies and practices relating to child sexual abuse. For example, sexually abused children were no longer accused of "leading on" their abusers, clearly a necessary shift. The movement also argued, however, that children deserved special protection because they are asexual and innocent, rather than because they, like all human beings, deserve to be free from abuse and harm.[37] As the sexuality scholar Steven Angelides convincingly argues, this newfound concept of children effectively erased children's sexual subjectivity. Based on this new conceptualization, children are not and should not be sexual subjects.[38] A child's interest in or knowledge about his or her body, particularly parts deemed "private," in itself became grounds for suspicion that the child was sexually abused.

Clearly, under no condition is child sexual abuse acceptable. The point here is that the anti-sexual abuse movement linked protecting children to the belief that children do not have a "natural" interest or curiosity about sex and sexuality, or at least they should not have such interests. Of course, the term "natural" is problematic in reference to sexuality, as sexual mores and norms vary across cultures and over time. But I use the term "natural" here to highlight Freud's idea that children are fundamentally erotic beings—and thus that sexual curiosity is a natural component of childhood—a notion that, due to the popularity of Freudian thought about sexuality, experienced a revival in Western culture during the twentieth century. This notion has been largely supplanted over the last few decades by the image of innocent, asexual youth surrounded by sexually predatory adults.

Based on inflated data regarding sexual abuse, and through the expanded definition of child victimization to include such events as talking to a child about sexuality, the efforts of the child anti-sexual abuse movement created a cultural climate where child sexual abuse seemed omnipresent.

Mass media also played a role in spreading beliefs in children's innocence and imperilment.[39] For example, sociologists Monica Casper and Lisa Jean Moore document the emergence in the early 2000s of what they call "pedophile entertainment"—a genre of reality television shows such as *To Catch a Predator* ostensibly aimed at documenting and curbing predation.[40] These programs suggest that pedophiles and predatory forces lurked around every corner, thus capitalizing on and reinforcing parental fears. In fact, physical and sexual assault rates against children declined in the early 1990s and have continued to do so throughout the first decade of the 2000s.[41]

Meanwhile, the discourse of childhood sexual innocence and vulnerability permeates the battles over sex education. "The seductive rhetoric of childhood sexual innocence"[42] is frequently used by both sides of the sex education debate because it meshes with the sense of an urgent need to protect children from sexual harm. Yet, as historians document, the discourse of asexual children in need of protection is a relatively recent one. It has also not been applied equally to all youth.

In examining the debate over sex education in North Carolina in the early 2000s, the sociologist Jessica Fields finds that abstinence-only proponents used childhood innocence to argue for abstinence-only instruction in order "to contain the corrupting influence of sexually unsalvageable adolescents."[43] This tactic suggests that, as children transition into adolescence, adults begin to think of some teenagers, at least, as sexual beings. In fact, alongside the notion that teenagers are innocent and in need of protection is a discourse of teenagers as highly sexually motivated *because* they are teenagers. This discourse is informed by the widespread belief that sex is an uncontrollable "drive" and that teenagers are hormonally fueled and particularly susceptible to that drive.[44] But it is also shaped by processes that project (hyper)sexuality onto Others based on race, class, gender, or sexual stereotypes. Social policy, discourse, and imagery construct a highly sexual and "sexually unsalvageable" picture of low-income, black, Latino/a, gay, lesbian, and bisexual youth.[45]

In fact, debates over sex education are profoundly shaped by racist, sexist, and heterosexist thinking about sexuality and adolescence, although rarely overtly articulated as such.[46] Fields, for example, notes that both sides of the sex education debate in North Carolina used code words such as "at-risk"—a racialized signifier of economic disadvantage—and "children having children"—a seemingly race and class neutral discourse that ignores the correlation between teen pregnancy, social class, and race—to "speak publicly of their private concerns for African American and low-income girls without claiming those concerns."[47] These debates, and sex education in general, also typically equate sexual activity with heterosexual intercourse and either dismiss other ways of being sexual or link homosexuality with perversity, deviance, or unhappiness.[48] In this way, heterosexuality is privileged as the normative and natural form of sexual expression. As sociologist Stephen Valocchi points out,

> [The dominance of heterosexuality is maintained in part] by preventing homosexuality from being a form of sexuality that can be taken for granted or go unmarked or seem right in the way heterosexuality can. As a result, the dominance of heterosexuality often operates unconsciously or in ways that make it particularly difficult to identify.[49]

Sexuality and social inequality have a long, intertwined history in the United States: "the use of sex as a form of domination—by race especially, but increasingly by gender and class—took shape in the seventeenth century and continued throughout American history."[50] In the early 1900s, for example, swayed by the eugenics movement, many state legislators passed sterilization laws to prevent "undesirables" from reproducing, and birth-control advocates pitched birth control as a way to reduce the number of births among those deemed "unfit," namely, the poor, immigrants, and people of color.[51] Revealing the continued linkages made between race, gender, and sexuality, southern racists resisted school integration in the 1950s by distributing pictures of white women embracing black men, playing on racist fears of hypersexual black men corrupting white women's purity and innocence.[52] Despite great advances by the Civil Rights, Women's, and Lesbian, Gay, Bisexual, and Transgender movements, the conflation of hypersexuality with those deemed Other still persists. Discussions about sex frequently draw and reinforce boundaries between normal, natural sexualities and deviant, nonconforming sexualities.[53]

The discourses of teen sexuality are thus highly contradictory, polarized, and reflect social inequalities. Sexuality is generally depicted as a perilous enterprise, even though it is a pervasive aspect of the American cultural landscape and is considered key to individual identity and personal fulfillment. At this historical and cultural moment, moreover, children are increasingly portrayed as young, innocent, and in need of protection, but some, especially black and Latino/a youth, are also constructed as sexually unsalvageable with their behavior construed as intentionally deviant. Adults are understood as children's protectors, yet they are also broadly framed as potential sex predators. The subject of sex education is embroiled in debates around whether young people should learn about contraception or be taught to abstain from sexual activity until they are married or old enough to handle the emotional and physical consequences of sex. This book examines how American parents navigate this complex and embattled terrain.

2

The Asexual Teen

Naïveté, Dependence, and Sexual Danger

Rosalia's days are long. As the sole family provider, Rosalia—a mother of five—works 6 days a week, 12 or more hours a day, at a dry cleaning chain. When I asked about her long hours, she responded: "It's supposed to be from 6 a.m. to 6 p.m. but more than likely it's until 7 p.m." She has a daily quota at work: "They tell me, to get paid that day I have to do this much, so I need to stay until I'm done with whatever they ask me to do so I can get paid." Her work is hard and performed in hot surroundings; her forearms are mottled with welts and scars from the machines she uses to clean and press people's clothes. Rosalia's five daughters, whose ages range from 9 to 22, keep her going. She described them as "happy," "intelligent," and "hard-working," although she is concerned that her 14- and 19-year-old daughters have some "lazy tendencies." The older daughters help out with the younger daughters—by, for example, getting them up and ready for school in the morning—and even though her two oldest are now moms themselves, they all continue to live together in a small apartment and share the housework and cooking. In a touching moment at the start of the interview, Rosalia's

22-year-old daughter brought her a towel, gently lifted her long, wet hair, and placed the towel around her shoulders, releasing and tenderly fanning her hair out to dry. It was Sunday, Rosalia's one day off.[1]

When her four oldest daughters were going through puberty, Rosalia's love for them grew stronger than ever, but her concerns also increased: "One of the signs of puberty is menstruation and when they have the first period, I worry so much when I'm at work. I'm constantly thinking about it, about that particular daughter moving on to new things in her life." Rosalia's main worry was that

> they may have bad influences that will give them ideas like drinking or using drugs and then again promiscuity—not necessarily promiscuity, but if they were to be abused then that brings on other problems like drinking and drugging and it could bring promiscuity into their life if they were to be abused.

She worries about the older men who hang around the courtyard of her apartment building, leering at her daughters and other girls. Afraid that these men might be sex predators, she orders her daughters to stay away from the courtyard and avoid talking to the men there. She is also "very concerned that people outside [the family], like let's say girlfriends at school or just people they know, may put ideas in their head, like go with this man or go here or go there." She knows she cannot control her daughters when they are in school and she is at work, but she can advise them about using good judgment. Although Rosalia still worries, she is "pleased with my daughters, the ones that have gone into that puberty or you know growing up, because they're not doing things I see other kids their age doing like drinking or drugging or being promiscuous."

Rosalia carries a notion of what the world is like for her teenage daughters—in a word, dangerous. She also knows that sexual teenagers are promiscuous partiers. She can identify the preteens in her apartment complex who are "heading in the wrong direction, they just don't have the direction [they need]." Her daughters "are not like them." But Rosalia feels somewhat overwhelmed by the daily task of giving her daughters the support and foundation they need to resist the temptations posed by their peers. She does not let her daughters date or go out alone until they are 18, because before that "they're gullible. They'll just believe anything. They're naïve, I guess." Even at 18, Rosalia thinks her daughters are prone to naïveté. As evidence of this, she told me that her two oldest daughters both became pregnant at the age of 18 and had their first child at 19. She suspects that these daughters were still too naïve and immature at 18 to withstand the tremendous peer and societal pressures to have sex, but at that point they were de facto adults, and she could no longer keep them at home all the time.

Rosalia is one of three parents I spoke to who has at least one child who became a teen parent. Like the other parents, she expressed dismay but most of all surprise about her daughters' pregnancies. To the extent that her teen daughters did not fit her stereotype of "the sexual teen," the pregnancies were completely unexpected. On the other hand, she believes that the pregnancies occurred because her naïve 18-year-old daughters were influenced by sexually active peers and today's hypersexualized world. The ideas Rosalia holds about teen sexuality are not unique. The parents I spoke with uniformly described their teens as sexually naïve and vulnerable to the pressures of the surrounding highly sexual and sexualized teen culture. Examining how and why parents maintain this notion reveals important beliefs and fears about teen sexuality.

Research on the role of parents in their children's sexual attitudes and behaviors generally falls into two camps: one wholly endorses the benefits of parents' involvement in teaching their children about sexual issues,[2] whereas the other questions whether parental involvement has more drawbacks than benefits.[3] Although both sides emphasize that parents play a critical role in shaping their children's sexual behaviors and experiences, much of this research is with teenagers or older youth and rarely delves into parents' motivations for talking or not talking to their children about sex. This research also does not capture parents' subjective understandings of their children's sexuality.[4] How parents perceive teen sexuality is important because these perceptions influence how they talk to their children about sex and try to manage their children's sexuality. Like Rosalia, the parents I spoke to did not, on the whole, describe their biological children as sexual agents with sexual desires, even though they view adolescents in general as highly sexually motivated. As we will see, parents prefer to understand their own children as young, naïve, and financially dependent. They also regard teen sexual activity as dangerous, are afraid for their teen children's safety and well-being, and feel responsible for protecting them. Based on my interviews with parents, I suggest that parents' attitudes about teenage sexuality are shaped by dominant ideas about—as well as contradictions and anxieties around—sexuality, teenagers, and modern family life.

Age and Asexuality

Parents consistently characterized their children as young, immature, and naïve. In doing so, they often compared their children to other teenagers.

Beatrice's comment about her 16-year-old daughter typifies this viewpoint: "One thing I've noticed is that she's probably a little bit more immature than some of her friends, and that's okay, I think it will come." Echoing Beatrice, Elena said her 16-year-old daughter "seems very young or immature at times."

When I first noticed parents consistently describing their teen children as young and immature relative to their peers, I thought it might have something to do with the parents who had agreed to be interviewed. Perhaps they volunteered because they have "good" kids who do not do all the "bad" things other teens do. Yet—as will become clear as the parents' stories unfold throughout the book—the parents I spoke with have teenagers who seem to have done virtually everything we define as bad for teenagers: some have become teen parents, and many smoke marijuana, drink alcohol, have unprotected sex, skip school, get failing grades, vandalize school property, sneak out at night, or watch pornography. Teenagers' actual behaviors, in other words, do not seem very significant in terms of shaping the sense parents have that their own teens are young, immature, and naïve. Why, then, do parents think of their children in these ways?

A number of compelling explanations come to mind. Parents likely see their children at times when the children's guards are down, and at these times they may behave in more youthful ways, giving the impression of immaturity. Like many Americans, moreover, the ideas the interviewed parents hold about the "typical" teen are often based on stereotypes; their own teenager's behavior complicates and defies these stereotypes. Reflecting a combination of these two explanations, Pamela said she does not like some of her 15-year-old daughter's friends. When I asked what she doesn't like about them, Pamela replied: "Oh just the way they talk, the way she is around them sometimes. You know, I can see her acting differently, like, I don't know, ruder or something. Maybe more like a typical teenager!"

Yet as I listened to parent after parent describe their own teen children as immature and young, regardless of the children's ages, it became clear that this also has a great deal to do with how parents think about teen sexuality and the anxieties they have about their children's sexual safety and well-being. For example, after describing their own teenagers as young compared to their peers, parents often went on to say that, in their opinion, their children's youthfulness means that they are not really that interested or knowledgeable about sex. Kirk, who described his almost 15-year-old son as "immature" and "a late-bloomer" added: "So he's not as interested sexually as some of the other kids [in his classes]." Referring to his 15-year-old son and 17-year-old daughter, Ron stated:

They're a little immature for their ages. Well, my daughter especially. She still acts a little younger than most 17 year olds. She looks younger than [17] to me too. Which, we really don't mind though. We don't mind that. Because, we can sort of regulate it a little bit easier when she gets little questions [about sex] and things like that.

Similar to Kirk's description of his son, Ron thinks that his daughter's immaturity relative to her peers has delayed her interest in sex, which relieves him. Parents, in other words, rely on their understanding of their children as young and immature in constructing their children as asexual.

Some parents linked their children's youthfulness directly to sexual innocence and naïveté. Kate believes that her 14-year-old son is too young to have sex: "I don't think it's safe for his age. Maybe it's just him, I don't know. But he's a little naïve." I asked Kate, "What is it about [your son's] age or his naïveté that makes you feel he wouldn't be safe?" After a long pause, Kate responded with a sigh, "I don't know. I . . . " She trailed off, so I prompted, "Is it that he wouldn't use protection?" Kate answered hesitantly, "Yeah? Or maybe, I guess, [that] he'd do something he didn't want to do. Get pushed into something or let himself be pushed into something. I think he would definitely do that. I'm not going to be cool if I don't do this." Kate's eventual answer suggests that she has a difficult time imagining that her son might experience sexual desire of his own accord, at least not at his age. She is concerned, instead, that he might succumb to sexual activity to appear "cool" in his peers' eyes. Her fears center less on whether he will use contraception and more on his being pushed into having sex before he develops an interest in it. Within this equation, his peers have a great deal of influence over him, a topic I take up in chapter 5.

Some parents find it difficult to think of their not-yet-adult teens as sexual subjects because they view sex as an adult activity with adult consequences. (When these parents talked about sex, aside from one parent who is a health educator, they referred exclusively to heterosexual intercourse.) For these parents, talking about sex is difficult, as it raises the possibility that their teen is growing up and this may upset the dynamics of their relationship. I began to suspect this after interviewing Paula, who has not talked with her 14-year-old son about sex, preferring to wait until he initiates these conversations.[5] As she explained: "Well again, it goes back to, is this too much information too soon? Does he need to hear about this stuff? I mean, he's just a kid and so—" Paula broke off, so I prodded, "Do you think too much information would be harmful?" Before replying, Paula sighed, "I don't know. Maybe I just don't want to go there yet or don't want him to grow up, 'cause sex is an adult thing." "In what way?" I asked. "Well, just in, it's not something you can even do until you've reached a certain physical maturity and the outcomes of sex—like pregnancy or disease—these are very adult consequences. They can stay with you for life." For Paula, then, discussing sex with her son implies that he is growing up. Because Paula conceives of sex as intercourse, and intercourse as an adult enterprise with adult consequences, talking about sex threatens to shift the dynamics of her relationship with her son.

The notion that sex is an adult activity and that having sex transforms a young teenager into a more mature, adult-like person was mentioned in one way or another by nearly every parent I spoke with. Referring to her 13-year-old daughter, Yolanda laughingly said, "She not interested [in sex] and for as long as she's not interested, I'm okay with it. You know, it's fine with me. The longer she'll be a baby, the better for me." Similarly, Beatrice, in discussing why she likely would not allow her 16-year-old daughter to have a boyfriend spend the night at their house, stated that it would transform their relationship:

> That would be—I don't know, wow! [Because] I guess [it would seem as though] we're condoning extramarital sex and she still is a minor. I mean, even though she's sixteen, to me, she's—. And I don't know if we're ready for that parent-child relationship to change, because she would be more grown up, *way* more grown up. I'm not ready for that.

Yet Beatrice is more conflicted than other parents who simply feel that teenagers should not have sex at all. She wants her daughter to have a safe and fulfilling sex life, even if she is still a teen, and she thinks that prohibiting a sleepover might contradict this stated aim: "I would rather them do it at our house than in a car or somewhere else. But I'd still have reservations about that." Thus Beatrice accepts that her daughter may have sex as a teen, but she thinks that teenage sexual activity should be covert, that she should not have to know about it.[6] Ultimately she said that her husband would never agree to a sleepover—"he would absolutely, absolutely not"—meaning she will never have to face the dilemma of whether to allow her daughter to have sex under her roof.

Based on their belief that sex is an adult activity, some parents are putting off talking about sex with their children until their teens leave for college. Gabriela is one of these parents. The summer before starting first grade, Gabriela's daughter, a precocious reader, found and read a copy of Judy Blume's *Are You There God? It's Me, Margaret*. In the book, published in 1970, Blume vividly details the pubertal explorations of sixth grader Margaret and her friends, including discussions about bras, breasts, and periods. After reading the book Gabriela's daughter asked, "Mom, what's a period?" Caught off guard, Gabriela replied: "'It's the punctuation mark at the end of the sentence.' And [my daughter] said 'No, I don't think that's what they're talking about.' I think I just blew it off, changed the subject or something, but I'll never forget that." After this incident, Gabriela found the book and "put it away for a couple of years." She did talk to her daughter about menstruation eventually, when her daughter asked a few questions "in fifth grade, when her school did the puberty program." She has not yet talked to her about sex, however. Gabriela thinks that her daughter, who is now 16, is still too young to talk about sex and contraception because she is too young to have sex. I asked Gabriela when she thinks her daughter will be ready to talk about these issues, and she replied, "I'm hoping that not until she's ready to go off to college." I asked, "How do you think the conversation will go?"

> Well the conversation will probably be that we will prefer that she abstain until she's older and she feels that she is in a very committed relationship, but here's the information just in case. I will probably present it as, here are our feelings and here is the information.

Parents such as Gabriela do not necessarily think their college-bound children will be adults when they leave for college, but college signals a slightly more adult status. Sylvia explained that she will consider her now 15- and 14-year-old daughters adults once they have graduated high school: "I guess [I'll consider them adults at] 18, when they graduate from high school. Because then they're going to college and they're off on their own and you're not going to be there to look after them." College represents a transformation of the parent-child relationship for Sylvia, because it is a time when she envisions her daughters as more self-reliant. College also signifies an achievement—it means that a teenager has made it through high school with decent grades, has done well enough on college entrance exams, and has successfully applied and been accepted to a university. In a culture that values self-reliance and individual achievement, college thus becomes an important milestone on the road to adulthood. Parents also pointed out that a college degree is a gateway to higher future earnings. Parents' anxieties about their teens' uncertain financial futures and chances for upward mobility may be better resolved once a child graduates from high school and heads off to college. Parents may also feel that the intensive parenting years will be behind them once their children are in college. Derisive terms such as "helicopter parents," "hover parents," and "Velcro parents" imply that parents should *not* remain heavily involved in their college children's lives—that the years of parental control should be over at that point. Of course, the very existence of these terms also indicates that this is not always the case. Some parents, however, anticipate experiencing a sort of letting go once their children are college bound.[7]

Like Gabriela, Sylvia thinks that college is the time when young people can become "sexually active," although she acknowledged that not all teens wait until college:

> SYLVIA: The way the teens are now, I—I know that they're out there doing it. But I wouldn't want it for my girls.
> SINIKKA: Why not?
> SYLVIA: I would rather they wait. I would rather they wait until after high school. Once they're in college, if they feel that they're in a serious relationship.

In addition to seeing college as a place where young people can start being sexual subjects, Gabriela's and Sylvia's responses reveal that college represents the time for young people to develop serious, committed relationships. In line with this understanding, some parents I spoke to actively discourage, and some forbid, their children from dating in middle and high school. Middle-class parents, in particular, encourage their teenagers to look upon dating as a casual enterprise and to avoid being tied to one person until they are older, or at least in college.[8]

College may not be the sexual and relational utopia that some parents envision, however. A National Institute of Justice study finds that college women "are at greater risk for rape and other forms of sexual assault than women in the general population or in a comparable age group."[9] In addition, despite profound changes in sex and dating on college campuses, college women still report being judged more harshly than college men are for similar sexual and relational behaviors and modifying their behavior in an attempt to negotiate sexual double standards.[10]

Nevertheless, for the parents I interviewed, teenagers are asexual until at least college or some other adult milestone, or until proven otherwise, and sometimes even after that. For example, when her 15-year-old son came to her with the news that his girlfriend might be pregnant, Portia tried to handle the news calmly and rationally: "I didn't want to dwell on it because I was really uncomfortable and they were kids exploring, the both of them were. Neither one was necessarily experienced. It's just an opportunity presented itself." The way Portia described her son's sexual activity is similar to how some teenage girls describe sex as something that "just happens," removing forethought and even desire from sexual activity. Studies suggest that girls may have difficulty acknowledging their own sexual desire in a society that often punishes girls for being sexually active.[11] This same dynamic was prevalent among the few parents I interviewed who know their children are having or have had sex. Like Portia, they did not describe their teenagers' sexual activity in agentic, positive terms.

As it turned out, the son's girlfriend was not pregnant. I asked Portia if they had been using contraception, and she replied that she was fairly certain they had not, as it was a spur-of-the-moment thing and she had not previously talked with her son about contraception, "Because he was such a young teenager and I really didn't think. And again, this is a really good solid kid, level-headed in a lot of ways, and had made pretty good decisions previously, so, no I—no, I just didn't." Prior to this incident, Portia saw her son as too young to need information about contraception. But her explanation also makes it clear that, as a responsible, high achieving, "good solid kid," her son does not fit her stereotype of a "sexually active" teen.

I later asked Portia if she has since talked with her now 16-year-old son about sex or contraception. Her answer clearly shows her reluctance to see her son as a sexual subject: "Well, since then he broke up with her. So, no, because he's not dating, we haven't talked about it." Portia and her husband have forbidden their son from dating until he graduates from high school. Once he goes to college, Portia feels he will be ready to date again and thinks that will be the time to discuss contraception. She emphasized to me many times that "he is a good kid who just got in over his head." She does not want one pregnancy scare to define her son and certainly does not believe it signals his continued sexual activity. Her reluctance to see her son as a sexual being because he is a "good kid," however, implies that she associates sexual activity with deviance and badness. Her statement dichotomizes good kids as asexual and bad kids as sexual and reveals that it is difficult for her to reconcile her feelings about her (good) son with his (bad) sexual activity. Parents' sense that their own children are asexual thus may also be shaped by the tendency to view ourselves and those close to us more favorably than we view those outside our social circle.[12] Social psychologists argue that this perceptual tendency helps us feel more positive and better about ourselves and those in our group.[13] We *want* to see those around us—our close-knit circle of friends and family—as good people. In a context where teen sexual activity connotes deviance and risk (as I discuss in more detail shortly), parents have few, if any, positive images of teen sexuality to draw on to construct a positive image of sexual teens.

Parents also link their understandings of their teens' sexuality to economic wherewithal. This rationale is in line with federal policy that poses financial independence as a precedent for sexual activity; the Personal Responsibility Act passed in 1996 emphasizes "the importance of attaining self-sufficiency before engaging in sexual activity."[14] Consider Beth's story, for example. When her 16-year-old son was in sixth grade, Beth's husband, whom she had recently married, discovered that her son had been downloading pornographic images onto his computer since fifth grade: "He had a ton, a *ton* of porno pictures." Later, after they confiscated the computer, Beth and her husband discovered that her son was recording pornography in the middle of the night, watching it during the day, and then erasing it. They have made it clear that watching any kind of pornography while still living at home is unacceptable:

> [My husband] doesn't come out and say that it's immoral, that you should never do it because he would probably be a hypocrite if he did. His thing is, "You're just too young to be looking at things like that right now. And in our house these are our rules and you're going to have to do what we say. When you're eighteen and on your own computer, you pay for your own computer and your own TV and your own service, you can do whatever you want. But whenever you're in our house you live by our rules."

Like her husband, Beth is not opposed to pornography per se: "I don't have huge objections to it. I feel the women who do it mostly are women who like the money from it. I'm sure there're situations where there are people who're forced to do stuff [that's degrading]. I just don't think that's what usually happens." Beth and her husband have managed to overcome their conflict about prohibiting their son's use of pornography, however, by asserting his youthfulness and economic dependence. Other parents, like Beth, also said that their children can have sexual desires when they are independent and financially self-sufficient but not while they are living at home and dependent on their parents. Thus, although age clearly plays an important role in how parents think about their children's sexuality—parents often indicated precise ages when their children may date; some, such as Beth, pinpointed when they may watch pornography; and many identified an age range during which their children are particularly naïve and immature—age is not simply about developmental trajectories: it is intertwined with economic dependence and a deep sense of parental responsibility to usher their children safely to adulthood.

Beth's strategic use of age and dependence also apparently helps her maintain the belief that her son is asexual and innocent, despite his interest in pornography. For example, she is fairly certain that her son is a virgin simply because he told her as much and he has not dated. She has no trouble talking to her son about waiting to have sex "telling him there's absolutely nothing wrong in remaining a virgin and not having sex, those things are easy to say" But Beth finds it harder to talk to him about contraception, and to date has not done so. She explained:

> It is harder to say if you're going to have sex, you need to make sure to have protection. It's harder to say that as a parent because you want to believe that they're not going to do it at that point in time, which probably, definitely is not a good attitude to have because I've been surprised a lot by what they're doing. He surprises me a lot. And I don't know why that is. As far as, like we have this selective forgetfulness about things that we did as kids. Because we thought we were so old at that age to go out and do those things. But when you look at your child, they're just so little and young. You just don't think of them ever even thinking about those things. It's hard to even think about what you should be saying to kids.

Beth expressed what so many parents I spoke with said: despite remembering what it was like to be a teenager, and even though her son "surprises her a lot" (in the past few years, he has been caught smoking marijuana, drinking alcohol, and downloading and recording pornography), she views him as "little and young" and cannot imagine him as a sexual being.

This understanding of one's own teen child as young and immature means that parents are often caught off-guard when they find out that their child is having sex. Some parents I spoke to learned that their children were having sex only when the child announced a pregnancy or pregnancy scare. Teresa's now 21-year-old daughter was 17 when she told Teresa that she was four months pregnant. Laughing, Teresa described her reaction: "I practically almost choked on a piece of chicken when she told me. She wasn't going to tell me! And she never hardly dated anybody, so it was just like an intense shock to me when she told me." Compounding Teresa's shock was that her daughter, in Teresa's words, had always been very shy and reserved. As a shy, quiet teenager who rarely dated, Teresa's daughter did not fit her understanding of a "sexually active teen": the pregnancy came out of the blue.

Talk about Contraception

I do not want to give the impression that all the parents in the book have not talked to their children about contraception. Despite being torn about how much information their children need *and* how much they can handle, more than three-quarters of the parents did say that they have talked about contraception. Of the eleven parents who have not done so, five said they avoided the subject for religious reasons (four mothers, one father). These parents expect their children to remain sexually abstinent until marriage and said discussing contraception with them, other than to point out that it can fail, would contradict that expectation. As chapter 7 will show, however, even self-identified highly conservative-religious parents experience some qualms about not providing their children with contraceptive information, and some do provide this information despite their strong religious beliefs.

The other six parents, all mothers, did not identify a particular reason for avoiding the subject of contraception except that they simply do not know how to broach the topic; their discomfort and sense that their children cannot handle or do not yet need this information have also prevented these conversations from occurring. Of note, five of the six mothers in this group either only have teenage sons or have a teenage son as their oldest child. As I show in chapter 3, gender is another factor shaping parent-teen discussions about sexuality, with mothers saying they find it especially difficult to talk about sex with their teen sons. In addition, five of these six are upper-middle class, and their privileged class location may influence their response. Because the problems associated with adolescent sexuality, such as teen pregnancy, are often framed as a consequence of poor family values among low-income families,[15] these upper-middle-class mothers may have felt more confident in telling me they have not talked about contraception. Or perhaps they think their class privilege in some ways buffers their children from the need for contraceptive information.

The parents who have discussed contraception with their children range from very religious to not at all religious,[16] from poor to upper-middle class, and have children at various teenage years. Yet all described their discussions of contraception in ways that underscore their reluctance to view their children as sexual subjects. These parents provide the information because they see it as a duty and as necessary to protect their children, but they do not necessarily see any immediate need for this information. For example, parents tell their daughters that they will help them with birth control *if* the daughters decide that they are ready to have sex, suggesting that regardless of their ages they are not there yet. Pamela was one of a very few parents who said she and her husband have told their 15-year-old daughter that they will not only support her decision to start having sex, but assume this will happen during the teenage years:

I tell her, and my husband tells her also, "If and when the time comes—and it will come—if and when you want to have sex with someone—not that we're saying go do it—let us know and we'll go get you on the Pill, we'll get you some protection." And so it's that kind of thing that we talk about.

Despite her seemingly pro-sex approach, Pamela takes care not to appear to encourage her daughter to have sex, even while she assures her that she will help her get on birth control "when the time comes."[17] Like Pamela, parents fear that by talking about contraception they may appear to tacitly condone sexual intercourse and are careful to explain to their children that this is not the case. Sylvia described talking to her 15-year-old daughter about contraception: "I have talked to her once where I told her that, 'I'm not saying that I approve or that I condone having sex at an early age, but, if you do,' I said, 'I expect you to either tell me or have protection.'"

Virtually all the parents also said that they would not make contraception available to their children without first being asked to do so. Parents think that providing contraception without their children asking for it sends a message that it is now acceptable to have sex. Yolanda, who has a 13-year-old daughter, is the only parent I interviewed who plans to get her daughter on birth control, whether or not her daughter requests it. Yet Yolanda agonizes over the timing: "I don't want to wait until it's too late. But I don't want to put her on it and let her say, 'Oh, now that I have birth control, it's okay.' So that's my biggest challenge right now."

Those who oppose comprehensive sex education usually argue that talking and teaching about contraception incites sexual activity.[18] A highly effective strategy used by proponents of abstinence-only sex education has also been to demonize and stigmatize sex educators and comprehensive sex education proponents, to cast them as depraved and even potential sexual predators.[19] Parents draw on these broader discourses in discussing contraception with their children, as well as planning when and whether to provide contraception. While they do not want their children to have unprotected sex, they also want to avoid the slightest impression that they approve of teenage sexual activity. Parents worry in part because, like many Americans, they associate teen sex with risk and consider it their responsibility to ensure their children's outcomes and well-being.[20] Delores explained why she will never allow her teen daughter to have a sleepover with a boyfriend:

That's just tempting her or tempting him to maybe experiment or be curious. That can lead to sex. And then later on down the road, you know, oh she's pregnant or something. Well how did it happen? Well Mom and Dad let her spend the night with the boy. So that comes back on me being the parent, being the one to set the rules. I am the guardian; I'm the parent. It's just for the safety of her and that boy [that I wouldn't allow that].

Parents believe that it is ultimately up to them to successfully guide their children through adolescence and into adulthood. In a context in which teen sexual activity is seen as inherently dangerous, parents may believe that a sexual teenager signals that they have failed this moral imperative. In talking about sexuality and contraception, therefore, parents try to protect their children, but also themselves, from any accusations of parental failure by carefully tailoring their message according to what they think their children are old enough to hear and process. This message largely appears to focus on the benefits of "waiting" and, as I discuss in chapter 5, on strategies to fend off their children's sexually active peers.

Ideas about age and maturity also influence parents' understandings of their children's contraception use. Two of the parents in this book who knew their teenagers were having sex and provided birth control expressed misgivings that they allowed their children to take on "adult" responsibilities. For example, Norma's 17-year-old daughter has been on birth control for two years, and Norma said this has weighed her daughter down with adult concerns:

On hindsight, I wish—I feel bad for her having to make adult choices so young in life, dealing with adult issues so early on. Having to go to the doctor every year like you're supposed to as a woman would. Having the responsibility of having to always take that contraceptive.

Similarly, when Nicole heard rumors that her 16-year-old son was having sex, she bought him a box of condoms. Buying her son condoms was "a hard thing for me to do. I told him that I prefer that if he was going to be active, be safe about it. I don't prefer that he does it, you know, 'You should be married. You shouldn't have to deal with this right now.'" Thus Norma and Nicole described their teenagers' sexual activity and use of contraception in primarily negative terms and spoke of their regret that their children did not delay sexual intercourse and now have adult worries and responsibilities.

Parents such as Norma and Nicole are clearly torn; they want their children to be responsible and are glad that they are using contraception, but they also want their children to experience a happy, carefree adolescence, not yet burdened by "adult" issues and concerns. During the middle school PTA meetings I attended while working on this book, parents also talked not just about the dangers confronting teenagers but about the joys of being a teenager. Many of the parents at these meetings (as well as those I interviewed) fondly recalled their own teenage years as unabashedly fun and exhilarating, and they want the same for their teenagers. From violent video games to the metamorphoses of Britney Spears and Miley Cyrus, parents worry that their teenagers are under relentless social pressure to grow up too fast.

Parents also think that their children face greater expectations to perform than *they* did as teenagers. Some talked about the stress of high-stakes standardized testing and lamented the increasingly competitive college and labor markets their children will soon face. Based on their own experiences, parents worry about the myriad challenges and potential sacrifices awaiting their children once they reach adulthood, and they want to delay as many adult burdens as possible—including the responsibilities that come with sexual intercourse.

So although many parents have talked about contraception and some have even provided their teenagers with contraception, the content of their talks tends to focus on possible future sexual activity and how to minimize risk. This focus avoids recognizing that their teenagers have sexual desires. By viewing their teenagers as potentially becoming sexual only through heterosexual intercourse, parents also reproduce heteronormative notions of heterosexuality as natural and inevitable, albeit plagued with threats of pregnancy, disease, and victimization, as the next section illustrates.

The Danger Discourse of Teen Sexuality

Parents' discussions about sex with their children largely revolve around a future time when they may engage in heterosexual intercourse and how they can guard against pregnancy, disease, and victimization. Kim emphasizes these possible consequences when she talks to her 17-year-old son, 12-year-old niece, and 10-year-old daughter: "[I tell them] 'Procreation is real. I don't care what anybody says, when you have sex, there's only the potential for a baby to pop up no matter what precautions you take.'" Parents focus on sexual peril and risk because they, like many Americans, think that adolescent sexual activity is a very dangerous undertaking: I term this the "danger discourse of teen sexuality."

Parents' belief that teen sex is inevitably and utterly dangerous means that other aspects of sexuality, such as pleasure and desire, seem unimaginable. Few of the parents interviewed, as I describe in more detail later, have talked about sexual pleasure with their children. Parents also typically said that they are too embarrassed to discuss masturbation with their children.

Those parents who have talked about masturbation often did so because they found their child (always a son) masturbating and felt it necessary to explain that, while masturbating is normal and may feel good, it should be done in private.

Some parents reported that their conversations about masturbation led to a broader discussion of sexual touching and the dangers of sex. Olivia, one of only two parents who talked to a daughter about masturbation, told her 14-year-old daughter:

> I said, "From time to time, you may or may not want to [masturbate]." I said, "But you may actually start washing yourself down there and it may feel good." I said, "No big deal." But that brought [us] into a whole other subject about knowing your boundaries when somebody touches you. I said, "If you feel something [when someone else touches you] then that means that that's bad. And you should never feel uncomfortable about someone touching you, especially down there." I said, "You've got to be honest with me, open and honest." She's like, "Okay, okay."

Olivia wants her daughter to feel that masturbation is "no big deal." But she also is concerned that if her daughter enjoys the sensation of touching herself, she may respond inappropriately if someone else touches her "down there." So she cautions her daughter—it's okay to masturbate, but it's not okay for anyone else to touch her. This introduces masturbation, but the conversation quickly diverts to danger, a topic all parents were comfortable discussing.

Although the subject of pleasure is often absent from parents' discussions of sex with their children, this is consistent with dominant discourses of sexuality in the United States, which view sex outside of marriage as a potential menace. In Gail's words:

> It used to be that getting pregnant was the scary thing of having sex before marriage. That's one of the nice things that can happen nowadays. I mean, there's some pretty snag nasty diseases running out there now . . . I saw a thing on the TV the other day that said three out of four HIV positive people do not inform their partner. *Three* out of four do not inform their partner! And then the next thing was, because a lot of them don't even know they're positive yet. I think the kids need to know that.

According to Gail, an unplanned pregnancy is now one of the happier outcomes of premarital sex as opposed to life-threatening sexually transmitted infections (STIs). For Gail, the stakes are too high in teenage sex. Her comment also highlights the role media play in shaping parents' understandings of the sexual dangers facing young people.[21]

After I interviewed Gail, I attempted to locate and verify, without success, the statistic she quoted—that three out of four HIV-positive individuals do not inform their sexual partner of their HIV status. The data I did gather, however, suggest that Gail's statistic is not necessarily accurate. The Centers for Disease Control and Prevention estimates that one in five HIV-positive Americans are not aware of their status. But even though there are more HIV-positive Americans today than ever before, the annual number of new HIV infections has remained relatively stable.[22] This means that Americans are getting better at avoiding HIV, probably because increased HIV testing has made more HIV-positive Americans aware of their status and they are informing their partners, and because those who do not have the infection are doing a better job of protecting themselves.

But, of course, HIV remains significantly prevalent, and parents are deeply troubled by thoughts that their children might contract it. Like Gail, parents frequently mentioned HIV as well as AIDS in their interviews. Numerous public health campaigns and education programs were initiated in the 1990s and have raised and maintained awareness about HIV, including information about infection rates and transmission. In this post-AIDS era, parents are still clearly aware of and concerned about the disease and, in line with a dominant discourse deployed by abstinence-only sex education,[23] some believe the risks of sex have been increasing since the 1960s and 1970s. Kirk expressed this when he said:

> There's more sexually transmitted diseases than when I was [young]. You know, I'm 45 that we didn't have—I mean maybe AIDS was out there but it wasn't something that people were too worried about. I never thought about it myself. You know, we had other types of sexually transmitted diseases but none of them killed you, so that's the thing that I warn [my son] about.

Some parents also discussed their fears about the human papilloma virus (HPV). Now the most common STI among young people, HPV has received a great deal of attention from the media and public health campaigns. Concerns about HPV have risen partly because of increasing rates of infection—although 90 percent of those who contract HPV do not develop symptoms or health problems[24]—but also because certain types of the virus are linked to cancer, especially cervical cancer. Melissa, who has three teenagers, raised the issue of HPV in her interview: "HPV is rampant. It is not [spread solely through] sexual intercourse; it is skin-to-skin. That's why we have twenty year olds that are dying of . . . cancer—at twenty years old! It is a *very* serious business." Melissa is right that certain forms of HPV can infect areas of the body other than the genitals and can be transmitted through bodily contact, not simply in exchanges of fluids. Only after fifteen to twenty years following initial infection, however, does invasive cancer develop and then only in some women. Meanwhile, abnormal cervical cells can be detected through routine Pap tests, and treatment at early stages has high cure rates.[25]

Around the time of my interview with Melissa, Gardasil, a vaccine that protects girls and women from the types of HPV that cause most cervical cancers and protects both males and females from most genital warts and other cancers linked to strains of HPV, became widely available in the United States.[26] The following year, in the spring of 2007, Rick Perry, the Republican governor of Texas, issued an executive order requiring all girls to receive the HPV vaccine prior to entering sixth grade. Although applauded by many public health officials, Perry's mandatory vaccination order also created a furor—conservative groups claimed it violated parents' rights and would lead to promiscuous behavior—and it was eventually overturned by the Texas legislature. Similar debates have occurred across the nation, and, as of 2009, no state government has successfully mandated an HPV vaccine, although Virginia and Washington, D.C. have enacted loose vaccination requirements for sixth-grade girls.[27] The controversy and consternation around mandating Gardasil vaccination is a vivid example of the political climate around teen sexuality in the United States.[28] Despite apparent widespread concern about young people's sexual safety, protecting the image of teenage female purity and parental rights appears to be more important than protecting teenagers' health.

Teen pregnancy, HIV, HPV—is sex more dangerous now than in the past? The answer is more complicated than a simple yes or no. American teens are engaging in sexual intercourse at about the same rate as their teen counterparts fifty years ago—in 2009 nearly half of all high school students reported having had sexual intercourse—but the teen birthrate has fallen dramatically (although it is still higher than the rate in most postindustrial nations).[29] Teens have more contraceptive options and sources of information than ever before. A greater incidence of sexually transmitted infections is found today than in the past, yet impressive advances in the screening, treatment, and prevention of STIs have also been made. And teens have gotten wiser about navigating the risks of sex: risky teen sexual behavior has declined over the past two decades, according to the nationwide *Youth Risk Behavior Survey*, conducted biannually since 1991 by the Centers for Disease Control in conjunction with local and state education and health agencies.[30] A majority of teens, for example, report using a method of contraception, most commonly a condom, at first sexual intercourse and the last time they had intercourse, although teens (like adults) do not use condoms consistently.[31]

On the other hand, the negative consequences of sex are not evenly spread among all Americans. Nationwide overall statistics may obscure the fact that, depending on race, class, gender, and sexual inequalities, Americans have varying access to social, material, and psychological resources to navigate and avoid sexual risk.[32] For example, despite comprising over two-thirds of the U.S. population, whites—the dominant and historically privileged racial group in the United States—accounted for only 35 percent of Americans living with HIV in 2006. In contrast, African Americans, a historically oppressed and disenfranchised racial group comprising about 13 percent of the U.S. population, constituted nearly half of all HIV-positive Americans in 2006.[33] To be clear, these striking statistics tell us nothing about the morals of white or black Americans, but they do offer insight into the consequences of an unequal society. Poverty and a lack of access to health care are major reasons for the higher HIV rates, as well as other health disparities, among African Americans.[34] Group differences in HIV infection rates by income and race remind us that the dangers of sex cannot be viewed separately from the structural, cultural, and political conditions shaping how people are exposed to and negotiate these dangers. Injustice and inequality are etched on the bodies of the dispossessed.

The risks of teen sexual activity also cannot be viewed apart from the interests that influence how risk associated with sex is researched, reported, and, in some instances, distorted. For example, an increase in teen births nationally in the mid-2000s led to sensational newspaper headlines, but a closer analysis of the data reveals that although the teen birthrate rose by 3 percent in 2006, it was still 32 percent lower than the peak rate in 1991. In addition, the increase occurred primarily among 18 and 19 year olds (i.e., legal adults), with only a negligible rise in births among 15 to 17 year olds. More recent data suggest that the teen birthrate has once again decreased.[35]

Whether for ideological reasons or financial gain, or both, in various quarters the risks of teen sexuality are often inflated and overblown. As sociologist Laura Mamo and her collaborators observe in their compelling examination of Merck's marketing campaign for the HPV vaccine Gardasil:

> With slightly fewer than four thousand U.S. deaths per year, cervical cancer was transformed from a relatively rare cancer with an effective health care

infrastructure for prevention and early detection into a death sentence, a "disease of innocence," *and* a major public health concern.[36]

Merck, of course, stands to benefit substantially if it can convince the American public of the dire consequences of foregoing the Gardasil vaccine. This is not to discount the potential health benefits of Gardasil. Mandating Gardasil would make it more accessible to low-income girls and women who lack health insurance, "precisely those most at risk for developing cervical cancer."[37] Yet Merck's promotional materials for Gardasil ignore the social class differences in girls' and women's sexual health and well-being and instead characterize all girls as "always and already 'at risk.'"[38]

As I discuss further in chapter 4, Americans often unquestionably embrace the notion that teen sexual activity is especially risky because it fits with current notions of teen vulnerability, inability to navigate risks, and irresponsibility. Relying on the danger discourse, parents are clearly frightened of the risks that sex poses to their children. They spoke poignantly of their fears about teen pregnancy and about lifelong and life-threatening sexually transmitted infections, often implying that these outcomes are inevitable when teenagers are "sexually active." These understandings play a powerful role in parents' desire to see their own children as asexual and therefore safe from the dangerous consequences of sex.

Other People's Children

That parents have a difficult time recognizing their children as sexual subjects became especially clear to me when I interviewed parents who are caring not just for their own children but for stepchildren, nieces, and nephews (six parents interviewed were in this category). Parents who are currently raising or taking care of children other than their own, or who have done so in the past, perceived these teens as much more sexual than their own children. Kelly's 16-year-old niece, for example, recently lived with Kelly and her two teenage sons for six months. During that time, Kelly said,

> I realized that my boys are pretty good, and I have no major complaints about how they act. Because this girl, she was very openly sexual and all she could think about was the next time she got to go see this guy. I would let the guy come in [her bedroom] and study with the door open. And it would get quiet and I would go in to check and she would actually be on top of him, kissing him. I was like, "Uh-oh. No. You go home. That was a test and you failed. Get out."

Kelly thinks that, in general, "kids are moving too fast these days." By contrast, her sons are not "even interested in acting like that. They have higher goals for themselves." Like Portia who has trouble viewing her good son as a sexual subject because she views sexual activity as deviant, Kelly separates her ostensibly nonsexual sons from other teenagers, such as her niece, who are "openly sexual." She thinks the primary difference is that her sons are goal oriented and will not be sidetracked by sexual activity. Kelly also indicated that her sons are more mature than she perceives other teenagers to be, including her niece. Although many parents described their teen children as immature relative to the children's peers (particularly sexually immature), a few, like Kelly, viewed their teens as mature for their age. Yet even these parents did not necessarily think that their children's maturity extended to sexual maturity and, instead, painted a picture of their mature teenagers as responsible, focused on future goals, academically driven, and capable of withstanding peer pressure.

Parents tended to attribute the problems and sexualized behavior of these non-biological children to a lack of proper adult guidance and supervision. Kim, who is caring for her 12-year-old niece in addition to her own two children, believes that the bad decisions her niece regularly makes, such as wearing "something that violates the [school] dress code and telling lies," stems from her lack of an authority figure: "My mother had [custody of] her from the time she was about six or seven years old and our parenting styles were a little bit different. So when I got custody of her, she had a couple of habits that I do not like." Kim worries that, unless she can redirect her niece's behavior, "it's only a matter of time before she starts acting out, you know, sexually."

Other parents also commented on children not necessarily under their care but who, they thought, exhibited problematic sexual behavior resulting from their upbringing. For example, Charles and Fern, a married couple I interviewed together, told me that five years ago, when they were living in the Caribbean and their 14-year-old daughter was 9, "she was accosted by a boy—a 9-year-old boy—[who] exposed himself to her and she came and told us." Charles and Fern made sense of this boy's decision to expose himself to their daughter in terms of his problematic family life. "[The boy] had some *major* problems," Fern explained, "where he would hit his mother and the father was very, very—he was terrified of his dad and his mother was *extremely* a religious fanatic." Charles added: "I think the problem in that relationship was the father was a heavy drinker. He owned a casino, or he ran a casino, and so he was away from the home a lot and he drank a lot and when he came home, he probably abused his wife. And so the child had some—." "There was all kind of problems in that household," Fern said, finishing Charles' sentence.

Charles and Fern's perception that their daughter was "accosted" in this incident also indicates a notion that young people *should* be asexual, and if they are not, they are predatory, or at least confused. Another illustration of this mind-set is Gail's description of her 15-year-old stepgrandson, her daughter's husband's child from a previous relationship whom she was caring for. Gail portrayed her stepgrandson's upbringing as chaotic:

> You know, he'd call crying. "What's wrong?" "Well, Mom left yesterday to go to 7–11 and she hasn't come back." And the kid's like nine years old. So they'd go get him. I mean, it was a very bad situation and because of that, he grew up with some pretty. He just doesn't have the standards that a child of his age should have already. He didn't have the stability and the guidance that he should have had. So now he's really struggling. He wants to be good. He wants to do what's right. He wants to do all this. And yet, he tends to fall into the patterns he grew up with.

Gail shared numerous stories about her stepgrandson's sexual escapades. She has seen him masturbating and, because he was doing this with his blinds open and his bedroom is at the front of the house, she suspects the neighbors have also witnessed this behavior. "So I said," Gail laughingly told me, "'You know what? If you have to, shut the blinds. Do it in private.'" She has also caught him making out with a girl who lives down the street, and found out he French kissed a girl he hardly knew on the school bus and has "fondled" girls at school.

I was startled by Gail's explicit stories about her stepgrandson. Gail was the fourth person I interviewed, and I had not heard such stories from any other parent. I asked how she knows so much about her stepgrandson's activities, and she exclaimed, "He tells me! [He will come to me and say], 'Grandma, I feel bad because, you know, I fondled this girl's butt twice today.'" Gail believes her stepgrandson discloses this information because "he's trying to be good. And he's starting to get there, that's why he comes home and tells me." She thinks her stepgrandson is confused about sexuality because he has not had proper moral guidance. Yet, as I interviewed more parents, I began to suspect that Gail is more aware of her stepgrandson's sexuality not only because she is willing to see him as a sexual being (albeit a confused one) but also because he is more willing to allow her to see him as one. Based on the stories Gail shared with me, her stepgrandson appears highly disposed to talk candidly with Gail about sexuality and about his sexual forays and confusions. Similarly, Kelly not only seems able to view her niece in sexualized terms, she also described how her niece talked openly in Kelly's presence about her sexual yearnings. The parents' stories made me wonder whether teenage children are conspiring with their parents to mutually construct a notion of their asexuality, an issue I explore in the next chapter.

Conclusion

The notions parents hold about "the sexual teen" do not square with their own understanding of their teen children. Parents instead described their teens as asexual, naïve, and immature. Several processes appear to be at play in explaining why parents think this way. Seeing one's own child as a sexual subject may be hard because it threatens to change or challenge the dynamics of the parent-child relationship, especially considering that parents view sex as properly an adult enterprise; if their children are having sex, parents told me, that means they are more grown up and the parent-child relationship is profoundly changed. Parents worry that with this shift in dynamics, their parenting might become unmoored; they would not know how to act toward their children. In addition to seeing sexual activity as an indicator of adulthood, however, parents also use financial independence as a marker of adult status. As long as a teenager is financially dependent, he or she is not an adult and is therefore not sexual. Parents said their children can be sexual when they no longer live at home and are paying their own bills (most prefer that this occurs when they are married).

Parents also equate sex with danger, and so their discussions about sex with their teenagers focus almost exclusively on the risks and negative consequences of sexual intercourse: pregnancy, sexually transmitted infections, and victimization. Parents' concerns, in this regard, are in line with the prevalent discourse of danger that dominates debates about, and depictions of, teen sexuality in the United States.[39] Based on this discourse, teen sex equals heterosexual intercourse and, by extension, danger, risk, and negative consequences. Although the sex education teachers I observed have expanded this discourse to include oral sex, they did so to point out that it is just as dangerous as sexual intercourse. Of course, the danger discourse of teen sexuality is about far more than the dangers of sex, as illustrated by the controversy over mandating the Gardasil vaccine for sixth-grade schoolgirls. The danger discourse is inseparable from political and cultural anxieties about teen sexuality—female sexuality in particular—as well as parental rights. This discourse, moreover, does not accurately reflect actual risk, as surveys have shown that child and teen sexual risks have been steadily declining since the 1990s.[40]

Meanwhile, parents also find it difficult to reconcile their teenagers' sexual activity with their belief that their children are innocent and good. For these parents, sexual activity suggests promiscuity and deviance, which they do not associate with their own children. Because parents are accountable for their children's behavior, they may wish to see their children as "good," not sexual, to prove that they are good parents. Indeed, parents who are caring for children they have not raised all by themselves appear more willing to perceive them as sexual subjects. These parents tend to view the sexual behavior of teenagers as signs of a poor upbringing. Within this understanding, a sexual teen is conflated with parental failure. In discussing the proper standards for raising children, I found that parents were very demanding of themselves and of other parents. Most parents blamed adolescent risk taking and problem behaviors, which, they said, includes sexual activity, on family breakdown and dysfunction. Hence parents may be better able to recognize as a sexual subject a child they have not entirely reared themselves because this does not raise the specter of their own parental failure.

It may also be difficult for parents to see their children as sexual beings because doing so can bring them into conflict with the government's child-protective agencies. One couple I interviewed was investigated by Child Protective Services (CPS) because a friend overheard them making what sounded like a sexually suggestive joke to their 11-year-old daughter. Denise's adult daughter had a similar experience. A kindergarten teacher reported Denise's daughter to CPS for possible sexual abuse because her son (Denise's grandson) used the words "penis" and "vagina" in class. Denise explained, "[My grandson] would actually tell the boys, 'You can't go in there [the bathroom]. There's a girl in there and that girl has a vagina, not a penis, so you can't go in the bathroom with her.'" Denise speculated that her grandson's teacher "figured, 'This kid knows too much, there's something going on with him.' And that's not always the case." Denise's daughter was indignant about the intrusion into her family life and parenting but willingly submitted to the CPS investigation because she wanted to be fully exonerated (which she eventually was).

In reporting Denise's daughter for possible child sexual abuse, Denise's grandson's kindergarten teacher, in addition to linking a young person's bodily knowledge to sexual abuse, may have been influenced by long-standing beliefs about black sexual deviance and hypersexuality.[41] At the time of this accusation, Denise's grandson was attending a predominantly white private elementary school where he was one of only two black students. When I asked Denise whether she thought race was a factor, she said she did not. As a result of this incident, however, Denise's daughter withdrew her son from the school.

It appears especially ironic that CPS investigated a parent because her son used anatomically correct terminology, considering that a major part of the sex education classes I observed involved teaching middle and high school students to use scientific terms for reproductive and sexual parts and processes. One middle school health teacher I spoke with, Ms. Blanton, distributes a four-page glossary of terms at the beginning of her sex education unit, and she quizzes her students daily on these terms (see Table 2.1).[42] Jessica Fields also finds in her study of school-based sex education that teachers adopt what she calls "a naturalist perspective," teaching about bodies, puberty, and sex just as they would teach any other scientific topic, such as human digestion or brain functioning.[43] Fields notes that teachers do so in part to protect themselves from charges of inappropriate teaching. Yet ironically, parents who teach and encourage their children to use these terms may be deemed potential child sex abusers precisely because their children are being equipped at an early age with this knowledge.

Although I was outraged when I heard stories from parents about being reported to CPS, after interviewing Charles I became aware that I too held an entrenched belief that parents should not view their children as sexual beings. During his interview, Charles described his 14-year-old daughter's blossoming young body as curvaceous, beautiful and "entertaining." My initial reaction to Charles' comments was one of shock and disgust, and I left the interview feeling remarkably disquieted. In line with dominant cultural assumptions, I construed Charles' acknowledgement of his daughter's attractiveness as a sign of possible child sexual abuse. It was only in reflection that I realized that I equated this father's comments with perversion and possible abuse rather than consider them a celebration of his daughter's development as a young woman.

Another aspect of the culture of sexual fear is therefore that parents who acknowledge their children as sexually attractive or whose children speak knowledgably about sex may face societal condemnation. Just as parents might feel uneasy seeing their children as sexual subjects, others in society might feel the same way about parents who acknowledge or celebrate their children's sexuality. This may be especially so for fathers, low-income parents, and parents of color who are typically already marked as overly sexual.[44] Thus in the current social climate, parents not only have a personal psychological investment in, but society also tacitly rewards them for, viewing their children as asexual.

Table 2.1. Ms. Blanton's Glossary of Sexual and Reproductive Terms

Amenorrhea: (a-men-o-re´a) Absence of menstrual periods.

Anus: (a´-nus) The outlet of the rectum (the lower part of the large intestine), through which solid waste leaves the body.

Areola: (a-re-o-la) The darker pigmented area surrounding the nipple.

Birth canal: Another term for vagina; the passage a fetus travels through during birth.

Bladder: The organ that holds urine, liquid body waste.

Bloating: Swollen beyond normal size due to retaining of fluid.

Breast buds: The first stage of breast development during puberty; small swellings directly underneath the nipple.

Cardiovascular: (car-de-o-vas´-cu-lar) Relating to the heart and blood vessels.

Cervix: (cer´-vix) The neck of the uterus, which protrudes into the vagina, and that has a small opening (about the size of a pencil point), through which menstrual fluid escapes.

Chromosome: (kro´-mo-som) A structure in the nucleus of a cell that transmits genetic information.

Cirumcision: (sur-kum-si´shun) Surgical removal of all or part of the foreskin of the penis.

Clitoris: (klit´or-ris) A small sensitive organ of erectile tissue located above the opening to the vagina, which responds to stimulation.

Corpus Luteum: (kor-pus lu´ti-um) A small yellow structure that develops within a ruptured ovarian follicle, and secretes progesterone.

Dysmenorrhea: (dis-men-o-re´a) Painful menstrual cramps.

Ejaculation: (e-jak-u-la´shun) Forceful sending out of seminal fluid from the penis.

Embryo: (em´bri-o) A name given to a fertilized ovum, from the second through the eighth week of development.

Endocrine gland: (en´do-krin) An organ that manufactures hormones and sends them out into the bloodstream.

Endometrium: (en-do-me´-tri-um) The mucous membrane lining the inner surface of the uterus.

Epididymis: (ep-i-did´-i-mis) A coiled tube through which sperm exit the testes.

Erectile tissue: (e-rek´til) Spongy tissue containing many blood vessels; it becomes rigid and erect when filled with blood.

Erection: (e-rek´shun) Hardening of the penis.

Estrogen: (es´tro-gen) Female sex hormone produced by the ovaries.

Excretory system: (eks´kre-tor-e) Organs that eliminate waste from the body.

Fallopian tubes: (fa-lo´pi-an) Tubes that convey the female sex cell (egg, or ovum) from the ovary to the uterus.

Fertilization: (fer-til-iz-a´-shun) Union of the ovum (female egg) with the sperm (male sex cell).

Fetus: (fe´tus) An infant developing in the uterus, from the third month to birth.

Flaccid: The relaxed state of the penis.

Follicle Stimulating Hormone: (foll´i-kel) The pituitary hormone that stimulates development of ovarian follicles.

Follicle: (foll´i-kel) A sphere-shaped structure in the ovary, made up of an immature egg and a surrounding layer of cells.

Foreskin: Loose skin covering the end of the penis.

Genitals: (gen´it-als) Reproductive organs.

Glans: The end, or head, of the penis.

Graafian follicle: (graf´-e-an foll´-i-kel) A nearly mature ovum, or egg, contained in a layer of cells, which ruptures when ovulation takes place.

Growth spurt: A rapid increase in height and weight, which typically occurs during puberty.

Heredity: The passing of characteristics from parents to child.

Hormones: Special chemicals secreted by endocrine glands, which cause changes in specific areas of the body.

Hymen: A fold of flexible membrane that partially covers the vaginal opening.

Hypothalamus: (hi-po-thal´(a)-mus) A part of the brain that, among other functions, secretes chemicals that controls the activity of the pituitary gland.

Labia (majora and minora): (la´bi´a ma-jor´ra, mi-nor´a) Two folds of fatty tissue that lie on either side of, and partially cover, the vaginal opening.

Luekorrhea: (lu´ko-ri-a) A thick whitish vaginal discharge.

Luteinizing Hormone: (lu´ten-i-zing) Pituitary hormone that stimulates estrogen secretion, ovulation, and forma-tion of the corpus luteum.

Membrane: A thin, soft, pliable layer of body tissue.

Menarche: (men´ark) The first menstrual period.

Menopause: (men´o-pawz) The stage at which menstrual activity ends.

Menstrual Cycle: The period of time measured from the beginning of menstruation (a period), through the series of regularly occurring changes in the ovaries and uterus, until the beginning of the next menstrual period.

Menstruation: (men-stru-a´-shun) The monthly discharge of blood and cells coming from the lining of the uterus.

Nocturnal Emission: (nok-turn´al e-mi´shun) The passing of semen from the urethra during sleep; a wet dream.

Nucleus: (nu´kle-us) The part of a cell that controls its functions and that holds the genetic material.

Ovary: (o´va-re) One of a pair of female reproductive glands, which hold and develop eggs and produce estrogen and progesterone.

Ovulation: (ov-u-la´-shun) The period release of a mature egg from an ovary.

Ovum: (o´vum) A female sex cell, or egg. (Plural: ova)

Penis: The male reproductive organ involved in sexual intercourse and elimination of urine.

Pituitary Gland: (pi-too´i-ta-re) An endocrine gland attached to the base of the brain, which secretes hormones.

Placenta: (pla-sen´ta) The spongy structure that develops in the uterus during pregnancy, through which the fetus derives nourishment.

Pregnancy: The condition of carrying a developing embryo in the uterus.

Premenstrual Syndrome: (pre-men´stru-al) Symptoms such as tension, anxiety, breast tenderness, and bloating, which begin several days prior to the onset of menstruation, and subside when menstruation begins.

Progesterone: (pro´jes-ter-one) A hormone that is involved with the menstrual cycle and pregnancy.

Prostaglandins: (pros´ta-glan-dinz) A group of chemicals produced in the uterus, which tend to stimulate contractions and may cause cramps.

Prostate gland: (pros´tat) A gland near the male bladder and urethra, which secretes a thin fluid that is part of semen.

Puberty: (pyu´ber-te) The period of life during which an individual becomes capable of reproduction.

Pubic hair: Hair over the pubic bone, which appears at the onset of sexual maturity.

Reproduction: The process of conceiving and bearing children.

Scrotum: (sko´tum) The pouch of skin behind the penis that holds the testes.

Secretion: (se-kre´shun) The process by which glands release certain materials into the bloodstream.

Semen: (se´men) A thick fluid, containing a mixture of glandular secretions and sperm cells, that is discharged from the penis during ejaculation.

Seminal vesicle: (sem´i-nal ves´i-kel) One of two glands located behind the male bladder, which secrete a fluid that forms part of semen.

Sexual Intercourse: The erect penis of the male entering the vagina of the female.

Sperm: Mature male sex cell.

Staphylococcus aureus bacteria: (staf(y)-lo-kok´us aw´re-us) The type of germ believed to cause Toxic Shock Syndrome (TSS).

Testis (Testicle): (tes´tis; tes´tik-el) One of two male reproductive glands, which produce sperm and the hormone testosterone. (Plural: testes)

Testosterone: (tes-tos´ter-on) A male sex hormone, which causes the development of secondary sexual characteristics.

Toxic Shock Syndrome (TSS): A rare, but potentially serious disease that has been associated with tampon use. TSS is believed to be caused by toxin-producing strains of the Staphylococcus aureus bacterium. The warning signs of TSS are: sudden fever of 102° F or more, vomiting, diarrhea, muscle aches, a rash that looks like sunburn, dizziness and fainting, or near fainting, when standing up.

Toxin: A poisonous substance that may be produced by bacteria.

Umbilical cord: (um-bil´-ik-el) The attachment connecting the fetus with the placenta.

Urethra: (u-re´-thra) A canal that carries urine from the bladder to the urinary opening. In males, the urethra is also the passageway for semen.

Urination: The act of eliminating urine, liquid waste, from the body.

Uterus: (U-ter-us) The small, hollow muscular female organ where the embryo and fetus is held and nourished, from the time the egg is implanted until the birth of the fetus.

Vagina: (va-ji´-na) The canal that forms the passageway from the uterus to the outside of the body.

Vaginal Discharge: A normal white or yellowish fluid (leukorrhea) from the cervical canal or vagina.

Vas deferens: (vas def´e-renz) A thin tube that transports sperm from the testis to the urethra.

Virgin: A person who has not had sexual intercourse.

Vulva: (vul´va) The external female genitalia, including the labia, clitoris, and vaginal opening.

Zygote: (zi´got) A cell produced by the union of a sperm and egg.

3

Negotiating the Erotic

When Parents and Teens Talk about Sex

When Gina—an affluent mother of three children—introduced me to her 19-year-old son Matthew, who had recently finished his first year of college, Matthew asked me to start my tape recorder. He wanted it on the record that "parents should never, *ever* talk to their kids about sex." As an example, he told me about his friend who "jumped out of the car when his mom popped the question."

> MATTHEW: He was in a moving car with his mom when she asked him—she's like, "I think it's time to talk to you about sex." And he just unbuckled, opened, and tucked, and rolled out of the car [laughs].
> SINIKKA: How old was he?
> MATTHEW: He was in the ninth grade. They were in the car together. He just literally was like, nuh uh.
> SINIKKA: So did you have the same reaction when your mom [brought up the subject]?
> GINA: He didn't want to talk about it.

MATTHEW: We don't go there. Why would you want to go there? I don't.
That's why I have school. That's what school teaches you. I don't need
to learn it from you.

GINA: Well, she's wondering if school taught you well. Did you get the information you needed there?

MATTHEW: Use a condom?!

GINA: Well, that's right. Well, we've talked to him.

MATTHEW: No we haven't.

GINA: I have talked to him.

MATTHEW: I don't listen. I just like la la la [holds his hands over his ears].

SINIKKA: You don't want to hear it from your mom?

MATTHEW: Oh yeah!

GINA: He thinks it's creepy from his mom. You don't want to even think that
your parents have sex. You know. That is the creepiest.

MATTHEW: I don't want to go there. Parents and sex talks just don't—
shouldn't ever happen. Ever!

Matthew's story of his friend hurtling himself from a moving car to avoid
discussing sex with his mother calls to mind an urban legend—it suggests
that teen boys generally are uncomfortable talking about sex with their
mothers and that a male teenage culture reinforces this dynamic. Toward the
end of our conversation, however, Matthew mentioned a friend who talked
to both his parents about his difficulties getting an erection:

GINA: Really! But you would tell us if that happened.

MATTHEW: No! No way! That's so weird!

GINA: Oh that's wrong because you had something going on and you asked
[your stepfather] about it.

MATTHEW: Well, yeah, but that's the man-to-man thing. He's like not techni-
cally my dad.

When I began this project I expected parents to tell me what they teach
their teens about sex, and although I learned a great deal about this, I also
discovered that these conversations are much more complicated than I had
anticipated. My initial thinking about parent-teen sex talk had been shaped
by popular and academic depictions of "the talk," which usually assume that
parents hold all the power and children are largely powerless. In this model,
parents are the active agents who either provide or neglect to provide sexual
knowledge. But this overlooks the fact that family sexual communication
involves interactions *between* parents and children, and may involve complex

negotiations over what is said and how it is said. Children are not passive recipients of information: "Parental power is always negotiated and routinely resisted by children and adolescents,"[1] as the above exchange illustrates.

Following the idea that family life is a collaborative venture, I believe that parental power, although considerable, is not absolute.[2] Rather than viewing power as hierarchical and repressive, I see it as relational and productive, and continually negotiated.[3] Whether it is giggling and acting immature, squirming and avoiding eye contact, or storming out of the room (or rolling out of the car), the parents I interviewed perceived their teenagers as actively resisting the parents' attempts to talk about sex. The perception of their children's resistant and evasive measures in turn supports the parents' notion that their teen children are young, naïve, and asexual. Parents often used examples of their teens' negative reactions to conversations about sex as evidence that their teen children "aren't there yet"—meaning they are not old enough to be thinking or talking about sexuality and are certainly not old enough to be having sex.

Because I did not interview teenagers, and, aside from Gina and Matthew, did not observe parents and teens talking about sex, I try to make it clear throughout this chapter that descriptions of any teenager's behavior does not refer to actual actions but rather to the parents' *perceptions* and *interpretations* of their actions. Parents' perceptions of their children matter, because they influence how and whether they talk to their teens about sex and also provide insight into how parents think about teenagers and sexuality. Parents' descriptions of conversations with their teen children about sex also expose how dominant ideas about adolescence, gender, and sexuality shape these interactions. Throughout our conversation above, for example, Matthew might be viewed as "doing gender"[4] by aligning himself with men and agentic sexuality ("use a condom") and repudiating his mother's attempts to talk with him about sex ("I don't listen"). Although he rejects his mother as a source of information about sexuality, conversations with his stepfather are appropriate because they are "man to man," implying that sex talk with a biological parent (especially a mother) is not only embarrassing but also emasculating. Indeed, this chapter demonstrates that, along with other currents flowing around parent-teen interactions, gender plays a central role in the dynamics of family conversations about sex.

Teen Resistance to Sex Talk

When I asked Rosalia how her daughters react when she tries to talk to them about sex, she replied, "They just don't want me to be telling them about this, any of it. They don't want to hear it." Mothers, especially, reported that their teenagers strongly resisted, even protested, such conversations perhaps because mothers are more likely than fathers to initiate these talks.[5] But overall both mothers and fathers who have introduced the subject of sex with their children said that they reacted with embarrassment and irritation. Shawna reported that when she talks to her 15-year-old son about sex, he "gets embarrassed and doesn't want to hear about it from me." Kirk's son, who is nearly 15, turns red when Kirk brings up sex. Charlene said that when she tried to talk about sex with her 15- and 17-year-old daughters they said, "No, you did not just say that!"

Some parents perceive their teenagers' negative attitudes toward talking about sex in developmental terms. Parents routinely told me that adolescence is a time when teens naturally withdraw from their parents—a widely held belief in America. Sharon, for example, described her 16-year-old daughter as moody and withdrawn, but she sees this as "typical." "[My daughter] says: 'You don't know anything about my life.' And yet I can say, 'Tell me about your school day.' [And she will reply], 'It was fine.' You know what I mean? A lot of that is typical [teenage behavior]." Nicole said that her 16-year-old son and 14-year-old daughter have acquired a know-it-all attitude:

> Because they weren't that a way [when they were younger]. No. They actually listened to what I had to say and they didn't think everything I said was crap [laughs]. Maybe it's because they did get older, but [now] if I tell them anything that I've been through, [they say], "No Mom, that's not how it goes!"

Nicole speculated that her children now reject her advice partly because she divorced their dad two years ago, but she also thinks that it is a natural part of adolescent development.

Parents hope that by the time adolescence arrives they will have established open communication that will allow their teenagers to come to them with questions about dating, sexuality, and their bodies. But these parents simultaneously believe that adolescence is the most difficult time for children, especially sons, to talk to their parents. Josephina thinks she has a "pretty good relationship" with her 14-year-old son but added, "Of course, with all the troubles that adolescents imply." When I asked Josefina about the changes she has seen in her son during his adolescence, she said:

> In my son's case, he's not as willing to ask certain questions. Certain questions he asks very directly, especially those that are technically oriented.

But those more about, what I'm going to feel? Or why do I feel this way? It's a little bit harder for him to approach even though I'm very open with him.

Josefina infers that her son has difficulty answering questions about his feelings because these are hard emotions for him to experience. She sees adolescence as a tumultuous time and believes that her son is confused by his bodily responses and emotions. Like Josefina, parents routinely depicted adolescence as a time when young people, overcome by raging hormones, are unable to conduct themselves rationally or responsibly. Parents such as Josefina thus understand their teens' resistance to sex talk based in large part on their beliefs about teenage development. In the United States adolescents are expected to be irritable, hormonally ruled, and draw away from their parents. Resisting family sex talk thus becomes part and parcel of being a teenager.

Mothers and Sons Talk about Sex

Despite perceiving both sons and daughters as mortified about and resistant to family sex talk, parents described this resistance as different for sons than for daughters. Parents tended to minimize and even infantilize their daughters' resistance. Sylvia, for example, said that her 14-year-old daughter did not handle discussions about sex well: "My little one giggles and gets real immature about it, so we'll just kind of let it go." This suggests that Sylvia views her daughter's reaction to the conversation as non-threatening, even cute. This perception was consistent with other parents' depictions of their daughters' resistance to family sex talk.

In contrast, mothers, in particular, described their sons' resistance as heightened opposition and defiance. Mothers gave the impression that they are shut out, discredited, and sometimes intimidated by their teen sons when the subject of sex arises; the mothers in turn back off and let their sons come to them when they have questions, whereas they urge their daughters to talk. Because mothers indicated extremely fraught and complex gender dynamics around the interactions with their sons, I focus here only on the mothers I interviewed who have teenage sons.[6]

Mothers of sons insisted that boys especially fall silent when given information that they are not ready or willing to handle, and saw this as a male trait. Kate, who described her 14-year-old son as "a man of very few words," explained that, because her son is reticent "to talk about just about anything," she leaves him alone and lets him come to her with questions about sex: "If [my son] asks me a question, I'll tell him and I'm honest. Other than that, I just leave him alone. I have to." She continued:

I have to. I really have to, yeah, because I don't go in his room. I don't search though his stuff. His privacy, it just *has* to be honored. So I just kind of let him approach me. Well, with him not being talkative, I can't just say, "Hey, we need to talk about birth control!" He'll just shut down [*laughs*].

Kate's discussion of the importance of honoring her son's privacy has an edge to it, as though she is afraid of her son's reaction if she violates his space. Rather than view her son's perceived reticence to talk as problematic, however, Kate accepts it as part of a larger truth about the characteristics of boys and men—namely, that men are stoical and independent, not passive or receptive—and this shapes her interpretation of her teenage son's behavior.[7] Similarly Penny, who has two sons aged 17 and 16, said that they "freeze up" when she attempts to talk to them about sex. She explained their reaction: "They're boys, and guys in general, I think, are just less receptive to being told stuff." To make sense of her sons' behavior, Penny, like Kate, relies on a notion of masculinity as active, not passive.

Some mothers think that sons need to be more independent of their mothers than daughters do. Ruth, for example, now a single parent after her divorce a few years ago, worried about "over-mothering" her 16-year-old son:

I remember reading this book that I thought was really interesting about how to create a scenario where your son is acknowledged as different than being female. Women have a tendency, I think, to over-mother. And in this book it was talking about over-mothering and how, sometimes, your son might rebel against over-mothering. And instead, you just have to put down some expectations about what you expect from your son and let him do it on his own time.

Ruth implemented the strategies suggested in the book she read about over-mothering and feels it has been a great success, giving her son more leeway and less structure. Her 14-year-old daughter, however, has expressed resentment, Ruth told me, "that I don't demand things of [her brother] at the same pace that I do of her." As Ruth's daughter observes, Ruth's strategy maintains a gender ideology of natural sex differences that buttresses male dominance.[8] According to this ideology, boys and men need autonomy and do not respond well to being told what to do and when to do it.

Ruth's concern about over-mothering also mirrors the prominent theme in parenting texts and popular discourses that dominant, overprotective mothers emasculate their sons.[9] This "expert" advice, coupled with cultural anxieties around masculinity, sexuality, and family structure—for example, mothers are often considered unable to adequately raise masculine sons on their own[10]—may encourage mothers to give boys more autonomy and less overall direction. In fact, some research suggests that boys receive less information about sex from their parents than girls do.[11] The mothers' accounts suggest that mothers, perhaps especially single mothers, may limit their sexual lessons to avoid impinging on their sons' development of normative masculine identities (which would in turn reflect poorly on the mothers' ability to produce masculine sons).

Mothers' understandings of their sons' communication needs are based not simply on the ideas they hold about masculinity, however, they are also shaped by their embodied interactions. Some mothers, especially mothers of older boys, described their sons as aggressive and intimidating in response to the mothers' attempts to talk about sex. Several of these mothers said that their sons have no significant male figure in their lives, and so the mothers assume the role of talking with their sons about sex. Rebecca, whose husband has been incarcerated for the past seven years, said she has been unable to talk to her 19-year-old son about sex because "he just shuts me out." Single mother Nicole, who said her 16-year-old son has been "real physically aggressive with me as far as wanting to push and be controlling" to gain status as "the man in the house," similarly finds it difficult to talk with her son about sex: "I did [ask] him at one point, 'Are you having [sex]?' He's like, 'Moommm!' You know, that was it. It wasn't no conversation. It was nothing. It was just, 'Moommm.'" Apparently Nicole's perception of her son's aggravation at this question, coupled with his physical aggression toward her in his bid to become "the man of the house," shut down the conversation before it even began.[12] Other mothers said that they pass the responsibility of talking about sex on to their male partners or their sons' fathers. Robin said her 14-year-old son brushes her off, sometimes hostilely, when she tries to talk with him: "I can have my feelings hurt by my youngest son in particular. I have times where I think he just doesn't like me. He doesn't want to talk to me about anything. He talks to his dad." This suggests that all mothers of sons may experience similar behavior when it comes to talking to their sons about sex.

Some mothers reported a sense that their sons devalue them as women and mothers. Kate feels that, because she is a mother, her 14-year-old son discredits the extent to which she knows anything and thus dismisses her feedback. On the few occasions when she has tried to give her son advice, "[My son will say] 'Oh, you're trying to be a mom again.'" Charlene, whose ex-husband is no longer involved in his children's lives, said that her 19-year-old son often rejects her attempts to discuss anything with him:

When things are bothering him, he won't say. And you will ask, "What's the matter with you?" "Nuthin'" You talk to him about your day or something, he likes to turn his back. He *loves* to do that. And if he's in one of his little moods, then he'll try to raise up like his voice or something. Because sometimes he gets like, "No, I'm gone. I'm a man."

Not only is Charlene's son unwilling to talk to her at times, but she hints here that he responds to her queries with aggression. On another occasion he threatened physical violence: "He just raised up like, 'Yeah, you're gonna be calling your brothers, 'cause you're gonna be going to the hospital.'" Although Charlene's story was more extreme than most, other mothers also recalled incidents where they felt threatened by their son's behavior, such as the son slamming a door, standing up abruptly and knocking over the chair, or, in one instance, punching a hole in the wall. All these mothers described their sons as physically intimidating. Charlene noted that on these occasions her son asserts his masculinity—declaring "I'm a man"—as a way of explaining why he should not have to talk or listen to her which, in itself, explicitly repudiates and devalues femininity. Yet Charlene sometimes stands up to her son, using "reverse psychology." If her son comes to her and wants to talk or asks for help, she does not respond: "[I tell him]: 'You didn't have an answer for me when I just tried to ask you what was wrong with you.' So sometimes I don't answer."

Obviously some mothers have a difficult time talking with their sons about sex, but their descriptions also clearly indicate that these interactions, and the mothers' perceptions of them, are profoundly influenced by dominant ideas about gender. In this context, where masculinity is associated with power, independence, and aggression and femininity is devalued, so-called experts advise mothers against "over-mothering" their sons. These inequities and discourses become naturalized and can become the conventional ways individuals conduct their lives and make sense of their own and others' actions. Yet the ideas mothers hold about masculinity, mothering, and "the talk" are not inevitable. We can and should think about ways to resist and challenge these notions—such as decoupling the links between masculinity, independence, and aggressive behavior and validating women's authority, in general, and mothers' authority with sons in particular. Challenging gender inequality will in turn make it easier for mother to talk with their sons about sex.

The Emotions of Family Sex Talk

Although parents consistently said that their teens resisted family sex talk, some also "confessed" that they, too, were not very enthusiastic about having these conversations, which call up awkward and uncomfortable feelings. The notion that family sex talk is embarrassing for all involved is not new—considerable research reports this finding—and, in most popular depictions, "sex education is uncomfortable and irrelevant, and the best anyone can do is to shake their heads at the silliness of it."[13] Yet my conversation with Gina and her son Matthew, related at the beginning of this chapter, led me to think that such difficulties might arise partly because these conversations evoke the specter of sexual intimacy. Matthew's choice of words in describing his friend's mother's attempt to talk about sex is illuminating. The way that Matthew put it—his friend's mom "popped the question," a phrase traditionally describing a marriage proposal—suggests that mothers asking sons to talk about sex introduces an apparently unwelcome sense of intimacy. Similarly Gina said, "You don't want to even think that your parents have sex. You know. *That* is the creepiest."

Just as parents have a difficult time viewing their children as sexual subjects, then, some suspect that their children are reluctant to see their *parents* as sexual beings and that family sex talks instigate these thoughts. Ruth, for example, said that she may have talked to her son and daughter, now 16 and 14 respectively, about the pleasure that can come from sexual activity when they were younger, but such conversations have become more difficult as they have gotten older:

> I think I did [talk about pleasure] when they were younger. And now it's a little bit more complicated. Even though I've been open with them, as kids they still don't want to know that I'm having sex. I think they still think it's something that their parents don't do really all that much. So even though my boyfriend spends the night a lot, they just don't want to think about the fact that we're sexual together. I think it brings it up when I talk about pleasure. It brings up—Eewww, are you doing that [*laughs*]?!

Meanwhile, parents themselves do not appear comfortable presenting themselves to their children as sexual subjects. They frequently said, for example, that their sex lives should remain private from their children. When Greg's oldest stepdaughter was in fourth or fifth grade, she overheard Greg and his wife having sex; the next day the stepdaughter told them "that she 'heard us sexing.'" I asked Greg how he responded to this. He replied, "I about died! Changed the subject. Next!"

Greg is still uncomfortable with the thought that his two teen stepdaughters might inadvertently see or hear their parents having sex. In fact, he prefers his previous home to the house the family now lives in because the former house provided more of a buffer zone between the master bedroom and the children's bedrooms: "The kids' rooms were way down on that end. There was a bathroom and a living room and a dining room and all that between our rooms. So that was nice." Similarly Josefina would rather not discuss her sex life with her 14-year-old son. Yet, unlike other parents who said their children do not want to hear about their parents' sex lives, Josefina's son has asked her personal questions: "Sometimes he dares to ask me about my own sexual life and that's where I said, 'Well, this is a very private matter. Let's not do it that way!' [*laughs*]."

Thus, despite hoping that their children will come to them to talk about sex, parents think it is inappropriate, unnecessary, or too uncomfortable to discuss their own sex lives with their children. They may feel that sexual disclosure makes people vulnerable; one consequence of self-disclosure is that it diminishes one's power.[14] By refusing to reveal aspects of their sex lives, parents maintain their authority and demarcate adult-child boundaries. By drawing boundaries around their own complex sex lives, they also maintain a good sex/bad sex dichotomy. Good sex is implicitly private and the terrain of adults; bad sex is public and the terrain of adolescents (and sexual deviants).

But as I talked to the parents, I came to think that their belief that their children are "grossed out" (Delores) when discussing sex may also stem from their own sense of sexual shame. Shame is a prevalent and, many argue, necessary aspect of social life that calls up feelings of rejection, embarrassment, and failure. "It is the 'social emotion' that arises from the 'monitoring of one's own actions by viewing one's self from the standpoint of others.'"[15] When feeling ashamed, individuals believe that others disapprove of them. With its underpinnings in Christianity, sexual shame has historically dominated American culture.[16] The parents I spoke with grew up "in a culture where compulsory heterosexuality and anti-sex attitudes reigned supreme";[17] indeed, they were highly critical of *their* parents' discussions of sex. Many recalled parents who never spoke about sex or encouraged negative and shame-filled understandings of sexuality. Yet, although parents criticized their parents' sexual lessons, these lessons, along with larger discourses of sexuality, constitute part of their emotional landscape and experiences.

More recently sociologist Arlene Stein observes that conservative groups have "mobilized to bring back sexual shame."[18] Joycelyn Elders, for example, was most famously shamed out of her position as Surgeon General in the Clinton administration in 1994 for suggesting that masturbation should be taught in sex education as a normal aspect of human sexuality. Dominant understandings of sex as shameful also partly explain the success of the strategies adopted by the conservative right in their movement against comprehensive sex education. Janice Irvine argues in her study of recent national debates over sex education that "much of the symbolic power of aversive rhetorics derives from the stigma historically attached to sex. Conservatives have drawn on the tenacious power of sexual shame and fear to galvanize residents to oppose comprehensive programs."[19]

Conservative opponents similarly invoked sexual shame to attack Barack Obama during the 2004 Senate election in Illinois and the 2008 presidential election for supporting school-based sex education beginning in kindergarten. "Learning about sex before learning how to read?" ominously intoned a John McCain campaign advertisement condemning Obama for supporting a bill introduced in the Illinois Legislature in 2003 that would have provided "age and developmentally appropriate" sex education starting in kindergarten and extending through high school.[20] Although Obama went on to win both elections, public figures who talk about sexuality in relation to youth all too often face shaming tactics, such as accusations of corrupting children's sexual innocence.[21]

Yet shame may also motivate conservative activists' fervor. Many of the anti-gay activists that Stein interviewed engaged in behaviors characteristic of shame, such as: speaking very rapidly and without cessation, rambling and getting off topic, and apologizing regularly.[22] I detected similar types of behavior among the parents when discussing the topic of sex. Some became flushed, or red in the face. A few confessed complete ignorance about aspects of sexuality and apologized for their lack of knowledge or for rambling. Some spoke faster and in a clipped way, as though they wanted to rush through the discussion. Most either stumbled over or avoided using words such as "sex" and "sexuality" and used euphemisms including "private parts," "down there," and "pee-pee," among others, referring to external genitalia. To be sure, I may have unwittingly contributed to the shame some parents seemed to feel. Even though I did my best to put parents at ease, I sometimes experienced embarrassment myself during the interviews especially when asking parents about their own sexual experiences. Parents may have sensed my feeling that asking people to talk about their sex lives is shameful, and this may have produced their responses in the interviews.[23]

Shame seems accordingly to be one of the "feeling rules" that govern talking about sex[24]—rules involving social cues and cultural norms about how an individual *should* feel in any given interaction or context. Rebecca, for example, who has been unable to talk to her 19-year-old son about sex because "he just shuts me out," laughingly said that she was so embarrassed when she found her son and his girlfriend in her apartment with tousled hair a year ago, "I was like, 'Can I get you guys a drink?' I just felt kinda funny around them, you know?" Rose is uncomfortable talking about sex not only with her children but also with close family members: "Some people don't care if they talk about sex, but I don't talk about sex with everybody I know. I mean, I don't even talk about it with my sister—who's my closest friend rela-tive—just because it's a private thing." Rose said that her discomfort around sex talk stems from her belief that it is a violation of the "private" nature of sex. She also establishes her adherence to this privacy mandate, thereby dif-ferentiating herself from Others who bring sex into the public realm.

These emotional norms can therefore reproduce social inequality by establishing affective expectations that regulate thought and emotion and that identify Others who do not perform the expected, culturally legitimated affect.[25] An individual parent or child who has no sexual shame may be deemed suspect and thereby discredited or stigmatized. As Rose disapprov-ingly put it, "Some people don't care if they talk about sex." In the context of thinking and talking about sexuality, parents may experience and establish affective and discursive boundaries around "what can be said, how it can be said, and who can say what to whom."[26] Even parents who want to have open conversations about sex with their children may signal otherwise through their emotional comportment.[27]

Who's Talking, Who's Listening? Schisms in Parents' and Teens' Reports of Family Sex Talk

The conversation I had with Gina and her 19-year-old son Matthew also revealed inconsistency between teens' and their parents' understandings and recollections of sex talks at home. Teenagers and parents do not always agree on how much talk about sexuality goes on in the home.[28] After Matthew left, Gina refuted his assertion that they have never talked about sex: "It's open communication, and so even though he says he doesn't talk about it him-self, we've talked about it. He just doesn't—the concept of it, when forced to admit it, I don't think he wants to admit it."

In fact, research shows that there is a significant gap between the extent to which parents and their children report having talked about sex, a gap that is greater for boys. Parents, that is, are more likely than their children, especially their sons, to report having family conversations about sex.[29] This suggests—because it is the mothers who predominantly have these talks—that mothers are not conversing with their children, particularly their sons, as much as they say they are. As we saw earlier, some mothers described encountering a great deal of hostility from their sons when they attempted to talk about sex, which consequently limited their sexual instruction.

Notably, however, this gap in family members' reports of sex talks may not simply exist because mothers are talking less often to their sons. A rare observational study of mother-teen sexual communication conducted by developmental psychologist Eva Lefkowitz concludes that mothers are just as likely to talk with their sons as with their daughters about sex, but sons are less likely to report having received this information. Lefkowitz and her colleagues speculate that "some gender differences in adolescents' reports of sexual conversations may be due to gender differences in their perceptions, rather than actual differences."[30] Simply put, boys may not be hearing their mothers' sexual lessons as well as girls are. Beth, who has a 16-year-old son, suggested that for mothers it is especially hard to talk to sons about sex— but also for sons to hear their mothers talk about sex—because it violates "a mother's role":

I'm his mother and I do motherly things. I provide lunches and I am the caregiver and I just have this role and that role doesn't encompass talking about strange things like that. And it kind of just goes against the grain of a mother's role to talk to her son about—about what he should and shouldn't do regarding sex, because you're involved and the nurturing type. I just feel like I have this role and it's very awkward for me to go outside of that role. I did it when I was a single mother but once [my husband] came around I just let him take care of it. I don't know if that's good or bad but that's what's happened. It's hard for both of us. It isn't easy for me to talk to [my son] about it and it's not easy for him to listen to me talk about it. And so sometimes I feel if that's the case then it's kind of not worth it, because you're too weirded out by it. You really don't absorb what the conversation is about.

Social roles, as Beth's comments illustrate, are highly complex patterns of living that many sociologists argue are at the crux of our individual identities.[31] Beth's assertion that a mother's role is a desexualized one may be shaped by her social position as a white, middle-class, and heterosexual woman. Some mothers, on the other hand, particularly those who fall into the "deviant" mother categories such as teen mothers and mothers on welfare, are frequently sexualized.[32] Beth's reticence to discuss sex with her son may thus stem from the notion that as a virtuous woman she should not know about "strange" things like sex. She may in turn convey great discomfort when attempting to have these conversations, influencing her son's ability to, as she put it, "absorb what the conversation is about."

Beth's statement captures the complicated gender dynamics and undercurrents in mother-son conversations about sex. Not only did Beth say that she did not enjoy having these conversations with her son, she thinks boys are so uncomfortable hearing their mothers talk about sex that, perhaps owing to the specter of sexual intimacy, they are unable to hear the conversation. This is precisely what Matthew said happens when his mom talks about sex: "I don't listen. I just like la, la, la." Teenage boys might also be motivated to actively block out their mothers' conversations about sex in order to project an image of masculinity as defined by popular ideas about manhood such as, for instance, that a "real man" does not learn about sex from his mother; he already knows all about sex.[33] Such a notion might also lead boys to deny having learned anything about sex from their mothers when talking with a friend, taking a survey, or responding in the context of an interview. As Gina put it, referring to Matthew's adamant denial of having talked with her about sex: "We've talked about it. He just doesn't—I don't think he wants to admit it." A boy's investment in masculinity may thus shape not only his recollection of family sex talk but also his willingness to acknowledge that these conversations even occurred and that he learned something from them.

Using School-Based Sex Education to Deflect Family Sex Talk

A common strand in all the interviews is that teenagers dismiss their parents' attempts to talk about sex by arguing that they have learned all they need to know in school. Although parents find sex education useful for sparking conversation about sex at home, they also said that, once children attend sex education classes, they use that experience to reject their parents' attempts to teach them about sex. This is typified by Greg's description of how his 18- and 17-year-old stepdaughters' react whenever he and his wife attempt to generate a family discussion about sex: "[They say] 'I know, I know, we learned all that in school already!'"

Rosalia is exasperated by her daughters' resistance to her attempts to talk about their bodies, relationships, or sexuality: "When I give [my daughters] advice they always tell me they already know because they've taken that class in school. But it's just too much to learn; the class just isn't going to do it. Even at my age, I'm learning." As Teresa put it, describing her attempts to talk to her 14-year-old son, "He'll say, 'Well, they teach all this at school.'"

Sex education teachers and presenters may contribute to this dynamic. In the sex education classes I observed, teachers and presenters frequently referred to parents as uninformed about sexual issues. This characterization may tacitly encourage young people to reject their parents' advice. Sex education teachers also typically described parents as sexual conservatives. For example, Ms. Fox, the health teacher at Taylor High School, told her students that their parents did not want her to talk about birth control but that she was going to do so anyway because she cares about their health and well-being. Similarly, in trying to get the students to think about negative outcomes of sex, Mr. Marks, an abstinence-only educator and guest speaker at Eastside High School's health class, asked rhetorically: "You come home [and say], 'Hey Mom, I had sex.' What do you expect? Clapping? No!!" His implication is clearly that *all* mothers disapprove of teenage sexual activity.[34]

Some parents are relieved, however, that their children have received school-based sex education because they do not feel equipped to talk about sex. Angie is Cuban-American, having immigrated to the United States with her two children seven years ago. She has never talked openly with her 16-year-old son about puberty or sexual matters, "Because at school, you know, in the classes they explain, you know. He learn very good in that class, I think so. They like this class because they have the answers [*laughs*]." Nicole also thinks that young people are more receptive to school-based sex education than they are to family talks about sex because they are with their peers in a learning environment:

> They spend their alive hours, is what I call them, at school. So they're going to learn and listen. And for me, they've got their friends' influence in the class while they're taking that, so I think they better absorb because they've got everybody's opinion around them.

So although parents said, in other words, that their children's school-based sexual lessons sometimes stimulate conversations in the home about sex, and although some parents are thankful that their children receive this information at school, parents also consistently claimed that once their children get some form of sex education at school, they use it to reject their parents' attempts to teach them about sexuality.

Conclusion

Clearly parents perceive a great deal of resistance from their children when they try to talk about sexual issues. The parents' stories suggest that family sex talk should not be viewed as a one-way interaction—with parents talking and children listening and learning—but as a relational and emotionally dynamic interaction. Parents and teens participate together in family sex talks. When it comes to talking about sex, parents often feel shut out by their teenagers. According to parents descriptions, when they raise the topic of sex, their teen children—sons especially—react with mortification, dismay, and anger; they also downplay the extent to which they need information about sex, actively reassure their parents that they are not interested in sex, and say they have learned all they need to know in school. In addition, family sex talks appear to conjure up not only teenage sexuality but also parental sexuality. It may require both parents *and* their children to see one another as sexual beings and to claim sexual subjectivity, a difficult feat to achieve in a culture characterized by sexual fear and shame.[35]

Parents' general uneasiness about sex is important here because, although early calls for sex education were predicated on the belief that parents are unfit to teach their children about sexual issues, since the 1980s official government doctrine has been that parents are their children's best sex educators. For example, abstinence-only sex education is often described as a form of sex education that increases parents' rights: parents who do *not* want their children to learn about contraception have the right to limit their children's sexual education to the in-school, abstinence-only curriculum. Those who *do* want their children to receive contraceptive information can provide it themselves or take their children to the family doctor or a clinic, such as Planned Parenthood, to receive this information. As the parents' stories exhaustively illustrate, however, it is difficult for parents to see their children as sexual subjects and to talk to them about sex. Whether parents do or do not talk to their children about sex is also heavily influenced by a culture of sexual shame and fear, along with cultural beliefs and structural inequalities around gender, age, and family life, such as the notion that teenagers resist parental input as a characteristic of their normal development. I continue to explore these dynamics in the following chapters as I move from parents' ideas about their own teens to the beliefs they hold about teenagers in general.

4

The Hypersexual Teen

Sexy Bodies, Raging Hormones, and Irresponsibility

As I have tried to demonstrate in the preceding chapters, parents do not view their own teen children as sexually agentic, desiring subjects but instead see them as young, naïve, and not interested in talking about sex. Parents think this way partly because they believe teen sexual activity is highly dangerous, linked to deviance and lack of proper adult guidance. But parents also stated in no uncertain terms that, because of their youth and raging hormones, teenagers are incapable of handling the responsibilities of sex, a belief shared by many Americans. In thinking this way, parents create a binary between adult and adolescent sexuality: adult sexual activity is safe, responsible, and mature; adolescent sexual activity is unsafe, irresponsible, and immature. This chapter examines how and why parents come to construct this binary, focusing on how their beliefs link to larger social discourses and inequalities that establish the boundaries of "normal," acceptable sexual expression. In doing so, I am influenced by scholars who urge us to consider how categories of difference are created and their consequences for the reproduction of inequality.[1]

Within each of the four major axes of inequality in the United States—race, social class, gender, and sexuality—numerous categories define difference, including, for example, black/white, rich/poor, male/female, and gay/straight. Social theorist Patricia Hill Collins refers to this categorizing of difference as binary thinking,[2] where difference is defined in oppositional terms, such as the "opposite sex." Binaries do not simply define difference but imply relationships of superiority and inferiority. One side of the binary is culturally privileged compared to the other. Men and women are not merely seen as opposites but, historically, masculinity has been constructed as superior to femininity. Thus binaries provide ideological justification for social inequality. If one group is better than others, it deserves social rewards to remain on top. The following examines how parents construct the asexual teen in relation to the dominant discourse of sex-crazed teens and to age and developmental narratives that dichotomize adults from youth. I also consider the implications of these binary constructions for parents' ability to recognize their teens as sexual subjects and provide them with a range of information about sexuality.

Teens on the Sexual Brink

Sandra, a white mother of two teenage sons, ages 15 and 17, is certain that both her sons are virgins. Moreover, she does not think they know much about sex compared to their peers: "I may be kidding myself, but I hope they are a bit clueless still." Although Sandra is relieved because, as she sees it, her sons have remained insulated from their hypersexual peer culture, she is still concerned. She worries that her 17-year-old, a senior preparing to go off to college in a few months, might "break loose when he discovers [sex]." She is afraid that if her son experiences sex in college, he may lose his way. Sex may consume him and prevent him from making good decisions about contraception, his studies, and his future. It would have been nice, she reflected, if he had dated in high school when she was still around to remind him to use contraception and to monitor his grades: "I almost wish that he would've had a girlfriend by now, before he goes off to college, but again I have got to cut that rope and let him explore that idea."

Like Sandra, other parents also worry that if their children have sex as teens, they may experience not only various negative consequences, such as pregnancy, sexually transmitted infections, or emotional turmoil, but they may "give in" or succumb to the pleasures of sex, as if to an addictive drug, and damage their futures in the process. So despite viewing their own children as asexual, parents frequently talked about sex, especially in adolescence, as "a natural libido yearning to break free of social constraint."[3]

Parents are not alone in this regard, as discourses and images of raging hormones and sexualized youthful bodies dominate U.S. culture. For instance, during the Texas State Board of Education meetings I attended to observe local debates over sex education, one speaker after another described teenagers as potentially sexually hedonistic and in need of social constraint. They differed only on how best to control teenage sexuality; some advocated information on contraception and others argued that teens should abstain from sex until marriage or adulthood. One speaker, in attacking the abstinence-only position, compared a teenage body to "a shiny red sports car sitting in the driveway. Do you tell them they can't drive it 'til they're married? No! They're going to want to drive that car." In this sense, teens are not only naturally motivated to have sex, but the motivation stems from the signals they receive from their attractive, youthful bodies.

In *Harmful to Minors*, Judith Levine observes that, while Western culture was framing young people as innocent and without desires, "it [also] constructed a new ideal of the sexually desirable object": the innocent child.[4] Indeed, in advertising and elsewhere, youthful bodies are often portrayed as the cultural epitome of sexiness reflecting, Levine argues, adults' "erotic attraction to children."[5] Following a similar thread, Casper and Moore contend that popular television programs about pedophiles do not just depict children as vulnerable to sexual predation, they revel in children's vulnerability while playing up their desirability precisely as vulnerable innocents;[6] the implication is that their predation is not only inevitable, as in damsel-in-distress stories, it is also titillating. In these ways children are not simply deemed innocent but are constructed as profoundly desirable precisely because of this innocence. These dual associations in turn magnify adults' fears about child and teen sexuality, as well as their children's sexual safety.[7]

And make no mistake about it: parents are very fearful about their teenage children's sexual safety. As we have seen, some of these fears center on disease, pregnancy, and deviance. But parents also think about teen sexuality in terms of hormones, hedonism, and irresponsibility. Running parallel to a notion of teenagers as young and sexually naïve is a dominant understanding of teenagers as sex-crazed *because* they are teenagers. School officials, educators, media, and other adults frequently construct teens as both too young to know about sex and too sexually driven to be trusted with sexual information: teens are discursively "made up" as sexually innocent but at the same time as hormonally fueled and sexually driven.[8] These polarized discourses are accompanied by heightened concerns about child sexual abuse and sex predators.[9]

As this chapter demonstrates, drawing on these discourses, parents frame their children as potential victims of sex—vulnerable to their own raging hormones and rash decision making but also to sexual predation and abuse. These depictions, I suggest, constitute "controlling images" of adolescents.[10] Controlling images are hegemonic ideologies and images that portray "faulty" aspects of marginalized, oppressed groups. Controlling images are fundamental to legitimizing and maintaining inequality in America. Media representations of young black men as thugs, for example, direct "attention away from social policies that deny black youth education and jobs"[11] and incite fear in many Americans, bolstering racism through the belief that racial integration of poor and working-class black youth is dangerous. I argue that controlling images of teenagers as irresponsible, controlled by their hormones and sexually vulnerable, promote the belief that young people need protection from themselves, other teenagers, and adults, and cannot be trusted with sexual knowledge and citizenship.

Raging Hormones and Irresponsible Teenagers

When I asked Delores, "How do you feel about teenagers having sex?" she replied, "Not great because it's just a bunch of crazy hormones." In line with popular understandings of adolescence, parents such as Delores depicted teenagers as irresponsible vessels of raging hormones. In doing so, they constructed a binary between adult (safe) and adolescent (unsafe) sexuality. Whereas adult sex is, or at least can be, responsible and rational, teenagers are incapable of making responsible, rational decisions around sexuality partly because of their hormones.

But it is not just about hormones. Like the speaker at the school board meeting who compared a teenage body to "a shiny red sports car," parents think that teenagers are particularly motivated sexually because of their hormones *and* their attractive teen bodies. Corina, for example, said that, "teenagers got their cute little bodies and their raging hormones. They're like raring to go." Similarly Sylvia described how she and her husband reacted to the news that their 15-year-old daughter has a friend whose boyfriend sometimes sleeps over:

> My oldest has a friend that has a boyfriend [who lives] out of town and he will come over and spend the night at their house. They're in separate rooms. And [my daughter's] asked me what I thought about that and I said, "Absolutely not! No, no, no, no." I mean, even my husband chimed in. I think he said something like, "It's like putting candy in front of a kid and saying, don't lick it or don't eat it" [*laughs*]. So, it's just no.

Just as young children cannot be trusted with candy, Sylvia and her husband believe that teenagers cannot be trusted with their bodies. Teenagers, parents told me, ooze desire and desirability; their bodies are sexy and desirable as well as hypersexual and desiring. This understanding among parents fuels a perception of their teens' vulnerability and the sense that teenagers are dangers to themselves. Of course, parents are not alone in this way of thinking; sex educators and other adults also hold this belief. Decrying her students' presumed risk taking, Ms. Fox—the health teacher at Taylor High—frequently chided them, "You think you got a force field or something." Young people, parents and sex educators told me, should be educated to fear their bodily desires because following their urges *will* lead to emotional and physical pain and suffering. As Sandra laughingly put it, "[Sex education should] just scare them to death!" Growing serious, she added, "There are diseases that will kill you. They will kill you." Melissa has a "zero tolerance policy—no alcohol, no drugs, no sex." She keeps her four children "on a very short leash. I mean, you're dealing with *life and death* issues from seventh grade on."

That parents described teen sexuality in terms of raging hormones may seem to contradict my argument that they do not consider their own children as sexual beings. But parents use the discourse of raging hormones either to connect it to their children's peers, as Sylvia does above, or to describe their own children's behaviors as entirely hormonally driven, thus ignoring their potential or actual sexual desire. Josefina, for example, who became a mother as a teenager, told her 14-year-old son that sex is largely instinctual and motivated by hormones:

I explained that [sex] it's very risky, in the sense that you are driven. A lot of your behavior is driven by your hormones. It's not that you're good or bad or you do this because you consciously want to do it and *decide* to do it, there's a lot of instinctive behavior and it's driven by your hormones. And it can drive you to very dangerous situations in which you can end up having AIDS or an unwanted pregnancy, which was [what] happened to me . . . I think I was lucky, in a way, because I got pregnant, I didn't get AIDS, which is a horrible disease and there's nothing you can do about it.

Josefina's tactics were shaped by her own experiences as a teenager, when her mother offered factual information about sex but never spoke about how Josefina might feel:

My mother was considered a little bit liberal for her background and she explained all the technical, biological processes of reproduction to me, but that was about it. I was never told, you will feel this when someone touches you. When someone approaches and kisses you, you will feel *all* these things. And you will end, probably, in having sex because it's just something so strong at that age. And there is a lot of guilt associated with having sex at a young age in my culture. So of course I had sex! But I never told my parents because I felt guilty about it. And every time I did it, I cried and it was just tragedy—it was—it was very hard. And I didn't want that to happen to [my son]. I really want him to feel in control of his body and making responsible decisions so no unwanted consequences will come out of that.

Josefina believes that sexual feelings are often missing from parents' discussions about sex with their children, and so she wants her son to know about these feelings so that he does not feel guilty, as she did when she had sex as a teenager. But she worries that even this information will not prevent him from getting carried away, and she fears that, in the moment, it is difficult for young people to make informed decisions about sex. Thus, despite Josefina's earnest hope that her son feels "in control of his body," much of what she tells him about sexuality suggests that it is out of his control. Paradoxically, her reference to raging hormones may make it more difficult for her son to develop sexual agency and responsibility, as this means that his hormones are thinking for him and he is not responsible.

Like Josefina, other parents also find it hard to imagine responsible adolescent sexual activity; for them, the phrase itself is an oxymoron mostly because they regard teenagers as irresponsible. As we saw in chapter 2, many parents view their teenagers as young and immature. By this way of thinking, parents also think teenagers are, because of their very youth and nature, irresponsible. Sylvia, for example, wants her 14- and 15-year-old daughters to wait to have sex until they are at least in college. I asked, "Do you think they might get more pleasure out of sex if they waited?" Her answer was blunt:

SYLVIA: No.
SINIKKA: Until they're more comfortable with their bodies, more knowledgeable about their bodies?
SYLVIA: I don't know if it's about pleasure. I think they would be more responsible rather than being a teen [laughs]!
SINIKKA: So in your opinion teenagers aren't responsible [laughs]?
SYLVIA: Yes [laughs]! What teenager is responsible?

As I did with Sylvia, I often asked parents if their concern about their teens having sex has anything to do with the amount of pleasure to be gained. I asked this in part because a great deal of research documents the absence of pleasure in U.S. discourses of teen sexuality,[12] but also because there is some evidence from more liberal Western nations, such as the Netherlands and Germany, that emphasizing pleasure can reduce negative outcomes of teen sex.[13] For example, educating youth that contraceptive use increases sexual pleasure by reducing worries—a dominant tactic in Germany—may be a more effective way to encourage teens to use contraception than simply stressing risk and (ir)responsibility.[14]

For this reason, I also explicitly asked all parents whether they have talked with their children about sexual pleasure. The most common response to this question was a flustered no, or a snort of disbelief at the apparent absurdity of the question. One mother started laughing so hard upon hearing this question that she could not catch her breath for several minutes. Parents said they would be mortified to discuss pleasure with their teens and, moreover, that it is reckless to talk about pleasure with teens given teens' irresponsibility and the rates of sexually transmitted infections and teen pregnancies. Some stated that, given our sex-saturated media, young people learn enough, if not too much, about pleasure elsewhere; a parent's job is to teach them about danger. Elena, who has a 16-year-old daughter, expressed this when she said, "You know how the TV is getting, everything is sexual. Everybody is already half-naked, almost. So I think she gets the idea [about pleasure], even from the movies."

Parents such as Elena firmly believe that teenagers know about sexual pleasure but that they must be taught how to refrain from sex or to safely and responsibly navigate the risks of sex.

Thus the subject of pleasure is one of parents' "evaded lessons" about sexuality—noticeable primarily by its absence.[15] Similarly Mr. Marks, an abstinence-only sex educator, asked a class of high school students at Eastside, "When we think about sex, do we think of positive or negative things?" Without hesitation he answered his own question, "Positive, right? Positives are easy to think about. We don't need to think about those. [In this class] I want you to think about the negatives. The outcomes of sex—how can it affect your life?" The assumption of this discourse of teen sexuality is that young people know all about the good things that accompany sex, but they need to realize all the bad things that go along with sex. For parents, educators, and community activists, the goal of sex education should be to teach young people to delay sexual activity until they are either married (abstinence-only) or are responsible enough to manage the overwhelming risks associated with sex (comprehensive and abstinence-based). Young people do not need to be educated in the pleasures of sex. In fact, because they believe teens are irresponsible vessels of raging hormones, parents said it is not only unnecessary but also imprudent to talk about anything other than the dangers of sex.

Although parents typically described teenagers as generally irresponsible, not all parents see their own teen children this way. Gabriela believes that her 16-year-old daughter is mature and quite responsible for her age. When I asked Gabriela why she thinks this, she replied: "Well you know part of her responsibility comes from her being scared. She's scared of harm. She doesn't want any harm to come to her. I think that's where a lot of it comes from." "Where do you think the fear comes from?" I asked. "I'm hoping it's something we instilled [in] her," Gabriela responded simply. Other parents I spoke with, like Gabriela, think their teen children are responsible and mature, not like other teens. These parents described their children as circumspect and careful, and often, as Gabriela does above, attributed this to fear. They also expressed relief that their children have learned to be guarded and cautious. Yet their stories suggest that their children may be afraid not just of external threats to their well-being but of their own bodies and desires.[16] In fact, as the next section illustrates, this seems to be the point of much "expert" advice around teenagers and teen sexual activity.

Scientific Discourse and the Construction of the Irresponsible Teen

Parents' conviction that teenagers are irresponsible is shaped by their perceptions of their children generally behaving irresponsibly—many parents shared stories of their teens acting in irresponsible ways—but current scientific, "expert" discourse also promotes this belief.

During the course of my fieldwork, I attended five PTA meetings at Hayden Middle School that featured guest speakers. A popular topic at many of these meetings was recent research suggesting that young people do not yet have the biological ability to regulate their impulses. At one PTA meeting, the guest speaker was a doctor who specialized in adolescent medicine. The gist of his talk, titled "Adolescence: The Brain, the Body, the Beast," was that parents need to act as their teenagers' prefrontal cortex, the part of the brain that regulates emotions and moods, and provides intuition and morality. It helps people choose between right and wrong and to control their impulses, sexual or otherwise. According to the expert speaker, the prefrontal cortex is also one of the last areas of the brain to mature. Thus, he explained, until young people develop the capacity to control impulsive behavior (which he estimated occurs some time in the mid-twenties) parents must stand between them and their poor choices.

This type of research suggests a huge divide between the behavior of adults and adolescents. Adolescents are impulsive, irrational, and emotional;

adults are cautious, rational, and in control of their emotions. Many of the parents at the meeting appeared to embrace this message wholeheartedly. They spoke poignantly about how the speaker's depiction of adolescence resonated with their own experiences raising a teenager and their memories of their teenage years. The parents I spoke with exhibited a similar binary understanding of adulthood as a time of maturity and rationality, whereas adolescence is a time of irrationality and irresponsibility.

Clearly, however, adults are also capable of engaging in impulsive, irrational behavior. One need only read newspapers or watch any number of television programs to see adults behaving irresponsibly. This binary between adult and adolescent behavior suggests a wide gulf between them that does not capture the complexities of everyday life. It is also historically and culturally specific: as social historians have chronicled, only recently has adolescence been designated a discrete stage in the life course.[17] The term "adolescence" itself was not coined until 1904 by the American psychologist G. Stanley Hall and was accompanied by a flurry of scientific "evidence" that this is a time when young people are neither physically nor developmentally suited for many adult responsibilities, including working, marrying, and bearing children. This body of scientific research also formed the backdrop for mandatory high school attendance, at least in urban areas, beginning in the 1930s.[18]

Understandings of adolescence are also culturally bounded. In her study of Dutch and American parents' beliefs about teenagers and sexuality, for example, sociologist Amy Schalet finds that the two cultures differ markedly in their beliefs about adolescence. American parents view adolescents as largely hormonally driven and potentially out of control. In contrast, Dutch parents construct teenagers as mature young adults capable of self-regulation.[19] These cultural beliefs influence parenting practices and the types of rights and responsibilities teenagers are afforded in each country.

Although today the notion of adolescence as a distinct stage in the life course is widely embraced in the United States, scientific studies continue to refine and reify the definition of adolescence. For example, an article in the *New York Times* reviewing research into teenagers' perceptions of risk concludes that, compared to adults, youth do not have the experience or practice to appropriately assess a situation and determine the best course of action. This research thus advises parents, teachers, and others who work with adolescents to train young people to recognize cues in the environment that signal possible danger. *New York Times* health columnist Jane Brody reports, however, that "younger adolescents" (although this term is never age-defined) do not learn as well from this approach and, instead, need to be closely supervised to be safe:

Young teenagers need to be protected from themselves by removing opportunities for risk-taking—for example, by filling their time with positive activities and protecting them from risky situations that are likely to be tempting or that require "behavior inhibition." A young teenage girl should not be left alone in the house with her boyfriend, and responsible adults should be omnipresent and alcohol absent when teenagers have parties.[20]

The article does not answer an important question, however: Why do "young teenagers" not respond well to a practice-based approach to decision making? Perhaps young teenagers do not do well with this approach precisely because they have not had the practice and experience researchers say are necessary to draw conclusions about the consequences of their actions. Ultimately, then, the advice to protect young teenagers "from themselves" may prevent youth from developing the experience they need to make informed decisions. Just as the discourse of raging hormones may prevent young people from developing sexual responsibility, this broader discourse of adolescence also may hinder their decision-making ability.

Along with representing a culturally and historically specific notion of adolescence, the article reveals heteronormative and gendered assumptions about sexuality: teenage relationships are heterosexual, boys are sexual predators, and girls' sexual innocence needs protecting. Brody also places the responsibility for young people's safety squarely on parents' shoulders. As her examples reinforce, it is up to parents to engage their young teenagers in "positive activities" and protect them from "risky situations." Brody's use of the term "responsible adults" is illuminating, however; it opens the possibility that there are good (responsible) adults and bad (irresponsible) adults—that irresponsibility is not simply the terrain of adolescents. In fact, parents themselves are highly fearful of the sexual dangers "bad" adults pose to their children.

Beyond Stranger Danger

Along with teenagers needing protection from their hormones and irresponsibility, parents consistently said that young people need protection from a broad array of adults. Beatrice, in speaking of the difference between her own upbringing and that of her 16-year-old daughter, raised the issue of sexual predators:

One of the really major differences between my childhood and [my daughter's], we didn't have to worry about sexual predators or being snatched, kidnapped. We played outside all the time and there weren't any mothers around watching and all that. And I just know that, for me that was a *major* thing when she was little. I mean, I never heard of sexual abuse, really, when I was a kid.

Beatrice suggests not simply that she did not know about sexual predators when she was young but that they were not even an issue. This hearkens back to a supposedly safer, more peaceful time when children were allowed to play outside unsupervised without fear of being snatched or molested. By contrast, when Beatrice's daughter was younger, she was never allowed to play outside unsupervised as Beatrice had done when she was a child. Instead, Beatrice organized and monitored all her daughter's play dates. She also described sexual abuse to her daughter and continues to caution her: "If you're in a group, you're safer." Even today, she keeps a wary eye on her 16-year-old daughter's whereabouts and friendships.

Although predators undoubtedly existed in her youth, Beatrice grew up in an era when the public had less knowledge, and therefore less concern, about child sexual abuse. Since that time, even though cases of child sexual abuse have actually declined substantially, considerable publicity has surrounded reported sexual abuse;[21] examples include the sex abuse scandals of Catholic priests, the emergence of sexual offenders registries, online sting operations with police officers posing as 13 year olds to nab pedophiles, and a spate of allegations of teachers having sex with their students. So, despite the reduced risk of sexual predation, parents today are still bombarded with information about sex offenders and child sex abuse.[22] And despite efforts by feminists, child protection lobbyists, and others to expose the "myth of stranger danger"[23]—the erroneous belief that most sexual assaults are perpetrated by strangers—parents continue to exaggerate the danger of sex abuse by strangers.

But it is not just strangers that worry parents. According to sociologist Janice Irvine, efforts over the last few decades to raise awareness about the dangers children face, sexual or otherwise, "had the ancillary effect of contributing to a cultural climate in which abuse seemed to lurk around every corner."[24] Indeed, many of the parents I spoke with broadly embraced the discourse of sexual danger to the point that they treat the behavior of predators as natural and inevitable. Anyone is a potential abuser, including family members. Sandra is pleased that her teenage sons have learned that sex predators are not always strangers, because "I never would have thought of my father or my uncle . . . molesting me." Sandra thinks the media and schools have done "a very good job of exposing [that predators may be known to the victims] and teaching that." Yet this information also makes it difficult for parents to gauge sexual threats, as the sexual danger toward their children may come not only from strangers on the streets but also from neighbors, family members, and, as the next chapter demonstrates, their children's peers and intimate relationships.

Some parents' sense that sexual predators are ubiquitous stems from a painful personal experience of sexual abuse. As a child, "a bad thing happened" to Lorena. First, she was molested by her babysitter's husband, and then later by this man's grandson. Lorena has not explicitly told her 16- and 9-year-old sons about the abuse; she feels it is too personal and she does not "know what they'd do with that information." Instead, she has told them "the reason they're not allowed to spend the night at anybody's houses is because bad things can happen." She does not want any harm to come to her sons and doesn't quite know how to keep them safe other than not to let them out of her sight.

Similarly, Sheila was "inappropriately touched" by one of her uncles when she was a child—an uncle who continues to be a part of Sheila's family and whom Sheila sees at family events—but she has not told her 16-year-old daughter about this. Instead she warns her daughter away from adult males in general:

> I had to start talking to [my daughter] early, to make sure that she understood that sometimes stranger danger isn't always strangers. Sometimes danger comes within a family too and you have to be careful. At six I told her, from now on, no sitting on any guy's lap unless it's Dad's. Dad's lap is okay, but no other man can hold you in his lap. And I would have to go and get her away, distract her from my uncle and stuff like that. So, we had to tell her stuff like that from the very beginning—that all people are not what they seem to be and even though something will feel real innocent to you, it might be feeling different to somebody else and that's disgusting [*laughs*].

Sheila regrets having to introduce her daughter to such adult concerns early on; she thinks it has severely eroded her daughter's trust in adults to where she is now uncomfortable around and distrustful of all adult men. Although Sheila's lessons, like Lorena's, stem from painful personal knowledge, she does not want to talk with her daughter about her own experience and instead paints a broad picture of potential abusers. Her lessons, however, are so broad and indistinct that her efforts to protect her daughter, though clearly heartfelt, may make it harder for her to develop the skills to distinguish good sexual encounters from bad ones and to fend off unwanted sexual contact.

But young people are not the only ones who may find it difficult to distinguish appropriate from inappropriate sexuality. Some parents revealed that they, too, lack these skills. Based on what she has heard on the news, Elena believes that anyone might be a potential sex offender, including her current live-in boyfriend, from whom she is in the process of separating:

> It can be anybody. It can be a family member. You hear about this on the news all the time. I mean, just recently there was the stepfather, then there was the stepmother. All of this goes through my mind, so it makes me more skeptical about any other relationships for me. And even so, I'm afraid like with [my 16-year-old daughter], I think that, I don't know, I had that problem, even with my boyfriend, having to move in with my boyfriend, I still had that problem, that constant supervision. Always, okay, making sure, okay, he's here, he's not over there. Of all the things I've seen and heard it's more of being more protective.

When I asked Elena what made her worry about her boyfriend, she shrugged and repeated, "It can be anybody." Elena doubts that she will get into another serious relationship once she leaves her boyfriend, as she does not feel that she can trust a man around her 16-year-old daughter. She worries that, because her daughter is shy and quiet, she might not speak out if Elena's boyfriend "tried something against her," revealing that Elena is most concerned about her daughter's lack of response. Yet she accepts her daughter's vulnerability as inevitable and, like other parents, sees no choice but to act as her protector. For now, until she can move out and live with her children on her own, she keeps a close watch on her boyfriend when her daughter is around.

The problem, then, with the discourse that proclaims "it can be anybody," that sexual harm can come from anywhere and everywhere, is that it does not provide boundaries around which to gauge sexual danger. For example, several of the single mothers I interviewed said that they have chosen to remain single partly because they want to focus on raising their children and do not have the time or energy for a relationship, but like Elena they are also leery about introducing an adult man into the family whose sexual history and proclivities are unknown. The broad, seemingly limitless "it can be anybody" discourse of sexual danger may thus prevent young people, as well as adults, from developing risk assessment skills as well as the skills to rebuff unwanted sexual contact. In this discourse, parents have the difficult challenge of preparing their children for an environment where anyone is a potential victimizer and everyone is vulnerable and a potential victim.

This discourse also dichotomizes sex as safe (implicitly good) in adulthood and unsafe (implicitly bad) in adolescence. The implication is that once young people reach adulthood or get married, they will have no difficultly achieving sexual happiness. Denise's story below suggests a more complicated picture.

Denise's Story

At a party recently I told a criminologist friend that I was investigating data relevant to sex education, and she asserted: "The problem with sex ed is they focus on stranger danger. That's not where the predators are. Most of the time, it's someone in the family who poses the danger. They need to teach kids that their bodies are their own. That *no one* can touch them without permission." I reflected that this is exactly what one of the parents I spoke to—Denise—learned from her parents when she was growing up and has taught her own seven children. Denise's story highlights the disconcerting aspects of these sexual lessons. Despite their focus on sexual danger in their lessons to their teen children about sexuality, parents assume that their children will have no difficulty achieving sexual and relational fulfillment in adulthood or marriage. Yet this contradicts the evidence that many adults find it hard to achieve happy, safe, fulfilling sexual relationships.[25]

Denise is black, with seven children ranging in age from 31 to 13. She is a nurse, works full-time, and lives in the home where she was raised, having moved there twelve years ago when she separated from her husband. Denise has made it clear to her children that their bodies are their own, no one else's: "I tell my kids, 'If somebody touches you, holds you, or grabs at you inappropriately, you need to tell them, back off, this is my body. That's it. No whatever.'" She believes this has been a highly successful approach. She proudly told me that her four adult children, ranging in age from 21 to 31, all made it safely through adolescence without unintended pregnancies or sexually transmitted infections. She is also proud that her three grandchildren were all conceived in marriage.

Denise thinks it is important for young people to hear open and frank discussions about sexual feelings and touching. Talk about touching is not simply a crucial component of parent-child conversations, she said, but should also be a cornerstone of sex education. She is upset that touching is not in the sex education curriculum: "They leave out the most important part. They don't tell them about touching. They go into detail with everything else but the touching. And the touching is what leads to sex!" When she talks with her own children, touching is front and center: "We'll talk about how they feel. 'How does it feel when somebody touch you in certain places or when somebody holds you too close, or if somebody's holding you close, or somebody hugs you?' Those type of feelings."

This approach has empowered her children, especially her daughters, Denise said, to own their bodies and feel agentic through them. For example, she said that her 16-year-old daughter spoke out in class when a student touched her inappropriately: "A guy put his hand on her leg and she said he was coming up her leg, and she screamed out, 'Get yo' hand off my leg!'" Her daughter was reprimanded for disrupting the class and sent to the principal's office, where she defended her outburst. Denise recounted her daughter's words: "She explained to the principal that she had told this boy, don't touch her no more, and he continued. And the only way to get the teacher's attention was to yell. And that's what I told her [to do]." Denise is proud that her daughter remembered her advice, stood her ground, and rebuffed the boy's unwanted touching. The principal also supported Denise's daughter and did not punish her for speaking out in class.

In another example, Denise's 13-year-old daughter told her that an uncle's hug had made her feel "nasty" and asked her mother to talk to him. In response, Denise validated her daughter's feelings and spoke to both her sister and her brother-in-law, the uncle, about the incident:

> I told my sister that I needed to talk to her about the way her husband was hugging my daughter. And she said, "Okay. You've told me how you feel, you need to tell him." I said, "Just so there's no hard feelings." So, I did. He said he wasn't aware that he had hugged her inappropriately but if that's the way he made her feel, he wouldn't hug her like that anymore.

Rather than downplay or chastise her daughter for her feelings, Denise took them seriously and followed through on her promise to speak to her brother-in-law about it. By consistently telling her children "nobody touches your body but you" and honoring their feelings, she hopes to encourage her children to carve out spaces of bodily integrity and, potentially, sexual autonomy. But her narrative also exposes a problematic aspect of this approach. This problem was brought out in other conversations with Denise where I observed that her children do not experience or are unwilling to talk about "positive" bodily and sexual feelings.[26] Even though Denise provides open communication and constant information, her children seem uncomfortable with their own bodies. For instance, in addition to her 16-year-old daughter's run-in at school and her 13-year-old daughter's discomfort over an uncle's hug, Denise provided several other examples of how her children, and even her grandchildren, have talked with her about their bodies and being touched. All her examples involved bad feelings—feeling uncomfortable or nasty—so I asked:

SINIKKA: Have they ever talked to you about something that felt good?
DENISE: [long pause] No not really. I remember one time, we were trying to get [my 16 year old] to use tampons instead of pads and that was the weirdest conversation we've ever had to have. Because all the girls were together.
SINIKKA: Your daughters?
DENISE: Yeah. And the older two were trying to tell her how to do it. [My 21-year-old daughter] even took her to the bathroom, gave her a mirror, and showed her how. And we could hear her screaming. She goes, "Oh Momma, it doesn't make me feel good. It's nasty, da-da-da." I said, "Okay, stop. If it doesn't make you feel good, if you think it's nasty, then you don't do it. You don't use the tampons. We won't go any further." And then we laughed about it and that was it. Finally, I guess about two months later, she learned how to use them and she came to me and she said, "Momma, I can use it on my own now and I don't need any help." I said, "How does it make you feel?" She said, "I'm okay after it's in." I said, "Okay."

Some of the stories Denise shared with me suggest that her children do not simply fear their own bodies but also their mother's reaction to their bodily functions. In providing an example of how close-knit her family is, Denise told me that when her 16-year-old daughter was 12 she started her period but did not initially tell her mother. Instead she told her oldest sister, Denise's 31-year-old daughter. Denise recalled this incident:

[My daughter] said, "Momma's going to be mad at me." And [my oldest daughter] said, "Why?" "There's blood in my pants and I wasn't doing nuthin'. You know how Mommy is. And I swear I wasn't doing anything. I didn't." So she said, "It's okay. You just started your period." She said, "Whew, I just knew Momma was going to say somethin' bad."

As we continued to talk, I began to understand that Denise experiences her own body in a fairly fraught way and does not have fond memories of her own sex life. When she was a child, her father, a Baptist minister, and her mother taught her that her body was her own and no one should touch her, the same lesson Denise now imparts to her children. Their lessons, and Denise's lessons to her own children, may reflect a politics of respectability centering on sexual purity and restraint—a strategy adopted by some middle-class African Americans in order to transcend stereotypes of black hypersexuality.[27] As with other discourses of sexuality, sexual respectability can "invade the body,"[28] shaping how individuals think of themselves, their bodies, and their sexuality. In Denise's case, it appears to have created discursive space to say no to sex but may have also made it difficult for her to say yes. Here Denise recalls her first night with her new husband:

DENISE: I can remember my wedding night. I told my husband if he touched me I was going to shoot him. He goes, "What's wrong with you? That's what getting married's all about!" [I said], "Pshaw, not my body."

SINIKKA: How old were you?

DENISE: I was 20.

SINIKKA: And you were pretty adamant. Did you have sex?

DENISE: Not that night! I packed my bag and came home [laughs]! And my brothers took me back the next day! It was awful! I was like, nuh uh. My brothers were hilarious. They told me, "No girl, nuh uh, you can't come back here. You married. You got to stay with your husband and that's part of life." [I said], "Not my part! Somebody else's got to do that part." And I'll never forget, my oldest brother said, "No, we can't do that part for you, you have to do it. You can tell him that you're not ready just yet. No, I'll tell him." I said, "Okay, you tell him." And it's like, he said [to my husband], "You have to start with the touching and the feelings first, 'cause she ain't gonna let you touch her body. So you have to work your way up." And, god, I bet you I didn't have sex for a month after I got married.

Denise had dated her husband for two years prior to marrying him. Their dating relationship was chaste. Her parents kept a close watch on both of them and would regularly remind her: "Nobody is to touch your body if you don't want him to." She said on her wedding night, "I didn't want [my husband] to [touch me]. That was that." Denise knew without a doubt what she was willing to do sexually (or, rather, not willing) and stood her ground. She experienced this as a small victory particularly when, once she started having sex, she found very little pleasure in it, confirming her initial reaction. I asked her: "Once you started having sex, how did you feel?" She replied with a sigh of resignation, "It was okay. And seven kids later—huh!"

Denise's children have asked her about her sexual relationship with their father. She has told them that of course they had sex, "'that's how you got here. When parents have sex, children are born.'" Her children then asked her:

> "Well, Momma, what was Daddy like?" I said, "A grizzly bear. Every time I sat on the bed, he woke up if he was asleep." And they said, "Oh, you so bad [*laughs*]!" I said, "Well, he could be asleep and I would come in and he'd say, 'What took you so long to go to bed?' And I would say, 'I was waiting 'til you went to sleep.'" And they would just laugh. I mean it's just—I didn't hide that from them.

Denise has told her children that she and her ex-husband had an active sex life but not because of her own desire. In fact, she tells them that she attempted to avoid having sex by coming to bed late, hoping her husband would be asleep. She also clearly ties sex to reproduction: a lesson her children seem to have taken to heart. When I asked her if she has dated in the twelve years since she and her husband separated, she laughingly replied: "No. Oh my [14-year-old] son says, 'Now wait a minute, you can't have no boyfriends.' I said, 'Shut up! I am grown.' He goes, 'Nah, because we can't be raising no more babies [*laughs*]!'" I asked Denise if she thinks she might date in the future. "Probably not. Nope. Because the only boyfriend I ever had was my husband and I married him and that was just it," she said poignantly.

Denise's story clearly reveals that she has gained little pleasure through her body, and the control she was taught to exercise has primarily involved fending off sexual interest, including her husband's and possibly her own. Also, sex often led to pregnancy in her life. "I love every single one of my children, but did I plan to have them all? No," Denise said, laughing. Although religion plays an important role in Denise's life, she did not say that her religion prohibits the use of birth control, and she has taught her own children about birth control. She has even shown her children how to put on a condom using a banana—something no other parent told me they did—and spoke quite knowledgeably about various forms of contraception during her interview. Perhaps despite being a nurse, Denise felt uncomfortable using birth control because it signaled intent to have sex. This is an explanation that many teenagers give—particularly teenage girls and those who have pledged to remain abstinent until marriage—for not using contraception.[29] Being prepared for sex and having sex in a responsible fashion (e.g., through the use of contraception) indicates an agentic form of sexual desire, suggesting that the person is actively seeking sex and simultaneously worthy of protection. Teens and perhaps adults like Denise who do not think of themselves as agentic sexual beings, or who do not want to think of themselves in this way, may experience a kind of cognitive dissonance around sex and contraception.[30]

The United States is a sex-saturated culture that sexualizes young people, sending them confusing messages about their bodies and sexuality. Many parents, like Denise and her parents, try to counter these messages by teaching young people how to establish and maintain clear sexual boundaries. The assumption behind this, of course, is that once a child has made it safely through adolescence without having sexual intercourse or being molested or harmed in any way, he or she will be capable of achieving sexual autonomy and pleasure. This implies, however, that adults are automatically capable of experiencing sexual joy or, at least, do not have their own difficulties in claiming a sexual self. Ultimately this ignores the evidence that many adults experience tremendous sexual struggles; some of these play out in their own lives, and some are directed outward and harm others.

Conclusion

Parents overwhelmingly emphasize the dangerous and negative consequences of teen sexual behavior, implicitly or explicitly dichotomizing adult sex as safe and teen sex as unsafe. Their ideas about teen sexuality are significantly shaped by beliefs about the differences between teenagers and adults: what I term the "adolescent/adult binary." Table 1.4 lists the binaries between adolescence and adulthood that parents articulated. These understandings are not unique to parents: over the past century in the United States, "adolescence has been defined as *not adult*."[31]

Parents view teen sex as risky partly because they think teenagers are irresponsible bundles of hormones surrounded by threatening sexual Others. In Constance Nathanson's words, "The very enormity of controlling adolescent sexual behavior leads adults to defend against the risk of transgression by stressing young people's responsibility—or irresponsibility."[32] This discourse

Table 4.1. Adolescent/Adult Binaries

Adolescent	Adult
Dependent	Autonomous
Impulsive	Rational
Irresponsible	Responsible
Immature	Mature

of teenagers as irresponsible, irrationally controlled by hormones, and vulnerable to numerous sexual dangers has become so entrenched in American society that it appears to have the status of a common-sense truth. As such, I suggest that it constitutes a "controlling image" of teenagers, serving to promote the belief that young people need to be protected from themselves and a host of sexual dangers.

The controlling image of irresponsible, irrational, hormonally driven teens also divides the adult world from the realm of adolescence, suggesting that when it comes to sexuality age represents an important axis of social inequality. Through their binary thinking, parents impose a wide gulf between adult and teen sexuality. According to this thinking, sex between consenting adults is automatically good; sex between teenagers can be good, and may be especially good, because teenage bodies are culturally paragons of sexiness, but still teenage sex is fraught with danger.

Teen sex *is* a risky enterprise in the United States,[33] but adult sex can also be both risky and unfulfilling, as Denise's story vividly illustrates. Characterizing sex as risky only during adolescence establishes a false binary. Similarly numerous other risky activities are associated with adolescence, as in all of life. For example, driving is risky. And whereas teenagers behind the wheel raise parental and societal alarm bells, fears about teens driving recklessly or getting into an accident do not seem to carry the same emotional and moral intensity as fears about teen sexuality.[34] Kelly, for example, compared teaching her 14- and 16-year-old sons to drive to teaching them about sex: "I can teach them how to drive, but I can't teach [them] how to—what they should know about sex." I suspect Kelly may have been about to say "how to have sex," but stopped herself, saying instead "what they should know about sex."

As we saw in chapter 3, parents view sex as private, and they may feel exposed and ashamed when discussing sex with their children. Like Kelly, some parents told me that because sex is private, it is beyond instruction. Similarly, parents who experienced sexual abuse have not told their children about their experiences but try to protect them from similar incidents through vigilance and scare tactics. This suggests that as long as sexual fear and shame permeate Americans' feelings about sexuality, young people as well as adults will find it difficult to access positive information about their bodies and sexual desires. The adolescent/adult binary ultimately prevents adults from offering youth information and skills to help them navigate both the pleasures and dangers of sex and to forge sexually agentic and empowered lives, perhaps because many adults cannot easily do this themselves.

5

Other Teens

How Race, Class, and Gender Matter

Parents do not simply view adults—whether strangers, known sex offenders, neighbors, or family members—as potential threats to their teenagers' sexual safety and well-being, but they also worry about their children's peers. Some parents, for example, described their children's peers as "openly sexual" and "promiscuous." Others spoke contemptuously about teens these days who lack sexual boundaries, who get pregnant (or get someone pregnant), and who spread disease and immorality. Overall, parents painted a picture of highly sexual and sexually active teenagers—just not their own. Teenagers may be complicit in all of this, however. A great deal of what parents claim to know about their children's peers comes from their own children; and teens seem to revel in telling their parents about their peers' sexual exploits. Sandra, who described her 17-year-old son as "not a big talker, but he is my ears," asks her son about "'the kids at school—do they talk about sex? Do they talk about having sex?' [He tells me], 'Oh yeah. They talk about it all the time.'" Teens are apparently not so forthcoming when it comes to talking about their own sex lives and sexual desires. The stories parents hear from their teens about their peers thus not only stoke parental anxieties but also likely contribute to their binary thinking.

But not all teenagers pose an equal threat: parents routinely used racialized, classed, and gendered imagery to construct their teen children's peers as more sexual than their own children. Recall, for example, that Ron (from chapter 2), a white, working-class father of a teenage son and daughter, characterized his children, particularly his 17-year-old daughter, as young, immature, and uninterested in sex. As Ron put it, "They're a little immature for their ages—my daughter especially." When I asked him why he thinks this, he said, "Well, because I can sort of compare her to other—you know, because of [this city] having a different ethnic background, it's a little bit different here than— you know, that's what I sort of look at too." It seemed that Ron was comparing his white daughter to her racial and ethnic minority peers, and so I asked him to clarify his view. He then explained that, whereas he grew up in an all-white community, his current neighborhood is highly racially and ethnically diverse:

> I was in the white area growing up. Okay? There wasn't different—I mean there was, but it wasn't [integrated]. Now that's changed. 'Cause where [we live now], they're living right there. You know, Hispanics and Asians and the poorest of blacks are right down the street.

Ron also expressed concern about the possibility that his daughter might date a black boy and about the phone calls his daughter has apparently received from older teenage boys who Ron thinks may be 18 or 19 years old: "'Cause they are adults. [Even] 17 year olds . . . when you go to jail, you go to jail; you're not a juvenile anymore."

This chapter examines how and why parents such as Ron call on race, class, and gender imagery and stereotypes in describing their own teen children as asexual relative to their teen peers. Parents' perceptions derive from the idea that teenagers are "getting older younger"[1] and from an increase in media coverage that exaggerates and distorts child and teenage criminality and violence.[2] But they are also shaped by the growing trend of "adultification"[3] of teenagers in the criminal justice system—that is, the prosecution of teenage defendants as adults, which has increased since the 1980s. As Barry Glassner observes: "The misbelief that every child is in imminent risk of becoming a victim has as its corollary a still darker delusion: *Any kid might become a victimizer.*"[4]

It is important to note that young people who are prosecuted as adults and deemed "unsalvageable" victimizers are often poor, black, or Latino/a, and their adultification extends beyond the criminal justice system. In her ethnography of an elementary school, sociologist Ann Arnett Ferguson finds that teachers and school administrators persistently viewed the behavior of African American boys as insidious, intentional, and adult-like but ignored or minimized similar conduct by white boys.[5] Teachers, sex educators, public discourses, and social policies also routinely construct black and Latina girls as "sexually opportunistic, excessive, and a drain on public resources."[6] The dominant American discourse of adolescence as a time of irresponsibility, when young people cannot be held fully responsible for their actions, not only constructs a false binary between adult and teen behavior but is selectively applied to young people and accompanied by a discourse describing some teenagers as willfully bad. Drawing on these discourses and stereotypes, the parents I interviewed described their children's peers as highly sexual and sexualized while hinting throughout that race, class, and gender play a role in this understanding.

Situating the Other: Race- and Class-Blind Discourse

Parents' depictions of their children's peers as hypersexual were often overlaid with race and class meanings, but rarely articulated as such; instead, parents skirted around discussions of race, ethnicity, and social class. For instance, when she talked about her fears for her 14-year-old son, Kate, who is white and lower-middle class, connected her concerns to her son's friends who live in a low-income neighborhood near her home. Kate and her son live on the edge of a middle-class neighborhood, but "you only have to go . . . a few blocks—half a mile—and you're in a really bad neighborhood, the projects." Children from "the projects" attend school with her son and have become his friends:

> He's hanging out with a bunch of kids that look really rough and they talk about gangs too, but I don't think they're old enough to be in gangs yet. But, I think it's actually a very glamorous thing to these kids. The rap stuff, and 50 Cent, and all those guys; Grand Theft Auto—it's really glamorous.

Kate described her son, in chapter 2, as sexually naïve and innocent and was concerned that he might be pushed into a sexual or other social situation before he is ready in order to appear "cool" to his friends. Given her description above, clearly Kate views her son's peers as a threat to his innocence. And though she did not explicitly talk about the racial, ethnic, or class backgrounds of these peers, her use of the terms "projects" and "gangs" evoked race and class. Thus, when discussing her son's sexuality, Kate identified certain friends of a different class and race as the objects of her fear and deemed these teen Others to be a negative influence.

I noticed that, like Kate, few parents spoke openly about race or class during their interviews but used veiled and coded language to refer to race and class. According to sociologists and race scholars Patricia Hill Collins and Eduardo Bonilla-Silva, as it has become increasingly taboo in modern America to discuss race openly, forms of overt racism have been replaced with the "new racism."[7] This is a colorblind racism that embraces certain aspects of black or Latino culture (for example, hip-hop music and fashion) while simultaneously casting black and Latino culture as deficient and the ultimate source of their lower socioeconomic position relative to whites and Asian Americans. Colorblind racism offers a new form of "racetalk," a way to talk about race that uses subtle code words to make racial references without using the standard vocabulary of racism. This "racetalk" also involves semantic strategies, such as indirectness or displacement, so that speakers can project an image of themselves as tolerant.[8]

Americans also commonly employ what sociologist Julie Bettie refers to as a "class-blind discourse," in which "class is often expressed through categories of difference . . . 'gender, race, ethnic origin, and so forth.'"[9] Bettie argues that class is rarely referred to directly; instead, class categories are spoken about and popularly understood as differences in "success, money, values, intelligence, gender, race, ethnicity and . . . sub-cultural styles."[10] Although use of this coded language may seem innocuous, it reveals and helps maintain pernicious social hierarchies and inequalities, as Penny's story illustrates.

When Penny and her husband married and started a family eighteen years ago, they decided that, despite the financial hardship, Penny would be a stay-at-home mom. They bought a house in a lower-income neighborhood and have lived frugally these past eighteen years on Penny's husband's salary. Their 17- and 16-year-old sons attend Eastside High School where nearly 90 percent of the student body identifies as black or Latino/a, and most are low-income. Penny, who is white, did not directly refer to the racial-ethnic or class composition of Eastside but described it as "one of the highest risk schools in the district." Risk is commonly used as a racialized code word for economic disadvantage.[11] Penny went on to say that there is a "cultural difference" between her and her neighbors: "Education is very important to us and I don't think it is for most of the families around here. It's just a cultural difference, I guess."

Stemming from her concerns about the student body at her sons' school and their peers in the neighborhood, Penny carefully monitors her sons' friendships rather than allowing her sons to choose their own friends. If one of her sons wants to bring someone to the house, she asks: "'How are his grades?' If he says, 'Not so great,' I say, 'Then I don't think that's the type of person you should be spending time with.'" I asked Penny how her sons respond to this request. "They agree. I think they know already," she replied. Penny and her husband also do not allow their sons to date, "and they won't be allowed to until they go to college." Again, I wondered whether her sons expressed dismay about this rule. Penny responded bluntly:

> No. They have a lot more aspirations than some others. I think that they have the ability to look around and see that there are many people who— there are mothers that bring their babies to school at Eastside. Or someone meets them there and takes their child to child care or whatever. They've been in school with young girls who are pregnant.

Penny shifts here from describing her sons' acceptance of the no-dating-until-college rule to differentiating her aspiring sons from their potential dating pool: girls at their school who get pregnant and become teen moms. In doing so, she semantically situates her white, middle-class sons as superior to their lower-income and racial-ethnic minority peers.

Although not directly articulated in terms of race and class, the anxieties of parents such as Kate and Penny are projected, by the use of code words, onto raced, classed, and gendered Others. Separating out their children's peers in this way preserves the notion that their own children are asexual and innocent. As Collins observes, in binary thinking one side of the binary relies on reference to its "opposite" for meaning. Binaries are relational: by referring to the Other, individuals define their place in the social landscape.[12]

A long history of binary thinking has shaped understandings of sexuality in American society. Poor people, new immigrants, blacks, Latinos, Asians, gays and lesbians, and those deemed mentally "unfit" to sexually reproduce, historically bore the mantle of "bad" sexuality; that is, they were seen as promiscuous, or "overly" procreative.[13] Many of these sexual stereotypes endure to this day and have become so entrenched that they are taken for granted. Some have been institutionalized, woven into the fabric of American social policy. The long-standing hypersexualization of black men and women, for instance, can be seen in policy makers' intense concern over and scrutiny of black teenage motherhood and in racialized stereotypes, such as the "welfare queen," all of which motivated the enactment of stringent and punitive new welfare policies in the mid-1990s.[14]

Given this history and that many Americans either use code words or avoid talking about race entirely, I asked parents directly how they would feel about their children dating someone who was not of the same racial or ethnic background. Some parents said that of course they would allow their children to date someone of a different race or ethnicity. Corina put it most emphatically when she said, "I don't care if he's *green*. If he take care of my daughter like she's supposed to be taken care of and treat her like the queen that she is, I don't care about color." Other parents, however, said they would prefer that their children not date and, especially, not marry outside their racial-ethnic group. These parents stressed that their preference stems not from personal prejudice but from societal prejudice, arguing that interracial relationships make life more difficult for people because of the way society generally views interracial couples—and children that result from an interracial relationship.

Yolanda was concerned about interracial relationships in terms of issues the offspring may face:

> My biggest concern is, because I went to school with a little boy who was a mixed race and he had *such* a hard time. This was probably the biggest thing that stayed with me. He had such a hard time fitting in because he was like, "The black guys think I'm Mexican, the Mexican people don't want to talk to me because they think I'm black." And he said, "I have such a hard time. Because it's like, 'Oh you want to be Mexican,' or 'You want to be a black guy.'" He said, "They call me Oreo and they pick on me. I've been picked on all my life. The girls, you know, they can't go out with me because the parents think I'm black or vice versa. And if I go out with a Mexican, the black people think, 'Oh, you're too good for your own.'" So that stuck with me. And he said, "I never want to do this to my kids." And I think to myself, I don't want my kids to go through that. I don't want her to have to go through the—just, the everyday, people talking smack.

Yolanda also discussed the familial difficulties her Latina cousin has experienced since she began a relationship with a black man. Yolanda's cousin has been ostracized by her family because of this relationship. "And I don't want them to look at my daughter that way. You know, I just—and it's probably a selfish thing, but in reality, that's the way I feel," Yolanda said wistfully. The stories Yolanda shared with me revealed the deeply personal racialized understandings concerning the romantic, sexual, and procreative relationships that structure parents' concerns for their children's happiness and well-being. These meanings, of course, are not merely personal; they are shaped by a long history of race politics, struggles, and inequalities.[15]

I also asked parents if they have talked with their children about whether they might be gay, straight, or bisexual. Although many parents said they have never had this conversation, some, especially those with gay friends or gay family members, said that it does not matter to them whether their children are gay or straight. Yet parents rarely strayed from presuming their children's heterosexuality.

Parents often based their acceptance of homosexuality on their belief that sexual orientation is not a choice. I asked Gina if she "would be okay" if one of her kids was gay, and she responded: "Well, what choice? Of course! It's like if they were born redhead." Gail, who unlike Gina considers herself fairly conservative, said she is evolving emotionally and coming to accept homosexuality largely because she is beginning to see that people cannot choose their sexuality. As an example, Gail mentioned *Brokeback Mountain,* a film about two secretly homosexual cowboys, which she thought was "superb" because "in the movie you see that they don't particularly want to be attracted to each other. And yet they are. And they cope with it the best they can." These parents typically were not as accepting of bisexuality, however. As Robin put it, "I think that suggests some confusion or maybe even a little bit greedy, you know—that you don't want to have to choose." So the belief now prevalent in the public discourse that sexuality is not a choice may encourage the acceptance of homosexuality, but it may do so by constructing a strict binary between homosexuality and heterosexuality that marginalizes bisexuality and, indeed, all sexual fluidity.

Other parents told me they prefer their children to be heterosexual but will accept and love them "no matter what." Nicole confided during her interview that her 14-year-old daughter might be gay: "I thought my daughter was leaning more to liking girls 'cause I never heard anything about boys last year, not a whole bunch." I asked, "How would you feel if she were gay?" Sighing, she replied: "I'd be okay with it. Yeah, I'd be okay. I'm not biased. I'm not going to say I'm, I'm—I wouldn't say I'm anti-gay, but, you know, my children are my children. I'm going to love them no matter what." Similarly, I asked Melissa, who has three teenagers, "How would you feel if one of your kids said they were gay?" and she replied, "Well, you love 'em anyway; they're your kids."

I found the phrases "no matter what" and "you love them anyway" troubling when used in relation to the possibility of a child being gay. Parents like Nicole and Melissa could have just as easily said the same about a child who has a drug addiction or who has been incarcerated for a violent crime. Despite parents' avowals of acceptance, their assumption and, in some cases, preference that their children be heterosexual reveals the operations of "heteronormativity—the mundane, everyday ways that heterosexuality is privileged and taken for granted as normal and natural."[16]

Parents were often quick to explain that their preferences for hetero-sexuality, just like their concerns about interracial relationships, stem not from personal prejudice but from their sense that, because of social stigma and discrimination, homosexuality (also bisexuality) entails a much more difficult life compared to heterosexuality.[17] "As a mom you don't want your child to be gay," Beth said. "But if he were gay I would love him no less. And I would deal with it. But it's a hardship later on down the road that you don't want to have to deal with." Similarly, despite Rebecca's belief that "there are cats and there are dogs. Some people are straight, some people are gay. It's just a fact. No moral judgment on there at all," she went on to say, "but if it's your own kid, it would be difficult to go through . . . Just because they have a rougher time in life . . . I would rather he be straight, just because it's easier."

Overall parents' biggest wish for their children is their future hap-piness and well-being. As Kelly said, referring to her preference for het-erosexual sons: "That is one of those things that you just really hope that everything in their life goes happily and joyfully." But parents who tie the future happiness of their children to same-race and opposite-sex relation-ships reproduce racist and heteronormative cultural logics. In other words, this tactic produces the very conditions that concern parents, creating and compounding the difficulties that children (and adults) may experience because they do not follow normative sexual and romantic paths.

Even though parents typically assume that their children are heterosex-ual and, in some cases, stated a preference for heterosexuality, most did not describe teen heterosexual relationships in positive terms. Binary think-ing does more than simply establish some teens as asexual and therefore good; it creates a scenario in which those teenagers are imperiled by their peers. Parents described their children's peers as not just sexual but *sexually predatory*, with gender, race, and class meanings often woven through their descriptions. Parents do not just worry about their daughters' sexual safety. Parents of sons see girls as potentially sexually dangerous and aggressive, and those with daughters described boys in the same light.[18] These assump-tions about their children's sexuality are heteronormative, as we will see, and yet they make teen heterosexual relationships sound quite unappeal-ing. Although teen heterosexual dating and sex can be unsafe, unfulfill-ing, and coercive,[19] I suggest that parents' warnings about the predatory "opposite sex" may not ameliorate this situation and may even help lay the foundations for it by encouraging teens to view heterosexual relationships antagonistically.

Girls as Sexual Aggressors

Parents consistently described their sons' female peers as hypersexual, sexually aggressive, or more sexually advanced than their sons. They said that girls mature faster than boys and often pressure boys to have sex to solidify a relationship, and many warn their sons away from girls. Sandra told me that her 15- and 17-year-old sons "recognize girls and things like that, but they are not panting after them, and [saying] 'I need a girlfriend.' I think it is more with girls." She continued, "Girls are like, 'Boys are important and it is important that you have a boyfriend.' So I remind my children: 'Okay, the girls are maturing a little quicker than you are . . .' And just forewarning them, 'Well this is what [girls] are aiming at.'" Similarly Kate cautions her 14-year-old son, "'Girls can manipulate you or be controlling.' Because [my son] is one that would let a woman walk right over him." One father, Scott, also voiced concern about sexually assertive girls, observing that his 14-year-old adopted son is "not the type to initiate sex, [but] there are girls out there that would. And he's not a 'oh no, I can't do that' [type of person]."

This understanding of female aggressiveness is contradicted by research indicating that girls often report feeling pressured to have sex before they are "ready"[20] and are more than twice as likely as boys to say that they have been physically forced to have sex.[21] Other research suggests a compelling explanation for how and why parents can frame girls' sexuality in such a negative light, however, finding that young women face an expanding but still limited range of acceptable sexual behaviors.[22] If they violate cultural expectations that girls are naturally less interested in sex than boys, they risk being labeled sluts.[23] As more young women have sought sexual pleasure and agency, many adults have responded with alarm, underscoring the tremendous anxiety about female sexuality that persists in the United States.[24] We see evidence of this in contemporary discussions of and panic over girls' participation in "casual" sex—such as hooking up, rainbow parties, sex bracelets, and "friends with benefits." Young women still navigate the good girl/bad girl dichotomy according to which either they are sexually innocent "good" girls or sexually lascivious "bad" girls. And, of course, these labels can adhere to young women regardless of their actual sexual experience.[25]

When parents spoke about their concerns for their teenage sons, some used the good girl/bad girl dichotomy as a way to establish their sons' sexual innocence. Casting "other" girls as sexual temptresses—as Scott put it, "there are girls out there that would [initiate sex]"—appears to help parents maintain the perception of their sons as asexual and innocent. Shawna was especially direct in this regard. Describing her 15-year-old son as "clueless," she said that he is not allowed to date until he's in college. Laughing, she added, "until about his junior . . . senior year of college." She worries that girls might take advantage of him: "You've got the nice girl and you've got the slut. You're seeing kids in elementary [school] pregnant, you know."

Parents' descriptions of girls as sexual temptresses often had class overtones, although rarely articulated directly in terms of class. For example, Rose told her 14-year-old son to "watch out for girls," and, around the time he transferred from a private to a public school, she initiated a conversation with him about the dangers of oral sex. She said: "I wanted to tell him, so he'll know, 'When a girl puts her mouth on a boy's pee-pee'—somehow, by saying pee-pee that kind of makes it more gentle to me, but he gets the idea—[I said], 'Boys really lose respect for girls who act like that.'" When I asked her why she felt it was important to have this conversation at that particular time, Rose explained that when her son attended private school, "there was talk among the moms that some of the kids at the public school, not our school of course, were meeting at the movies and having oral sex in the back row." Now that Rose's son is at a public school, she worries that he may confront this situation, suggesting that the girls Rose deems sexual (and sexually threatening to her son) attend public not private school, and are from lower-income families (relatively speaking).

Renae, like Rose, also instructs her 19- and 13-year-old sons to watch out for girls: "[I say], 'You better stay away, stay away. Sometimes girls trap you.'" Renae had been telling her sons this for many years, but last year her worst fears appeared to be coming true. Her financial situation is modest—she is a teacher's aide and her husband works in a door factory—but her oldest son, Cameron, a bright, focused student, had been awarded a full college scholarship in his senior year of high school. Then he had a pregnancy scare. His girlfriend—like Cameron, she's black and from a low-income household—claimed she was pregnant. Renae was immediately suspicious and insisted that Cameron accompany his girlfriend to Planned Parenthood to take a pregnancy test. The test came back negative, confirming Renae's suspicion. To this day she is certain that Cameron's girlfriend faked the pregnancy either to prevent him from going to college or to attach herself permanently to a young man with a promising future. As soon as she knew the test results, Renae demanded that Cameron break off the relationship (which he did).

Cameron is now a freshman in college and tells Renae that this experience "'really kind of woke me up to women. I'm scared of women.'" Although she is pleased that Cameron is not dating and is focusing on his education, Renae hopes he will remain open to women in the future:

[I tell him], "Get your education. You going to meet a whole lot [of women] out there in different careers and different, well, attitudes and all that. Educated and everything. And on your level." Because I didn't feel [his ex-girlfriend] was on his level to be honest. She wasn't on his level education-wise at all. She was more streetwise. She didn't graduate. They were supposed to graduate at the same time and they didn't. She had to go to summer school to finish up.

Renae does not think that Cameron should stay away from all women, just certain kinds of women. Like other parents, she did not overtly talk about social class but used code words such as "streetwise" that have strong class overtones, imbued with allusions to gender and race. Her warning evokes the discourse of the female gold digger.

The gold-digger narrative, prevalent in mainstream hip-hop, meshes with contemporary and long-standing stereotypes of working-class and poor African American women, making them the objects of parental (and social) anxieties.[26] Anticipating that her son will become a member of the professional class, Renae's advice is also probably shaped by the precarious status of the black middle class[27] and by a dominant discourse that suggests there are few eligible black men compared to a surfeit of single black women.[28] By encouraging her son to find girlfriends who share his career aspirations and intellectual abilities, Renae implicitly urges him to seek out women—and she suggests there are many—who will share his future social class.

Boys as Sexual Aggressors

Parents of daughters also saw boys as sexual aggressors. Exemplifying this concern, Greg frequently tells his 18-year-old stepdaughter that she is better off in a group than paired up with a boy:

> If the news has something about date rape on it or these girls turn up missing or dead and, not that it only happens on dates, we're not telling her that, but it's like, there's safety in numbers. [I tell her], "If you're with a group of friends and you stay with a group of friends, there's less chance something's going to happen to you . . . If you're in a group you are better protected." And I just hope she honors that. So far, I think she has.

In addition to relying on the news and other information sources, Greg, who has a biological teen daughter as well as two teenage stepdaughters, bases his belief about predatory boys on his own experience as a male: "I feel like I have to protect my girls. You know, I was a guy and I want to protect my girls from that." Here Greg establishes himself as a sexually predatory teen boy and then moves to identify himself as his daughters' adult sexual protector. In both cases, girls are passive and vulnerable.

Overall, parents' descriptions of the discussions they have with their daughters about dating and relationships paint a fairly grim picture. Parents view relationships, in general, as a hindrance to their daughters' well-being. Gabriela tells her three daughters, ranging in age from 7 to 16: "'Take care of yourself first then seek out a relationship with someone else. Make sure that you're taking care of yourself first. Be self-sufficient, have your own job, your own career, travel, have your own interests.'" Some fear that even a responsible, trustworthy daughter might be lured in over her head by a boyfriend who is less focused, less responsible, and more sexually driven. Some parents feel this way because their daughters have expressed regret that they were pushed by a boyfriend into doing something they were not ready to do. For example, Shawna's 20-year-old daughter had sex as a teenager because, according to her, the boy she was with pressured her: "Yes. She's over it, but she's very, very cautious. She hasn't had a boyfriend [since]. She's just like 'I don't even want the pressure. I don't want a boyfriend.'" In addition to avoiding the sexual pressures that go with dating, Shawna also stated that her daughter does not need to spend the time and endure the emotional pressures accompanying dating: "She's in college. She needs to concentrate on some things right now. She got in a little bit of academic trouble so she needs to concentrate on that." Shawna is not convinced her daughter can be safe *or* focused if she is in a relationship. In this way, parents described heterosexual relationships as potentially dangerous for their daughters, as well as an added demand on their daughters' already demanding lives.

The ways parents discussed their daughters' potential dating relationships were often not only gendered but were also colored by race and class. Race was especially salient for some parents, especially white parents, suggesting the continued linkages between race, gender, and sexuality.[29] For example, Beatrice stated that she will allow her 16-year-old white daughter to date whomever she chooses without showing disapproval because she thinks "it's important to explore." She added, however, that she would feel some disapproval if her daughter were to date a black or Latino boy:

Boys I think at this age don't have a lot of social skills; meet the parents kind of thing. And, I don't know, just from my observation, that may be especially true for Hispanic and black boys—just they have a different family background or cultural reference. I mean, I have thought of that and I would not discourage her or anything. I would try to encourage her to talk to me about it.

Although Beatrice claims she would not discourage her daughter from dating black or Latino boys, she perpetuates racist assumptions by stereotyping them as lacking the social skills of other boys. In saying that she would want to talk to her daughter about dating outside her race, she also suggests that she may introduce her stereotypical attitudes to her daughter.

Depictions of hypersexual black men corrupting white women's purity and innocence have historically ignited racist fears.[30] Some narratives of the white parents I interviewed suggest the persistence of this trope. Pamela was blunt about the prospect of her white 15-year-old daughter dating interracially: "[My husband and I] do *not* want her to go out with a black person. I would be okay with the Hispanics. I just, the issue with a white person and a black person, I just think there's a lot of issues with that and so we won't let that happen." Pamela explained her feelings in this way: "Where I grew up, people were shunned and bad names were called to the girls that were going out with the black guys. And it was mostly white girls with black guys, not the other way around." Pamela's explanation reflects a legacy of racial and sexual politics in which white women who dated men of color risked being deemed race traitors and fallen women.[31]

Other parents, however, were not as direct as Pamela in voicing concerns about interracial dating. Sheila is conflicted about the black boys her 16-year-old white daughter dates:

SHELIA: She never has had a white boyfriend. Never. It's always been black guys. Always . . . Even if we're driving down the street, she does not ever do a double take on a white guy. Always on a black guy. Always.

SINIKKA: Have you asked her why?

SHEILA: She likes their bodies. Physically they just seem to her to have more—she's more attracted to the muscle. And I keep telling her, "That's okay, at this point in your life, to be obsessed with that, but to think that that's a good long term thing [laughs]?" Because, like I said, their value system, she does not embrace. But she likes the music. She likes the look. And last year, if she answered her cell phone, you could not tell that she was not black, she went full into the dialect.

The way Sheila described her daughter's attraction to black boys' bodies may reflect the extent to which Americans have sexualized African American men and boys, depicting their bodies as hypersexual and hypermasculine.[32]

Sheila thinks her daughter is just going through a phase, and she frequently emphasized that her daughter "does *not* embrace their cultural values as a whole," implying that blacks have different, possibly inferior, values compared to whites. She also told me a story about one black boy who apparently exposed himself to her daughter two years earlier, suggesting Sheila wanted me to see that her worries about black boys are not unfounded. The story reveals the particular dilemmas parents face and how their interpretations are shaped by race, gender, and current understandings of teen sexuality. The boy and her daughter, who were schoolmates, were standing outside the house talking when Sheila's husband, who was watching them from a window, saw the boy "acting suspicious." Her husband bolted out of the house and "ran the kid off our property." Their daughter admitted that he had exposed himself to her and said it was "gross." In response, Sheila's husband "sat out in our driveway in the back of our van for two nights with a rifle in his hand [*laughs*]." This occurred over Christmas break. In their efforts to keep their daughter safe, Sheila and her husband tried to transfer her to another school for the following semester:

> [We] couldn't get her in the school where we could get her back and forth in time and stuff. So she had to go back to the [same] school. And we really contemplated calling her school and telling them what had happened. Or calling the police that night. But she would only tell us his first name. She wouldn't tell us his last name.

Although it is difficult to say whether Sheila and her husband would have responded in a similar manner if the sex of the teenagers in this story had been reversed—that is, if a girl had exposed herself to their son—or if the boy in the story had been white, it seems that racialized and gendered sexual politics and discourse shaped their reaction. Female sexuality, especially white girls' sexuality, is often associated with, and may be experienced in terms of, vulnerability and victimization.[33] Meanwhile, the sexuality of African American boys and men has historically been framed as excessively dangerous and out of control.[34] Under Jim Crow segregation, these framings worked in tandem to justify racial inequality and anti-miscegenation laws. Sheila's husband's effort to protect his daughter with a rifle is, in fact, reminiscent of lynching, an institutionalized mechanism of segregation. The attempt by Sheila and her husband to transfer their daughter to another school further underscores their sense that she could not be safe near this boy. Their daughter, however, was unwilling to divulge the boy's full name, suggesting that she resisted her parents' efforts to characterize her as a victim.

Conclusion

Parents routinely constructed their children's peers as hypersexual Others who pose a threat to their own children's sexual innocence and safety, as well as their promising futures. Table 5.1 lists the binaries parents articulated between their own asexual teens and their hypersexual peers. Social inequality clearly plays an important role in parents' binary thinking. In understanding teen sexuality and talking to their children about it, parents rely on long-standing sexual stereotypes to project their anxieties about teen sexuality onto gendered, raced, and classed Others. This othering of their children's peers seems to preserve parents' notions of their own children as asexual and innocent. But it also means that parents see their own children as potential victims in their intimate relationships. Parents of sons expressed concerns about sexually voracious girls seducing and trapping their gullible sons. Parents of daughters worry about sexually predatory boys using and sullying the reputations of their vulnerable daughters. Parents' discussions about teen heterosexual relationships appear to be primarily intended to keep their children away from intimate relationships until they are older. This tactic, however, suggests that adults have a monopoly on good relationships and may prevent parents from having frank discussions with their children about the complexities—the good, the bad, and the ambivalent—of romantic attachments.

Through their binary thinking, parents also contribute to the notion that teen sexual activity is bad, and hence teens who have sex are bad and blameworthy for any negative consequences that befall them (unless, of course, it is their own children). For example, Beatrice, in talking to her 16-year-old daughter about a pregnant girl at her school, told her daughter, "She made a choice and her life's going to be harder because of that." In line with a prevalent American discourse of personal responsibility, parents assign agency to other teens' sexual behavior but conceive of their own teens as sexually vulnerable and potential victims. This way of thinking effectively creates an excuse for their children: if they behave "irresponsibly," their peers are to

Table 5.1. *Asexual Child/Sexual Peers Binaries*

Asexual Child	Sexual Peers
Naïve	Knowledgeable
Focused/Goal-oriented	Lack of Focus
Passive/Follower	Aggressive/Leader
Victim	Predator

blame. The scapegoating of Others may thus be an unintended consequence of legislation such as the Personal Responsibility Act of 1996 that is designed to promote individual responsibility in a society marked by inequalities.

Yet parents did not invent the binaries, so it is worth asking: Whose interests are served by the binaries? Why do the sexual binaries and hierarchies exist in the first place?

I suggest that the asexual/sexual binary buttresses the social order, and hence social inequality, by blaming teen Others and their parents for the problems of teen sexual activity. According to this binary thinking, good parents maintain and protect their teenagers' sexual innocence, and bad parents have teenagers who have sex and whose behavior is typically characterized as predatory, dangerous, and agentic. This way of thinking absolves society of responsibility for negative consequences of teen sexual behavior. It diverts attention from the cultural ideologies, institutional arrangements, and social inequalities that structure parents' and children's lives—including the conceptual and practical obstacles to contraceptive information and services in America—and shifts the onus for negative outcomes of teen sexual activity squarely on both the teens and their parents.

So while parents' binary thinking about teen sexuality may help bolster social inequalities, it must be understood in the context of a larger, highly unequal society that lacks a strong social safety net and presents a limited range of acceptable life trajectories. Young people are supposed to graduate from high school, go to college, get a good job, marry, and have children, in that order. Parents are expected to orchestrate and facilitate these outcomes.

The parents in this book feel accountable for their teen children's present and future well-being; but they are also pessimistic. They worry that their children's lives will be hard. Some parents spoke dispiritedly of the extreme competition to get into college. Some described the limited options facing their children without a college degree. Through their binary thinking, then, parents are not simply trying to preserve their children's innocence; they are also expressing anxiety about the ability of their children to successfully navigate their way through adolescence and young adulthood in order to secure a piece of the pie.[35] Moral panics such as those around teen sexuality "mine rich seams of anxiety."[36] The panic over teen sexuality particularly resonates with parents' fears for their teenagers' futures in what parents perceive to be an increasingly competitive environment. By desexualizing their teen children relative to their children's hypersexual peers, parents present their teenagers as deserving, worthy citizens, ultimately pointing to the role sexuality plays in notions of good citizenship in a highly unequal society like that in the United States.[37]

6

Anxious Monitoring

Strategies of Protection and Surveillance

A petite, divorced mother of four, Melissa views teen sexual activity and other aspects of adolescence as "life and death" issues. She tells her children: "'I trust you, but if you slip off in the sense that you say you're somewhere where you're not then you will be checked on every two hours. So, I'll trust you and then we'll see.'" Melissa carefully monitors her children's activities and has gained a reputation among their friends as a hard-nosed parent. "I'm known as the strict mom," she wryly commented. She reads her children's e-mails and text messages, periodically reviews their Web history on the family computer, and regularly checks postings on their and their friends' MySpace sites. She is always waiting up when her older children come home at curfew to quiz them on where they were and what they were doing.

To maintain this vigilance, Melissa stays up past midnight and begins each day "at four-thirty or five every morning." Indeed, she seemed frenetically busy on the day I interviewed her. She met me in the parking lot of a coffee shop, invited me to hop into her SUV, and explained that we first had to take her 16-year-old son to football practice. She also cut our interview short, because she had to take her youngest child to a scheduled appointment.

I examine here how the danger discourse of teen sexuality informs the strategies parents employ to protect and safeguard their teen children. Discourses do not simply articulate particular worldviews; they also guide people's actions.[1] The danger discourse of teen sexuality informs parents' sense that their teenagers, facing constant sexual pressure and threat, need to be kept busy and carefully monitored. Uniformly parents believe that the best way to keep teenagers safe is to enroll them in extracurricular activities, know their friends, keep track of their whereabouts, and establish parameters delineating what they can and cannot do.

Despite their common belief in the need to protect their children, however, parents' strategies are shaped and constrained by the resources at their disposal. Middle-class parents such as Melissa can access a range of supervised extracurricular activities which they hope will keep their children safe. The more affluent parents I spoke with also described using and providing their children with tools and technology to keep track of their whereabouts. Lower-income parents, in contrast, literally use their bodies to safeguard their teenagers. I delineate these strategies in this chapter and discuss their consequences for parents' and teenagers' well-being.

Extracurricular Activities

In interviewing Melissa, I was reminded of sociologist Annette Lareau's study involving families of fourth graders.[2] Like Melissa, the middle-class families Lareau studied had hectic lives. Between work and school, these parents ferried their children to and from numerous organized activities—sports practices and events, dance and music lessons, tutoring, and more. According to Lareau, organized activities are an important means for middle-class parents to cultivate their children's talents, whereas working-class and poor parents believe that children's development unfolds naturally, with parents simply providing the necessities of food, shelter, comfort, and other basic support. In fact, some of the lower-income parents Lareau studied expressed pity for middle-class children's highly structured and organized lives.

Unlike Lareau, I did not find a class difference in parents' support of extracurricular activities, as all parents interviewed said that they wanted their teen children to participate in organized activities. I suspect this is because they view extracurricular activities as a way to occupy their teenagers' time more so than as a means of cultivation. Parents told me that extracurricular activities can help to cultivate their children's skills but, at their age, mainly function to keep teenagers safe by ensuring that they are in controlled environments, have a "focus," and are surrounded by "positive" peer groups. Outside activities also keep teens from being bored—something parents believe encourages "experimentation," sexual or otherwise. Kelly, whose sons are 16 and 14, put it this way:

> It's a little scary for me, because I am like, you know, what would happen if they came home and said, "Mom, this girl called me up today and we have got to go figure stuff out." I don't want to have them come home pregnant. You know. I don't want that. I'm just glad that their interests are in different places, like basketball.

Paula described how she and her husband responded when their 14-year-old son wanted to drop out of his swimming program: "We're like, 'Well that's fine, but what are you going to do instead?' And we just asked him, 'You pick the activity, but we want you to do something.'" Nonparticipation is not an option. Parents want their teen children to be involved in extracurricular activities.

Middle-class parents I interviewed, however, had greater resources to draw on than lower-class parents to occupy their children. Many casually described their children's numerous organized activities. Kim, whose 17-year-old son is heavily involved in dance, outlined the weekly schedules of her 12-year-old niece and 10-year-old daughter:

> On Mondays and Thursdays we go to tutoring. And that's been happening for the last, say, two years. [My daughter] goes to dance Tuesday, Thursday, and Friday. Acting on Wednesdays and Saturday mornings. Choir and voice lessons on Sunday. I mean, it's just, everything is set.

Ruth also spoke about her children's many activities. Her 16-year-old son is less active than her 14-year-old daughter, but he is on the basketball team at his private school and serves on the student council. "And, my daughter plays soccer. She's starting [public high school] this year and she's also going to be in musical theatre." Ruth's two children also attend enrichment summer camps annually, something they have consistently done since they were little. Sharon's 14- and 16-year-old daughters have participated over the years in band, choir, volleyball, rowing, and numerous church-related events and trips; and her oldest daughter regularly attends private therapy sessions.

Many of the working-class and poor parents I spoke with also encourage their children's participation in extracurricular activities, but they rely on activities tied to their children's schools; even then, they said it is often difficult to purchase the required equipment. Kelly, for example, who earlier talked about her teenage sons' interest in basketball, is a single mother who works full-time. Her sons ride the bus to and from school daily and are expected to be home when not in school or in transit until Kelly gets home from work. The exception is when they have basketball practice or when one of their coaches, whom Kelly described as completely devoted to their players, telephones: "[Their coach] will call up some of the kids sometimes, 'Hey we're getting together at the middle school and we're going to have a scrimmage.' Or, whatever; stuff like that, that keeps these guys in focus with having a social kind of atmosphere." Kelly is thankful that her sons have such caring, involved coaches. She reflected on the importance of basketball in her sons' lives:

> I don't know what all the other people do, if they go bowling or what they do, but my kids do basketball . . . When they go on the Internet, they look up shoes, basketball shoes. I have even gone to the history and looked to see what they look up. They look up shoes.

The problem is that Kelly's tight budget makes it difficult for her to purchase the shoes that her sons so desire: "When they say, 'Mom, why can't we go out and buy me some new basketball shoes?' I say, 'Let me look at my bankbook. Let me see how much I have. Sorry dudes. It's either food or shoes.'"

Corina also firmly believes in the importance of extracurricular activities but said that when she was a single mother she often found it difficult to buy track shoes for her two older daughters, who are now in their twenties. She recently told her daughters that she sometimes had sex with men for money in order to support her daughters' activities: "I'm not saying that I sold myself but hey—if I had to do it for my girls, yeah. And not putting them in any danger. I didn't bring no men to my house." I asked how her daughters' responded to this information:

> They didn't believe me. It was like, "Mom, you're kidding. You was always with us. You ain't had time to do stuff like that." I said, "Well you got those tennis shoes, didn't you? Or you went to that track meet that I couldn't afford to get you to, I got you there." You know. Sacrifice.

Like other parents, Corina views her daughters' participation in organized activities when they were teenagers as an important part of their development and a way to keep them safe. She could not, however, take for granted the ability to purchase the equipment and entrance fees required for their participation. Instead this required, as she put it, "sacrifice." Sacrifice is a central narrative in poor women's accounts of mothering.[3]

Even with formidable middle-class resources, however, children cannot be involved in extracurricular activities at all hours of the day. In their efforts to keep their teen children safe, parents engage in various other forms of protection and surveillance, including making sure they know their children's friends.

Friendships and Autonomy

Teresa, a mother of five, has rules for her children, but she also allows them a fair degree of independence. For example, she said that her 14-year-old son has "his own liberty, you know, to be able to make his own choices, and try to learn from them. And hopefully as he's growing up he learns right from wrong and who's good and what's bad." I asked her, "What is something you would let him choose on his own?" She replied matter-of-factly, "Picking out his own friends. He chooses his own friends."

Teresa has not always liked her son's friends: "He's had experience[s] where his girlfriends or boyfriends would try to get him in trouble and just leave him hanging there, like, hey, with his hands in the cookie jar." Yet she believes these negative influences have taught her son some important lessons, consistent with her warnings:

> Be cautious of the friends that you have because there's a lot of times that they may say, yeah, they're your friends, but when it really comes down to it, they're not gonna be there. You know, they're gonna get you in trouble quickly, but they're not gonna be there to help you out of it.

Despite these warnings, she thinks he has figured this out on his own: "I let him see for himself and I think he's done pretty good about it. He's pretty good at distancing himself." Teresa believes that the company her son once kept was responsible for the minor trouble he got into in the past. She is delighted that he has learned to pick his friends more carefully since those "cookie jar" incidents, particularly because she worries that the trouble he can get into over the next few years will have greater and longer-lasting ramifications, such as a criminal record, a sexually transmitted infection, or an unintended pregnancy.

I was somewhat taken aback initially by Teresa's matter-of-fact statement that she would allow her son to choose his friends. Do parents really think they can control who their teenage children befriend? As it turns out, some do. Many parents spoke of their concerns about their children's friendships. Some, such as Penny—who, recall, quizzes her sons about their potential friends' grades and vetoes friends with bad grades—go even further than Teresa: these parents do not just voice concerns about their children's peers but actively scrutinize them. Parents try to achieve a balance, however, between giving their teen children some degree of autonomy and monitoring their behavior and choices. This effort was particularly apparent when parents talked about their teenagers' friendships. Pamela said she is not happy about her 15-year-old daughter's friends. I asked, "Do you say anything to her about some of the friends you're not so sure about?" "Yeah, I'll tell her," she replied. "But, you know, [I also tell her] 'It's your choice. They're your friends. I may not like 'em, but you may not like some of my friends.'" Parents such as Pamela said that they do not control their children's choice of friends and would not even consider this. But clearly they do let their children know which friends they like—and which they do not.

To be sure, friends matter in terms of the kinds of activities—and trouble—that youth get into, and peer groups become increasingly important in adolescence.[4] Yet in keeping with their binary thinking, parents consistently expressed concern that their "good" kids will be led astray by peers. In reporting a story about her son skipping school a couple of years ago, Kelly said: "One day he hid from the bus and he stayed home from school with his little bad buddies." Kelly's description of this incident indicates that she thinks her son was in some ways tricked into skipping school by his "bad" peers. Norma also described some of the mischief her 15-year-old son had gotten into over the past year as "giving in to peer pressure," such as taking her car for a joy ride in the middle of the night. Norma believes this even though it was the friend who told her about her son having taken the car.

Nicole recently learned that the best friend of her 14-year-old daughter "is [sexually] active. That's what [my daughter] told me. She told me and I wasn't thrilled because they're the same age, they're 14, and that just blows my mind, even though I was a 15-year-old mom. Still, you know, that's an influence on her." Nicole was so worried when her daughter told her about her best friend that she "blurted out, 'Hey, are you interested in those type of things?' She was like, 'Oh my god, no Mom!'" Nicole trusts her daughter's response, because she thinks they have a fairly open relationship. But, similar to other parents who link teen sexual activity to danger and deviance, she also believes that her daughter has plans for her future and is motivated to avoid sex in order to avoid getting pregnant: "[My kids] know that I was a young mom and I don't want that for them. And she don't want it for herself either. She wants to go to school. She wants to be a neurosurgeon."

Because parents view their teenagers' peers as potential bad influences, they are vigilant about the company their children keep. Beatrice has always made sure to be on a first-name basis with her daughter's friends and their parents. Even now that her daughter is 16, Beatrice keeps close tabs on her friends:

> We got pictures back from her [last] birthday and I'm looking at them and I'm like, "Who's that boy? He's sitting in my living room!" And she's like, "Oh Mom, that's Samuel and Felipe." And I went, "When were they here? I didn't even see them!" She goes, "Well, they came in really fast." I was like, "Hello, I think I need to know if somebody comes into my house and there is time enough for you to take a picture."

Beatrice already knew Samuel, but she had not yet met Felipe and was outraged that he was in her home without her knowledge. She has chided her daughter since, "'No kids in our house I don't know!'" Given that Felipe is likely Latino, and given the negative racialized stereotypes Beatrice expressed about black and Latino boys in chapter 5, her anger over Felipe's presence in her house without her knowledge may also reflect her racist concerns.

One of the most touching stories I heard from parents about their attempts to supervise their teenager's friendships came from Hector and Juanita, a young couple with six children. Hector and Juanita came to the United States from an impoverished rural area of Mexico several years ago. Hector speaks limited English, and Juanita knows no English. When I arrived at their house with a bilingual translator, their oldest child, a 14-year-old daughter named Eva, came outside to greet us, brought us into the home, and introduced us to her parents.

Juanita and Hector both admitted that they are frequently confused and overwhelmed by American society and the bustling city where they live. Juanita has a third grade education, and Hector completed fifth grade. They blame their lack of English-speaking skills, education, money, and knowledge about how to navigate American society for what they perceive to be Eva's increasing rejection of them. Lately she has occasionally talked back to her parents and has made it clear that she dislikes that they travel by bus when going out as a family. She has told her parents repeatedly that she would rather they all squeeze into the family truck than ride the bus. Juanita quietly said, "She is ashamed and complains about not having more things, like new shoes or clothes. We tell [our children] when we were young we didn't have anything; not even one pair of shoes, not one toy. We started working at 8 or 9 [years old]." Juanita believes that Eva would be satisfied with what she has if she did not compare herself to peers and did not want so desperately to fit in with them. In what sociologist Allison Pugh terms the "economy of dignity," consumer goods in America's consumer-oriented yet deeply unequal society are often fraught with meanings and desires around belonging and status.[5]

Hector and Juanita are ambivalent about what America can offer their children: "there is more freedom in this country [but] more temptation," Hector stated. He and his wife were both "dutiful children; there was no fun," he added, and they are glad that their children can enjoy a childhood different from their own. But they want their children to be responsible and are worried when they hear about American teenagers, as Juanita put it, "doing bad things and being disrespectful." They do not allow their children to go to other people's houses "to do their homework or whatever." Instead, the children are instructed to invite friends home so they can be properly supervised—neither Hector nor Juanita think that they can depend on other parents for supervision. The problem is that Eva no longer wants to bring friends to their home—an impeccably neat, sparsely furnished, tiny house that Hector has meticulously repaired and renovated over the years, using leftover building materials from his carpenter friends' job sites. Eva is apparently embarrassed about the house because it is so much smaller than her friends' houses and is constructed of mismatched building materials. Hector and Juanita do not want to deny Eva a happy childhood, which they were denied, but they also do not want to lose her to her peers. For now, the "friends at our house only" rule remains in place but they are not sure how much longer the rule will last. They don't want to drive their daughter away, especially as they anticipate her living with them until she is married.

Hector and Juanita's story also illustrates how the scarcity of resources can affect parents' abilities to monitor their teen children's friendships. The more affluent parents I spoke with typically have larger houses with spacious public rooms where teens can gather in semi-privacy. These parents go to great lengths to encourage their children to spend time at home with their friends, turning parts of their homes into teen-friendly destinations—from remodeled basements to fully equipped game rooms to family dens with couches and surround-sound TV—largely because they don't think other parents are as attentive as they are. Delores, for example, is dismissive of her 13-year-old daughter's friends' parents "because a lot of them let their kids kind of like wander the streets . . . just kind of let them go."

According to Portia, some parents go too far to keep their children at home, however. Portia said that wealthy parents in her neighborhood "have their house and the guesthouse—I hear about this from the kids—and the guesthouse has a fully stocked liquor cabinet and the kid can have a party in there with no adult ever being present. There are big get drunk parties." These stories fuel parents' concerns about their children's friends, and their friends' parents, as well as their children's safety outside the home. Parents said they keep a watchful eye—but not annoyingly so, in their estimation—when their children's friends spend time at their home. They do not believe they can trust their children's friends' parents to be as vigilant.

Cell Phones, Caller ID, Cars, and Protective Bodies

In addition to using various supervised activities and keeping tabs on their friendships, affluent parents use tools and technology to monitor their children. Middle-class parents, for example, discussed the importance of their children having their own cell phones, and Sharon told me that her key household rule is that her two teenage daughters must call regularly: "Nobody goes anywhere without letting us know where they go. If they move from one location to another location, we get a phone call about what that move is." Beatrice bought her 16-year-old daughter a cell phone in sixth grade so that she could "keep up with her and stuff. And sometimes I get mad if I call it and it's on voicemail or whatever. I'm like, 'You should have this phone on!'"

Kim also uses cell phones to monitor her 17-year-old son, a young black man with braided hair and baggy clothing. However, her fears center less on what her son might do and more on how her son might be perceived in their wealthy, predominantly white neighborhood:

> The biggest thing [I worry about] is other people's reactions. One night he wanted to come home from the dance studio and he wanted to skate home, but it was late. And, I said, "I really don't want you out there skating in the middle of the night . . . I'm always afraid that you're going to be picked out for the wrong reasons and something's going to happen as a result of that." [In the end], I let him skate, but he was on his cell phone periodically and I was behind him [in my car] [*laughs*]! Because you never know, there are instances of mistaken identity. [My son] has hair down to here [indicates her shoulders] and it's braided. He has to keep it braided because of his dance. And he wears the baggy [clothing]. He wears big pants. He's never liked wearing—even when he was young, he always liked his clothes big.

And when you look at him—I told him, the way he looks and the way he acts is different. He's real polite, "Yes ma'am, no ma'am, yes sir, no sir." He's real polite. Unfortunately, society's—we don't take a good look, we can't get past what we see on the outside. So that's what I worry about—that in itself.

Kim worries that in her well-off, white neighborhood her son might be judged as a young black thug because of his appearance, not for the person he is, "an intelligent, artistic, free-spirited kid." She encourages her son's self-expression but worries about his ability to survive in a society that fears young black men.[6] In trying to balance his independence and his safety, she carefully monitors his behavior and whereabouts, employing the resources at her disposal, such as a car and multiple cell phones.

Cell phones of course, being mobile, do not indicate the user's location (unless a parent is trailing them in a car!), so Beth has adopted other technologies to keep track of her 16-year-old son: "He has to call me from place to place. And then has to prove that he is there. Like calling me from a house or something so I can see it on caller ID." In addition to paying for her son to have a cell phone, Beth can afford a phone with a caller ID display so that she has visible proof of her son's whereabouts. Although none of the affluent parents, of those interviewed for this book, described using Global Positioning Satellite (GPS) technology to track their children,[7] some evidence points to the growing popularity of these products, particularly in high-end vehicles, and many retailers market these products to parents as a way to keep their teenagers safe.[8]

Some middle-class parents are conflicted about how far to go to protect their children. Portia's husband wants their 16-year-old son and 14-year-old daughter to learn how to be resourceful and self-sufficient. To that end, they both have summer jobs and are supposed to save their money to pay for the things they want. To reinforce the message of self-sufficiency, her husband does not want Portia to help them out when they run low on money. Portia frets:

My view is that things are very different because when we grew up, you could spend a thousand dollars on a car and it—I was in a small town, so if my car broke down, it wasn't that big a deal. There really weren't any bad parts of town and a relative could come help me. We don't have relatives. We're out here on our own . . . So I want him to have a reliable vehicle. I want him to have enough money for fuel so that he doesn't run out of gas and enough money to make sure that he eats enough. That does take money!

Portia believes that the world is a more dangerous place for her children than it was for her, because they live in a big, diverse city and have no relatives nearby to watch out for them. Although her husband wants the children to be more resourceful, Portia gives them money to protect them from danger. She has insisted on buying her son a new vehicle, as it will be more reliable and safer than a used one. She also pays for her children to have their own cell phone and reminds them constantly to keep the phones charged. Against her husband's wishes, she secretly gives her son additional money to pay for gas, and helps her son and daughter out with money for food and other incidentals.

Lower-income parents also think the best way to keep their children safe is to closely monitor their whereabouts, but they have different resources to do this. Instead of equipping their children with cell phones and other technology, working-class and poor parents described using their bodies and physical presence, whenever possible, to ensure their children's safety.

In line with previous research, dangerous neighborhoods featured prominently in the stories of lower-income parents.[9] Corina, for example, spoke extensively about her concerns for her daughters' well-being in their neighborhood. At the time, Corina was married and living in a sparsely populated "frontier" state. When her oldest daughter was 5 years old, Corina considered allowing her to walk to the school bus stop on her own: "The bus stop was on the same block with the house. And I could watch her from the house." Even so, Corina was reluctant to take that step and voiced her concerns to her then husband:

> I said, "But I'm scared because I don't know the neighborhood." We just had moved into the neighborhood. And I didn't know who was in the neighborhood. And, actually we was the only black family in the neighborhood. Everybody else, of course, was Caucasian. And so I said, "Well, I don't know if I want her to walk up there by herself."

Corina worried that her daughter might encounter racism in their neighborhood, but her fears were nebulous, and she had not fully decided whether to allow her daughter to make the one-block journey to the bus stop on her own. Her husband suggested that they check the Internet to see if any sex offenders lived nearby:

Well I'll tell you, we pulled it up. The guy who lives next door to me right here; the neighbor on the corner where the bus stops; about seven of them in and around there was child molesters. On *my* block alone. So of course, no I'm not about to let my baby walk by herself. So, I told her, I said "Oh no, we can forget about that." She's not walking out there by herself.

The data gleaned from the Web solidified Corina's concerns. Throughout her oldest daughters' schooling, even when they were seniors, Corina "never let them catch the bus, I transported them." She did tell her daughters about the sex offenders in their neighborhood and even "posted the pictures on our walls in our house," but she was not convinced that this information alone would ensure their safety. Instead, she practiced extreme vigilance.

Charlene, like Portia and Corina, believes she stands between her children and a very scary world. Charlene, who was homeless at the time of her interview and renting a room in a run-down hotel, described her neighborhood as the kind that Portia fears her children might drive through. Charlene especially worries about her 17- and 15-year-old daughters' safety in the neighborhood:

Like, where I stay, it's like a lot of Hispanic guys and a lot of them look like, I don't know, I ain't going to even say, but them are mainly the ones that are chasing them little girls or they're telling them something. They'll be like, "Hey, say little momma." And when I'm with [my daughters I tell these men], "Keep your eyes over there because you're not going to go to jail 'cause they're underage, *I'm* going because I'm going to whoop your tail!" So I have to be the protector of my girls, you know what I'm saying?

Because Charlene does not own a car, her daughters must walk to the bus stop or to their part-time jobs. Charlene tries to make a point of walking with them, placing herself between the men in the neighborhood who whistle and make catcalls at her daughters, whom she described as attractive and curvaceous.[10] She does this at what seems to be an enormous cost to her own well-being. Despite having to get up very early to get her children off to school and go to work herself, she often stays up until past midnight or, if she is asleep, gets up so that she can escort her 17-year-old daughter back to their hotel room from her part-time job at a nearby fast-food restaurant. As Charlene put it, "I'm by myself raising them, taking care of them. And sometimes it get stressful. It get hard. But I can't concentrate on that. I just have to keep my eyes open. I tell them to watch their surroundings." Charlene teaches her daughters to monitor their surroundings, but she also literally uses her body to shield them from danger.

Charlene's story also shows how parents' personal vigilance, as a solution to the discourse of sexual danger, has different consequences for young people depending on social class. For example, Charlene carefully monitors her daughters' clothing choices to ensure that nothing they wear is too tight or too revealing:

> They hate for me to go [clothes] shopping with them, 'cause I have to do the finger thing. Stand up, do the finger thing. You know, bend over. And they don't like that. So they'll go shopping without me. But when they come in and I say, "Let me see your clothes." They'll be like, "Oh, Momma, ugh." [And I will say], "Let me see them or we're going back and exchanging them." So they know how to get clothes that are not revealing.

By carefully monitoring their clothing, Charlene hopes to minimize her daughters' vulnerability to sexual danger. Her strategy, however, is consistent with the notion that women are ultimately responsible for preventing and controlling their own potential victimization by behaving and looking like "good girls."[11]

Charlene's efforts to physically protect her daughters have other consequences. When Charlene's 15-year-old daughter failed ninth grade and had to attend summer school, Charlene got up every weekday morning at 6:00 a.m. to walk her to the bus stop. But then Charlene got a temporary job at a computer warehouse and had to be at work at 5:00 a.m. At first she would get to work late or miss days to walk her daughter to the bus stop for summer school, but eventually she was in danger of losing her job. Charlene was in no position financially to bargain with her employer and so, as she put it, "I canceled summer school. So [my daughter] had to repeat [ninth grade] . . . she was upset about it, but she got over it."

Charlene's decision to "cancel summer school" may have been shaped by welfare reform. In 1996 the welfare system was radically altered. Along with other changes, mandatory work requirements and a five-year lifetime limit on benefits were instituted, effectively redefining what it means to be a good mother, at least if one is poor.[12] To be a good low-income mother today is to be a working mother. The realities of Charlene's life mean that, in order for her to maintain her status as her children's protector *and* the family breadwinner, her only option was for her daughter to drop out of summer school.

The Internet and Online Dangers

It is important to note that I interviewed parents in the mid-2000s, before Facebook was a mainstream factor outside college campuses, before Twitter and iPads were popular, and before Apple introduced the iPhone in 2007, making so-called smartphones increasingly commonplace. At the time, however, the social networking site MySpace was popular and teen safety in cyberspace was a significant topic in the media.[13] Three of the PTA meetings I attended at Hayden Middle School over the course of my fieldwork included a session on how to monitor, track, and control children's online activity. That these sessions were even offered, and that attendance rates were high at all three, suggests that this was an area of great concern to parents.

Parents exhibited a complicated relationship with the Internet. As Corina described earlier, some went online to identify and locate potential dangers to their children, and others used the Web to research subjects such as human anatomy and sexually transmitted infections so they could talk with their teens about sexuality. Delores was panicky when she thought about having "the talk" with her 13-year-old daughter, so she turned to the Web: "I just remember searching on the Internet . . . [to see] what books are out there that I can really feel comfortable talking to my daughter about. We found pictures that the doctor had [used] and I was able to show her that."

Parents with computers at home worry about their children spending too much time online, but some depicted these computer activities as relatively harmless and preferable to numerous other activities teens could be doing. Barb said that her teenage sons and daughters are constantly on the family's two computers "instant messaging and communicating. And, it's probably nothing wrong with it, but I get tired of seeing it sometimes . . . The Internet was down the other day and they didn't know what to do with themselves. So I think it's very easy to get out of balance with it."

Paula said that devising rules around "computer use" was something new for her: "Because I didn't have that growing up and it's not something my parents had to deal with." Like other parents, Paula is vaguely concerned about the amount of time her 14-year-old son now spends online:

> I used to worry about the TV and how much they watched and now it's the computer and how much they're on the computer. And he's on things that I don't know a lot about, like MySpace. And, you know, I assume he's just talking mostly with his friends 'cause that's what he says. And our computer is in a public room, so at least he's not locked away. But it's a fine line

of trying not to look over the shoulder and be respectful, but at the same time be concerned about his safety.

In her study of twenty-first-century parenting strategies, sociologist Margaret Nelson calls this "monitoring (with a small 'm'), which entails open conversation and taking a look at what . . . children place on social networking sites." Nelson contrasts small "m" monitoring, favored by elite parents, with "Monitoring (with a capital 'M'), which entails actually going out and purchasing a piece of technology," such as a keystroke-reading program, that tracks and creates a record of an individual's every online move.[14] Working- and middle-class parents are far more enthusiastic about Monitoring, even as they doubt they can afford these technologies.

Regarding computers and the Internet, the parents interviewed mostly engage in small "m" monitoring. Having the computer in a public space in the home is especially important, parents told me. When I asked Sylvia if her teen daughters have a computer in their room, she laughingly responded, "No way! We want to be able to monitor what they're doing on the computer." Portia and her husband considered allowing their 16-year-old son to have a computer in his room because he kept complaining that "everyone else had one." They eventually decided against it, preferring to keep the family computers "in public places" in their home. Portia said it was a difficult decision "because we were like, well, [when] he goes to college, he's gonna have a computer in his dorm room, but even then he'll have a roommate and a RA [Resident Advisor]."[15]

Parents sometimes use their Web browser's history feature to keep track of the sites their teens are visiting. Penny's husband checks the online history periodically on the family computer to make sure that their 16- and 17-year- old sons "are using it [the Web] appropriately." About six months ago, Penny reported, "he found some [porn] sites on there that we were able to trace back to when another little boy was over. And we talked to that little boy and we talked to that little boy's parents, too. I [told them] that as long as he was going to come over and access those things on the computer, then he wasn't going to come over anymore. It's not what our computer is for."

Penny wasn't forthcoming about how she and her husband viewed their sons' participation in accessing the pornographic sites, so I asked: "Did [your sons] say, 'Yeah, we were looking at that too'?" She replied testily, "No, they didn't say they were looking at it [and] we knew because *he* [the friend] did this. He did this. He was doing this very frequently. And the only time they'd been on the computer was when this other little boy was over." Consistent with parents' view of their own children as asexual compared to their peers, Penny is vehement that her sons' friend was responsible for accessing the pornography online and believes her sons took no part in it. As proof, she said that her husband continues to routinely monitor the Web history on their home computer and has not come across any pornographic sites since the boy in question was banned from their house.

Some parents, of course, discover that their own children (mostly sons) have accessed pornography online, typically as a result of finding links to pornographic websites in the Web history or because the family computer is infected with a virus that is tracked back to a pornographic site. In line with monitoring strategies, these parents forbid their children to access online pornography and increase their involvement in and knowledge of their children's activities online. The parents I spoke with generally do not want their children to view pornography, although mothers were more uniformly opposed to this than the few fathers I interviewed. Some mothers worry that pornography will distort their sons' ideas about women's sexuality and the role sex plays in heterosexual relationships. Others described pornography as a kind of "gateway drug." If youth are allowed to watch pornography, in other words, this may lead them to watch more, and more extreme, pornography or even have sexual intercourse. Mothers feel morally responsible for protecting their children from these outcomes and attempt to do so by restricting their access to pornographic material. Also, once a mother knows her teenager has viewed pornography, allowing this to continue is tantamount to acknowledging that her child is a sexual subject, which, as we have seen, is difficult for parents to do. Thus the discovery that a child has accessed pornographic images is generally followed by prohibitions on viewing pornography and heightened monitoring.

Lorena is an exception. Two years ago, when her 16-year-old son was 14, "he crashed our computer from downloading porn." In turn, Lorena "cut off the Internet" at home: "We don't have it no more. And then he did it on the cell phone, so then we cut that off too. So now he has no access to the Internet or the cell phone."

Most parents who have Internet access at home, however, see it as something to be managed and monitored, not something that can or should be turned off because it is so central in people's lives and is a valuable resource. For example, Yolanda, whose oldest daughter had just turned 13 a few months earlier, spoke extensively of her fears for her daughter's safety in relation to the Web but also indicated some conflict about her daughter becoming so scared of Internet dangers that she no longer goes online:

> Right now she's not even old enough to be on MySpace, but everyone has
> a MySpace and she went over to a friend's house and created a MySpace

account. And I had her delete it and she did it again. And I said, "Fine, you can have a MySpace, but I want to be able to access it whenever." So I can. I monitor her photos and I monitor what's being read and written and so forth. And . . . it's scary because you hear so many things. And, I mean, we've even had a big blowout because at one point earlier in the summer, she received a phone call and, I mean, I'm an adult and the kid did not sound *anything* like a kid. And, I got on the phone and I asked what his name was and I said, "Do not call over here again. I don't believe that you're 15 years old." And I said, "Even if you are 15 years old, what do you want with a 12 year old?" She was 12 at the time. . . . And I told her, "There's a big age gap there—a 15-year-old's mentality is beyond a 12-year-old's." I was in tears. I was freaking out because I was ready to just yank the computers. And I didn't know what to do. It's just so scary. So I had her get online and read horror story after horror story of what could happen in any of those instances. There's so many articles because it's happened so much already that it was an eye-opener for her and now she's a lot—she rarely gets on the computer now. She's kind of [scared] and I didn't want to scare her away from [it] you know, because I know the kids get on there and chat and so forth, but it's just scary.

Similarly Renae told me that the lessons her 13-year-old son received at school about "predators and all this type of stuff," along with the information he has gleaned from "watch[ing] the news with us," has scared him so that now, like Yolanda's daughter, he rarely goes online. Renae stated, "That's a good thing I guess. I don't know." "You don't sound so sure," I prompted. "Yeah, 'cause I mean some kids look for [information to complete] homework on the computer, educational stuff like that," she replied. Parents such as Renae and Yolanda are torn: they do not see computers and the virtual world as simply an inevitable, negative influence on their children's lives; they also spoke of the numerous benefits of the Internet as an important resource as well as a means of communication.

Other than Rose's reference to a female classmate who emailed her son a "suggestive" picture of herself, parents did not mention sexting or cyberbullying.[16] Greg did, however, talk extensively about the "vulgar" sexual letters his 15-year-old stepdaughter received last year from a boy at school "telling about all the neat things he would like to do with her." Greg discovered the letters because his daughter was saving them, and Greg came across them in her room. In confronting his daughter about the letters, Greg said: "'Does he say these things to you also?' And she's like, 'Oh, yeah.' You know, and I'm like, 'You do realize that if he says this to you this is sexual harassment.'"

Greg handled this incident in line with a *New York Times* article suggesting that aggrieved parents respond to sexting by reporting it to the school principal:[17] "We called the school to let them know that, 'Look this is going on between this young man and my daughter, and we're not at school so this is your problem.'" The principal arranged for the two teens and their respective parents to meet with the school counselor. Greg described the meeting:

We met [his] mom and dad. They were embarrassed. 'Cause they go to read the letters and, you know, I told the counselor, "I speak Spanish but I'm not going to be the one translating for his mom." Not at all. He can do that. So Mom and Dad were very apologetic.

During the meeting, however, the boy's parents told Greg that "[their son] was getting phone calls at night. So we checked the phone bill and found [out] he was getting the phone calls from [our daughter]." As a punishment, Greg grounded his daughter "from the phone." But despite his daughter's apparent complicity, Greg still views the boy as the aggressor and his daughter as the victim. Along with gender, Greg's reaction may have relied on racialized and classed sexual stereotypes. From Greg's description, the boy in question was low-income and Latino; whereas Greg and his daughter are white and middle-class.

Conclusion

Despite viewing them as "good" kids, parents are uncertain whether they can trust their children given peer pressure, temptation, and the scary world of sex offenders, and so they engage in various forms of protection and surveillance. The strategies parents use to keep their teenagers safe are clearly draining and distressful for parents. To be sure, parents expressed great love for their children and revel in their activities and in being part of their lives, but many also admitted a profound, gnawing anxiety and sense of exhaustion. Some look forward to the time when their children leave home. I asked Beatrice, "When do you think your daughter will be ready to move out of the house?" Her response was swift and vehement:

Oh god! Never! She wants to go to [a local university] and live at home! I'm like, argh! "Hello! Okay, Mom and Dad are moving. We'll move to the country. We'll rent you the house [*laughs*]." [Our daughter] tells everybody, "My parents are going to abandon me!"

By holding themselves responsible for protecting their children—through organized activities, vigilance, constant contact, and their physical presence—parents tire themselves out. But they see no other choice—they need to protect them from a scary world. And apparently some teenagers have grown accustomed to this and expect their parents' omnipresence in their lives.

Parents' strategies of protection and surveillance, however, constitute a private solution to the discourse of teen danger; the amount of resources available for parents to enact protectionist strategies depends on their social class and therefore so does the viability of these strategies in terms of keeping the children safe. Moreover, as Portia's story in chapter 2 suggests, protectionist strategies are not foolproof. Portia is affluent, and her children participate in a number of enrichment programs. In addition, Portia uses her formidable resources in an effort to buffer her children from harm. Yet when Portia left her son for nine weeks in order to stay with her daughter at an eating disorder clinic in another city, her son had unprotected sex.

All this suggests that ideas about teenagers and teen sexuality need to be radically reenvisioned. The discourses and policies dealing with teen sexuality that hold sway in U.S. society today deny teenagers full sexual citizenship; they construct false dichotomies of responsible versus irresponsible teenagers, adults versus children, sexual autonomy versus sexual danger, trustworthy versus untrustworthy, and good versus bad, all of which deny young people a full range of feelings and experiences and reproduce social inequalities. They also create a heavy burden for parents trying to keep their teen children safe.

7

Uncertainty in Parents' Sexual Lessons

I met Corina, who had been a teen mother, on a sunny fall day at the nonprofit center where she works using her own experiences with teen motherhood to help teen mothers in her care. She has also worked tirelessly over the years to ensure that her three daughters "[don't] have to go through what I went through." Her first daughter was born when Corina was 15, and, as she put it, "by the time I was 17, I had two babies." Her parents died when she was 14, and she was living with her grandmother when she became pregnant the first time:

> I got away. My mother was dead. My grandmother couldn't chase me around, you know, so I had too much freedom. And I don't want my girls to do the same thing. And I always told my girls, I don't want them to be like me. I want them to be better than me.

Two of Corina's daughters are now in their early twenties and married, with children of their own. Her youngest is 14 years old. When her two oldest daughters were in high school, Corina had them sign a contract promising to abstain from sex until marriage. She pledged to give them each five hundred dollars upon graduating high school if they could abstain from sex, as measured by their not becoming pregnant. To reinforce the abstinence message, she took them to witness a friend's childbirth—what she called "the child-birthing class"—so they could see for themselves, "Look it hurts! This is what happens." Corina was also extremely vigilant, "never" leaving her daughters' sides:

> I would go with them to the movies. I would go with them to the mall. I went to the dances. I was the chaperone at the prom [*laughs*]! I can just go on and on about all the little stuff I did. If there was a track meet, I was there. Everything they did, I did with them.

Corina also had several male friends talk to her daughters about the "male point of view." One friend in particular—Corina described him as "a player"—told her daughters "the truth, 'I just want women for their body. I'm using them and if any other man tells you that's not what they're doing then they're lying to you.'" Corina hoped that these talks would help her daughters realize the pitfalls, especially for women, of having sex outside marriage.

In addition to her vigilance, the contract, the child-birthing class, and the talks, Corina also offered her daughters information about contraception, even taking them to Planned Parenthood for a consultation. When I asked her why, she explained:

> Because things happen, you know? I was a teenage girl. I snuck out the window. And I figured my girls will slip up and they'll do something crazy too. So they need to know the right methods to take. [I tell them], "Make sure you use protection. You protect yourself. You protect him. You don't want to get no disease. And if he's out messing around then you'll most likely catch something." Plus, Planned Parenthood, they show videos. They talk to you. They teach you about contraceptives. They tell you about the venereal diseases, what they all do to your body, how to prevent you from having children and everything else.

Corina wanted her two oldest daughters to have "something left to save for your husband on your wedding night." Based on her own recollection and understanding of her teenage experience, however, especially having been surrounded by "lying boys saying all the right stuff," she was deeply torn about whether her efforts would succeed. As with many of the parents' stories in this book, gender distrust is woven through the very fiber of Corina's sexual lessons. Because boys cannot be trusted, Corina believes, her daughters *must* be prepared to protect themselves. Wanting to give her two oldest daughters the best chances in life, Corina did everything possible to help get them through high school without incident and, when they graduated, she gave them each the promised five hundred dollars. With one more daughter to get through high school, she plans to have her 14 year old sign the abstinence contract this year, and she is organizing another child-birthing class and a trip to Planned Parenthood.

Corina's story reveals a great deal of conflict and ambivalence, especially about abstinence. She fervently wanted her daughters to abstain from sex until marriage, partly because of her convictions about the sanctity of marriage, but also because of her own experiences as a teenage girl. Yet based on her experiences—especially her memories of being attracted to boys, pressured by them, and eventually abandoned—Corina was not convinced that this would happen. Like Corina, many of the parents I spoke with promote abstinence when they talk about sex with their children, even as they doubt its practicality. Parents articulated a love-hate relationship regarding abstinence: they believe that abstinence promises physical and emotional safety and well-being, and they like the simplicity of telling their children to abstain, but they are also deeply skeptical that abstinence is a realistic course. They fear that by advising abstention, they are not adequately preparing their teens to deal with issues around sexuality. Parents' stories expose a deep angst and confusion about this subject, and so it is important to examine parents' ambivalence over the advice they give their children about sex as well as the sources of their ambivalence. In this pursuit, the following pages demonstrate that American parents are not nearly as polarized in their thinking about sex education as they are so often characterized.

Why Ambivalence?

Sociologist Kristin Luker's study of skirmishes in communities across the United States over sex education finds that, when it comes to teen sexuality, Americans are polarized: sexual liberals disagree with sexual conservatives fundamentally regarding tradition versus modernity, values, and the role of information in people's lives. Sexual liberals believe that young people need information about sexuality so they can make good sexual choices, whereas sexual conservatives believe that too much sexual information can be confusing, even dangerous, and they worry that equipping young people with knowledge about sexuality, including contraception, jeopardizes the institution of marriage by removing a major incentive for young people to get married—namely sex.[1]

Although this research helps us to understand the heated fights over sex education, it depicts reality, by its predominant focus on the activists and the communities involved, as "divided into people who are for or against someone or something."[2] These positions do not accurately represent the everyday issues parents face in their attempts to teach their teenage children about sex. Instead, as we will see, ambivalence and ambiguity reign.

I use the term "ambivalence" more in a sociological than psychological sense. Psychologically, ambivalence broadly refers to "the simultaneous existence of attraction and repulsion, of love and hate."[3] Psychologists tend to focus on individuals' contradictory states toward people, objects, or symbols. A sociological understanding of ambivalence emphasizes that contradictory feelings or attitudes are often rooted in structured social relations.[4] Ambivalence, sociologically defined, is "the result of pressures imposed by contradictory demands or norms placed on an individual in a particular social location, role, or relationship."[5]

Sociologists examine how social conditions can encourage intense conflicting emotions. Ambivalence tends to arise from interdependence and often entails a sense of obligation, for example. The parent-child relationship is rife with ambivalence given the extent to which parents' and children's lives are intertwined and interdependent. A parent might profoundly love his or her child but might also feel deep resentment about the child's dependence and neediness. Ambivalence may also be rooted in contradictory cultural discourses, such as those associated with teen sexuality. Teen sexual activity is routinely linked to a host of negative outcomes, even as notions and images abound of teenagers as highly sexual and sexualized.[6] Sexuality is itself associated with strong emotions. Sexual intimacy can invoke feelings of vulnerability, desire, shame, and love, even simultaneously. Nor are parents able to face this issue simply and straightforwardly; indeed, their own feelings often leave them deeply conflicted.

This chapter describes parents' ambivalent feelings about how best to guide their children's sexuality but also discusses the discursive and material social conditions that contribute to those feelings. Their uncertainty arises from their own life experiences and their emotional investment in and feelings of accountability for the safety and well-being of their children. But inequalities (especially gender related) and contradictions connected with teen sexuality also guide parents' emotional states.

Ambivalence is often ignored in research, but paying attention to it can provide important insight by introducing complexity to the sex education debates and showing that, among typical parents, the so-called divisions between sexual conservatives and sexual liberals are not as clear-cut as research suggests. Examining parents' ambivalent feelings also underscores how parents' social status, beyond simply their political, religious, or moral beliefs, shapes their understandings and management of teen sexuality. Finally, ambivalence is itself a significant component of how parents think about their children's sexuality.[7]

Although the focus of this chapter may seem disconnected from the preceding chapters, ambivalence and the previously discussed binary thinking are linked in an important way in that contradictory feelings may be resolved by splitting them, separating the good from the bad, and engaging in "othering."[8] Parents' binary thinking—constructing their own teen children as asexual compared to their children's hypersexual peers—may arise partly from their efforts to resolve ambivalent feelings about how to ensure their teen children's sexual safety and well-being. Splitting and othering are also evident in the parents' stories in this chapter; for example, in Corina's decision to provide her daughters with information about contraception because boys are untrustworthy.

The Context and Contours of Parental Uncertainty

Many parents are conflicted about how to talk to their children about sexuality, simply because contradictory sexual messages dominate the cultural landscape. Sex is often vaunted as a powerful drive in life, key to personal fulfillment and happiness, and important for self-development, but it is also depicted as a risky enterprise, particularly for teenagers, and as immoral outside marriage. Parents are whipsawed by numerous competing discourses. As abstinence-only sex education has become the dominant discourse around teen sexuality, the discourse of teenagers as sexually driven and teen sexual activity as inevitable increasingly competes with the discourse that abstinence is best—the moral and rational choice.

Reflecting a combination of these two dominant discourses, most of the parents interviewed professed that they prefer sexual abstinence until marriage (or adulthood), but they also expressed deep misgivings that abstinence may not be terribly realistic. As Josefina put it, "Abstinence is best. It's the only way where you're one hundred percent *not* going to get pregnant; you're *not* going to get any sexually transmitted diseases. But it's not real." Josefina's statement, and her anguished tone, suggests she desperately wants abstinence to be a realistic option, even as she is not convinced of its practicality. Rose also encapsulated this stance when she said, referring to her 14-year-old son, "even though we're Catholic and you're not supposed to have sex 'til you get married, I know, in reality, that's probably not going to be the case. But I want—I hope it won't be until he's in his twenties." Rose fervently wants her son to abstain, ideally until marriage but definitely until adulthood, yet she worries that if she pushes abstinence too hard, her son might develop guilt about sex if he does, indeed, experience it outside marriage.

In contrast to Rose, Beth does not anticipate that her 16-year-old son will remain abstinent until marriage, but she still tells him that this is what she expects:

> BETH: I will say things like half-kiddingly, but he knows I'm not kidding, like "Now remember you cannot have sex until you're married." I just know that's not going to happen. I think the no-sex-until-marriage thing is a religious thing and we're not that religious, so I don't have that expectation of him.
>
> SINIKKA: But you tell him anyway?
>
> BETH: Yeah, because you don't know what else to say.

Beth tells her son to abstain not for religious reasons but because she lacks a cultural repertoire to talk about sex outside marriage in any other way.

As I have noted throughout the book, teen sexuality is routinely framed in negative terms: popular discourse and media accounts tend to focus on teen pregnancy, sexually transmitted infections, "casual" sex, and victimization. Moreover, although debates over sex education are often based on the notion that abstinence programs differ from comprehensive sex education curricula, both approaches typically rely on the danger discourse of teen sexuality, emphasizing the risks and negative consequences of teen sexual activity.[9] A positive discourse of teenage desire and sexual pleasure, especially female desire, is notably absent in both popular discourse *and* sex education.[10] Abstinence holds great allure in this context yet doesn't fully resolve parents' concerns.

Although Beth has not yet talked with her son about contraception, there are some parents, like Corina, who likewise stress abstinence but nonetheless provide contraceptive information. Lorena, for example, prefers that her 16-year-old son wait to have sex until he is married *or* until he has found the right person: "I always instill in him, 'You have to have somebody special. It has to be somebody special. Hopefully it will be the person you marry. But these days I can't expect that, but that's what I prefer.'" Because she feels she cannot expect her son to abstain until marriage, Lorena has discussed contraception with him but remains conflicted. When I asked if she thought it was acceptable for teenagers to have sex, she responded, "I don't know. I think it depends on the individual. But my son? No. I don't think so." Like other parents, Lorena is torn between her strong sense that sex is not safe for her teenage son and her feeling that he may be driven to have sex because of his hormones or peer pressure.

Parents' own experiences critically shape their uncertainty about what is best for their children. Lorena wants her son to abstain partly because she was a teenage mother. Although she attributed many positive things in her life to having been a teen mom, including becoming more responsible and goal oriented, she also said that becoming a mother at 16 made it harder to achieve her goals. She currently works full-time in a low-wage job and takes college classes in the evenings, hoping to someday become a probation officer. She would like her son to have an easier life.

Based on their own experiences, however, some parents wonder whether sexual abstinence until marriage lives up to the claim that it is the route to happiness. Sheila, who has two sons in their twenties and a 16-year-old daughter, articulated this uncertainty:

> I will always discourage a teenager from having sex before marriage, period. But really what I would want is that they wait to have sex until they're about 25 and figure out what they want first [*laughs*]. If I could really say that and get away with it! But instead, I define it as wrong before marriage. I don't necessarily—with my own experience and my experience with my husband, I don't think our life would have been any better or worse if we had waited. It developed along the way. And you can wait until you get married and then hate the sex with the person you're with, even though you love them dearly.

Sheila and her husband of twenty-eight years both had active sex lives as teenagers and had sex with each other before they married. She doesn't think this harmed her in any way, and yet she would not feel comfortable saying this to her children and is annoyed that her 16-year-old daughter's sex education class at school "did the condom route." As she continued to talk, however, it became clear that she has told her children to wait to have sex until marriage *or* adulthood. She described the conversation she and her husband had with their daughter about the sex education class:

> We interjected our own values and told [our daughter], "Well, this is what they're going to be teaching you, here's how we feel about it." And my thought on that has always been, "I would prefer you wait 'til you're married. However, if you decide, *as an adult*, that you're *not* going to do that, be careful. Take these precautions."

As Sheila's interview progressed, however, she let it slip that she told her daughter she will help get her on birth control in high school:

> I did tell her, "I don't want to put you on the Pill because I don't want you to think, at 16, that I've given you permission. But, if you're going to do that anyway, I'd rather have you on the Pill than—" Because at that point . . . if she's made up her mind, I'm not going to talk her out of it. And that's why I say on that [background form] thing, I'm somewhat conservative—I would rather it be like that, but I also know the world we live in. Yeah, it's been a while since I was young, but I do remember.

Shelia considers herself somewhat conservative because she thinks abstinence is probably best, but at the same time she is unsure. Like many parents I spoke with, she relies on her own life experiences to figure out what is best for her teenage daughter. These experiences are often more nuanced than the sex education debates might suggest. Sheila had sex as a teen and still remembers how it felt. She does not feel she was permanently scarred by it and in fact remembers it fondly. Nor does she believe her teenage sexual experiences have prevented her from having a fulfilling sex life as a married adult, as the abstinence-only position asserts.

But Sheila is conflicted and voiced accountability for safely ushering her daughter to adulthood. As she put it, when she said she would like to tell her daughter to abstain until she is an adult rather than until she is married: "If I could really say that and get away with it!" Similarly Beth, who has told her son to abstain from sex until marriage even though she does not really expect this, indicated that she feels accountable for not yet teaching her son about contraception:

> I try to do what I'm supposed to do as an obligation as a parent and just for society in general so I don't put this kid out there who doesn't know anything about the consequences of his actions. It's probably long overdue—I haven't talked to him about contraception. I have friends that have [talked to their children], I just haven't.

Referring to her 16-year-old son, Nicole said, "Even though I know my son has probably had sexual activities, I have not known, I have not seen, I have not heard. You know?"

Overall, parents said that *they* are responsible for guiding their children through the teenage years and into adulthood. As the above comments suggest, a parent may feel complicit in and perhaps responsible for any negative outcomes as a result of giving their teen child "permission" to have sex, inadequately teaching their teenager about the "consequences" of sex, as well as knowing their teen is having sex or acknowledging to an interviewer that they know. But also, because parents' and children's lives are deeply interconnected,[11] whatever happens to children naturally affects their parents' lives as well. Fern, referring to her hopes for her 14-year-old daughter's future, put it this way: "[Her father and I] we won't be happy if she's not happy."

Case Studies in Uncertainty: Strong Opinions, Conflicted Parents

It might seem obvious that some parents, especially those with moderate or conflicted political views, such as Sheila, would express uncertainty about their sexual lessons. Surprisingly, however, I found ambivalence even—and, in some cases, especially—among parents who articulated strong opinions about politics, religion, sexual morality, and healthy sexuality. Parents do not simply have a rigid set of convictions that they doggedly stick to but instead take their cues from their children, their own complex desires and memories, and their understandings of how society generally works.

In what follows I draw from two interviews to further explore uncertainty and contradiction in the parents' narratives. Following the sociologist Ken Plummer, my goal is to use "deep stories" in order "to see more clearly that lives are not simply straightforward in their genders, bodies, sexualities, or relationships."[12] One parent interviewed is a mother of two teenage daughters who defines herself as "very liberal" and who works at the college level in health education and outreach; the other is a father of one teenage son and two younger sons, and identifies as a "very conservative," active Catholic "who follows the Church's teachings."

I have chosen to focus on these two parents because they represent ideological extremes from opposite ends of the political spectrum, and both expressed strong opinions about sex education and teen sexuality. In this way, their stories provide insight into the ways that parents with deeply held convictions about teen sexual activity attempt to guide their own children's sexuality; such insight introduces additional complicating dimensions into the existing research, which narrowly focuses on activists involved in the fight over sex education. These two parents also share the same biological sex as their children. The mothers I spoke with tended to say that they feel more competent and authoritative when talking to their daughters about sexuality, whereas fathers said they are better equipped to talk with their sons.[13] Hence some parents—mystified by their children's sexuality, which they view as "other" than their own—may feel conflicted regarding what to teach their children about sex. Focusing on parents who share their children's biological sex avoids confusion in differentiating parental ambivalence from these other gender dynamics.

Sharon's Story

Sharon is a married, white, 51-year-old mother of two teenage daughters, ages 14 and 16. With a total household income of just over $150,000, Sharon is one of the highest-income parents in the book. She identifies as very liberal and has a postgraduate degree. A few years ago she declined a promotion and sought a new job that would be less stressful and time consuming so that she could spend more time with her family.[14] The new job also allows her to use her expertise in sexuality research and education. Prior to her interview, Sharon explained that because of her job as well as her upbringing she is very knowledgeable about sex and feels comfortable talking to her daughters about sexuality.

Sharon was frank about sex in her interview. Whereas I typically had to warm parents to the subject by first talking generally about their children and their daily schedules, she brought up the topic of sex in response to my first question: "How would you describe your daughters?"

> They're very different from one another, both physically and personality wise. The older daughter, the 16 year old, doesn't act out—other than mouthiness—but doesn't act out in any way that I'm aware of in terms of sexual involvement or sexual intercourse. But she may be sexually active, I don't know. We certainly talk about it.

Sharon not only raised the subject of sex early in her interview but also offered a glimpse into some of her conflicted feelings. In her description of her 16-year-old daughter, she refers to teenage sexual activity in terms of acting out, suggesting a conservative stance on teens having sex. As we will see, however, Sharon wants to cultivate her daughters' sexual subjectivity—a sense of pleasure and agency in their bodies[15]—and is convinced that teenage sexual activity is "unavoidable."

Sharon grew up in a fairly liberal household. As a teenager, in the 1960s, "there were still messages about not having sex until you got married and

I never even listened to any of that crap and my parents certainly didn't shove that down my throat." She is critical of a great deal of the information available about sex in the 1960s, describing it as "condescending:" "They just assumed that you were heterosexual and assumed a whole lot of things. People didn't talk about STDs." Sharon instead tries to provide her daughters with diverse information about sexuality: "My kids, they don't hear—if I have anything to do with it anyway—homogenous messages when it comes to sex and sexuality." In contrast to parents who simply assume their children are heterosexual, for example, Sharon has actively surrounded her daughters with affirming images and messages about gays and lesbians. She specifically asked a close friend who is a lesbian to be her oldest daughter's godparent because "I want to have homosexual adults in my child's life so that if they grow up with that orientation, if that's their way to express themselves sexually, that they don't feel shunned or feel that that should be hidden or act out in self-destructive ways."

She and her husband have also made it clear that they do not expect their daughters to get married or to be heterosexual: "When the girls were little, when we talked about marriage we would say, 'When you get older and if you *choose* to get married.' We try to use [the word] partner. And every once in a while I say, 'When you get older and you settle down with a girl or a guy.'" As Sharon put it, "we're not . . . disgusting PC [politically correct] people at all. But we just want it to be safe for them." She and her husband hope that their daughters feel safe to express their sexuality in a variety of ways, within or outside marriage. Moreover, they are openly affectionate in front of their daughters because, "[in a relationship], you need to enjoy each other physically and we do and I want them to see that. Sex isn't this dirty thing you hide away; it's part of life."

Sharon is also pleased that her daughters are exposed to other happily married couples through friends of their family and members of their church: "they just have great role models . . . I think that I'm not seeing any kind of white trash influence on them." I was intrigued by Sharon's use of the term "white trash," and so I asked her what she meant by it. Clearly annoyed by my question, she replied, "Well, you know what I mean. Just like, just like—. You know, when I say white trash I mean like fighting and fussing and screaming and bad divorces and battering. That sort of thing."

Indicating that class is as much about cultural as economic differences here,[16] Sharon explicitly distances her middle-class behaviors and attitudes from those of the lower classes. The lower classes, not the middle class, engage in domestic violence, "bad divorces," and corrosive emotional interactions. Her use of class stereotypes constructs her own middle-class gender and sexual subjectivities "as enlightened and progressive."[17] By stating, "you know what I mean," she also stresses that this belief is a kind of cultural logic—widely known, understood, and assumed to be common sense—and she positions me as a fellow member of the enlightened middle class and thus someone who shares her worldview. Sharon believes that, through her privileged class status and her daughters' exposure to others who share a similar class standing, she can bestow important social resources, including "good" relationship skills, on her daughters.

Through all these strategies, Sharon hopes her daughters develop a healthy sense of relationships and of their own sexuality. She also wants to instill in them a right to sexual pleasure. In her previous job as a health educator, she traveled around the state lecturing about sexuality education: "I'd talk about, just say yes. That we need to educate young women to just say yes. So that they could say yes without all the come here, get away sort of stuff." In other words, Sharon hopes to cultivate in her daughters what sociologist Karin Martin terms "a positive sense of self and sexual subjectivity."[18]

To that end, Sharon was among a minority of parents interviewed who have talked to their children about masturbation (and one of only a couple of parents who talked about it with a daughter). Moreover, the handful of parents who talked to their children about masturbation typically did so after "catching" them masturbating, and their conversations focused on masturbation as something that may be enjoyable but must be done in private. Sharon, in contrast, has spoken to her daughters about masturbation as something explicitly pleasurable. She also openly explained how masturbation helped her find sexual pleasure: "We've talked, very lightheartedly, about masturbation. And I told them, 'If I hadn't done it, I don't know how I would have enjoyed sex with somebody.' [So we didn't talk about] the specifics of it, just that it's normal and that it might help out." Sharon hopes these talks will encourage her daughters, if they have not already, to masturbate. Her goal is for them to learn about their bodies and what is sexually pleasurable now, rather than wait for the moment of intercourse to provide sexual fulfillment.

But Sharon also spoke cogently of the dangers "sexually active" women, indeed all women, face in a sexist society, particularly one that privileges male sexuality. In talking to her daughters about sex, she tries to emphasize both their sexual agency and right to sexual pleasure *and* the sexual difficulties young women may encounter in a sexist society.[19] Her struggle to balance sexual pleasure with sexual danger reveals the complexity of this endeavor. It also shows that parents' sexual lessons are not as straightforward as the polarized liberal versus conservative sex education debate suggests.

Despite her sex-positive perspective, for example, Sharon has made it clear to her daughters that she prefers that they wait to have sex: "Because there's lots of time to do that, why do it now? I mean, yes exploring bodies, yes, kissing, but you have your whole life to have sex." Sharon worries that, because they are young women, her daughters may be sexually victimized or pressured into being sexual when they are not really interested or ready to have sex. She described, for example, talking to her daughters about oral sex. From what she has seen and heard, Sharon thinks girls often participate in oral sex not for their own sexual pleasure, but because it's "the thing to do now. And if I truly felt that they were getting a lot of pleasure doing that, well go. But that's not what's happening in the majority of those cases. I mean, it's a statement or whatever." Thus, she has stressed the difference between "doing something that they want to do and something that they felt obligated or pressured into doing. And that only they can make decisions about what's right for them and I'll support them however they choose to do that. But I don't want them to feel obligated or pressured."

The above quote captures the conflict Sharon has in her effort to raise sexually agentic daughters. She wants her daughters to feel empowered to actively learn about and seek out sexual pleasure, but she also believes that many girls feel removed from a sense of themselves as sexual beings, are vulnerable to sexual violence, and face societal condemnation for being sexually knowledgeable (if only allegedly so). Her daughters, for example, have talked disparagingly about girls at school who are rumored to be "sexually active:" "You'll hear them say just horrible things about other girls. Like, 'She's such a skank.' 'Well, what's a skank?' So we kind of talk about those things when they come up. 'Oh god, she has a bad reputation.' 'What does that mean?'" Although Sharon encourages her daughters to question the sexual double standard, she is also aware that it is a continuing dynamic in her daughters' lives that could negatively affect them, given that all girls in a sexist society risk the label of a "slut," "easy," or a "skank."[20]

How is Sharon's thinking about her daughters' sexuality influenced by her desire that they develop sexual agency and her coupled fear that it will be difficult if not impossible for them to do so until they are older? She is highly conflicted about how and whether her daughters can exercise sexual autonomy and agency. From reading her oldest daughter's diary, she found out that her daughter gave a boy a "hand job in the church van on the way to a ski trip."[21] She voiced uncertainty about the incident:

If she was doing it because she wanted to and if she got something out of it, I guess I don't really have a problem with it. But if she feels like, she *has* to—I hope that's not what it is. I don't want her to feel like she's got to sexually service some boy in the back of the church van! I honestly don't think that's how she felt or I might have said something. I think she's got a good head on her shoulders when it comes to that.

Sharon hopes her daughter freely chose to explore and pleasure this young man, but she is concerned that she may have felt pressured to "sexually service" him. In the end, she has not talked with her daughter about this incident because doing so would reveal that she read her daughter's diary, which might damage their relationship, [22] but also because she has decided to frame the incident in terms of choice, not victimization.

As Sharon talked, I saw that some of her conflict about teen sexual activity generally, and her daughters' sexuality specifically, comes from her own experiences as a heterosexual woman. For example, Sharon conveyed some ambivalence about her first sexual experience:

SHARON: It was a good one. It was planned. I knew where I was in my cycle. I knew my roommate was out. It was not heated. I mean, it was not rushed. It was not back seat of a car. It was great.

SINIKKA: What do you attribute your sensible first sexual experience to?

SHARON: Well, I'm not even sure it's the healthiest thing. It would be nice to have a little bit more abandon I guess. But I kind of like to be in control. The thought of being taken advantage of just argh!

Sharon's concern that, as a woman, a man might try to take advantage of her sexually required that she carefully plan and stay in control of her early sexual experiences. Yet she feels torn about this: although she *was* in control and experienced sexual pleasure in a safe environment, she believes her desire for control led her to hold something back. Reflecting a dominant cultural understanding of sex as something that people "give in" to—a notion that "good" sex involves complete and utter abandonment[23]—she would have liked to let go more. Despite her conviction that heterosexual sex is often a contest in which men struggle for dominance and women are punished for being easy, she is not immune to the prevalent cultural discourse of sex as an uncontrollable force that overwhelms all rational thought as it sweeps lovers up in passion and ecstasy. Similarly, while Sharon is glad that her daughters get "a ton of information about sex" from various sources, she also wistfully said: "I wonder if it might just take some of that exploratory kind of learning as you go kind of stuff away, which is kind of sweet."

Recent studies of sex education indicate that activists and sex educators are divided about the role of information in people's lives. Sexual conservatives seek to maintain the mystery of sex, and they believe that too much information robs sexuality of its mystery. Sexual liberals, in contrast, stress the importance of demystifying sex and emphasize that it is a natural drive.[24] Sharon's narrative suggests greater uncertainty and an intermingling of these diverse positions on the role information plays in young people's lives. Sharon grew up in a liberal household and is proud that she has gone beyond her parents' sexual liberalism in her own household. She feels she is providing her 14- and 16-year-old daughters with diverse information about sexuality and hopes to equip them to enter adulthood as sexually knowledgeable, agentic young women. Yet even though she wants them to be informed about sexuality, she also wishes they were slightly sexually ignorant. Her use of the word "sweet" suggests that she would like her daughters to approach sex with a touch of innocence and lack of knowledge, rather than as a calculated enterprise. Her statement above also implies that sex may be more rewarding when it involves a mysterious unfolding, that too much knowledge about sex can be a spoiler. Sharon wants her daughters to be informed, but she also wishes they could experience sex in a fumbling, mystified fashion.

Sharon also ruefully acknowledged that she sometimes does not like her daughters' cavalier attitudes toward dating and relationships. Her older daughter, whom Sharon described as so attractive she "will make men walk into shelving in the supermarket looking at her," only recently had gone on a couple of dates with a young man. Her younger daughter, who is "kind of straight up and down, totally different build," has a group of friends where "there are a lot of hugs. There's a lot of handholding and a lot of back rubs. With people that they would each say, 'Oh god, I wouldn't date him, he's my friend!'" Sharon expressed exasperation with her daughters' lack of dating and dating styles. As she put it, "I wouldn't mind seeing each of them just sort of June Cleaverish get a crush on a guy." By this, she explained, she would like them to follow a more "traditional" dating trajectory: "get a crush on a guy," go out on "car dates," and be monogamous.

Yet even though Sharon wishes her daughters could experience "traditional" (heterosexual) dating, she does not want them to be tied down to any one person. She hopes that her older daughter does not get serious with "the guy that she now occasionally goes out with" because the boy is a senior and planning to go to college in the fall. Sharon worries that if the relationship continues her daughter may miss other dating opportunities: "I would hate to see her feel obligated not to date if she was in a committed relationship and he was not here." She explained, "He's a great kid, but it'd be nice if she wasn't tied down, if she had some freedom."

Sharon wants her daughters to follow a normative relationship trajectory—meet someone, fall in love, and have a monogamous dating relationship. She worries that what she calls "their aloofness" may interfere with this path, and yet she also wants them to maintain their freedom and not be tied down. The notion that relationships weigh young people down was particularly prevalent among the middle-class parents I interviewed. Sharon worries, as do other parents, especially with daughters, that her children may lose their identity and autonomy in a relationship. Yet she would also like them to be less savvy and hard-nosed about dating. Just as she wishes they could experience the mysterious unfolding of sex, she yearns for them to innocently embark on a relationship, even as she fears it.

It's not surprising that Sharon is conflicted about her daughters' dating relationships and attitudes toward dating. Her dissonant feelings reflect a particular cultural moment, with Americans bombarded by contradictory discourses about femininity and heterosexual relationships. The reported high divorce rate and the increase in single parenting signal that relationships, in general, can just as easily be fleeting and corrosive as fulfilling. People are more aware of the prevalence of domestic violence and that these dynamics extend into dating relationships. Terms such as "date rape" and "codependency" have entered the common lexicon. But also young women, and especially middle-class, college-bound young women such as Sharon's daughters, are expected to be independent, have a successful career, and be self-supporting.

On the other hand, single life is routinely portrayed as unfulfilling and depressing, even despite middle-class girls' "self-development imperative"[25] and greater awareness of the dangers of intimacy. Relationships are still viewed culturally as superior to the single life, which is deemed a second-class status.[26] According to this dominant discourse, true fulfillment can only be achieved in blissful communion with a loved one. The imperative to be in a relationship may be particularly strong for women who are supposed to "always want love, romance, relationships, and marriage."[27] Seen in this light, Sharon's ambivalence is an inevitable reaction to the competing discourses around what it means to be young, female, and in a relationship in the twenty-first century.

Scott's Story

I interviewed Scott and his wife, Miranda, at a restaurant near their workplaces. They have been married eight years and dated for four years before that. Once married, Scott adopted Jamie—Miranda's son from her first marriage—who was 6 at the time and is now 14. Scott and Miranda have since had two sons together; one is 7 and the other 3. Miranda is white and, at age 37, a few years older than Scott, who is 34 and also white. They both wore necklaces adorned with small gold crosses to affirm their Catholic faith. Miranda identified her political views as somewhat conservative, whereas Scott identified his as very conservative.

Both work for the government—he as an engineer, she as an accountant. Even though they have a combined income of $130,000, they live modestly. Both are from working-class families and have had to work hard, they said, for everything they have. Describing their lifestyle as frugal out of choice, they reject the "spend it now, pay for it later" ethos embraced, in their view, by too many Americans. They own a house in a subdivision far outside of town to keep their mortgage payments low, meaning they both have long commutes to work. And Miranda does all the household shopping at Wal-Mart, where the family also gets haircuts, clothing, and other items. "That's our store," Miranda proclaimed cheerfully.

I interviewed Scott and Miranda together, but Scott dominated the interview. We frequently returned to Scott's conflict over how to raise a son to follow Catholic teachings on contraception when he realizes that this is probably an unrealistic goal. According to Scott, "The moral values that we're trying to instill are not being supported by what you see in society." In spite of the strength of Scott's religious beliefs, his story, like Sharon's, underscores his profound inner conflict and uncertainty, and highlights the role gender plays in shaping his advice about sex.[28]

Scott was raised in a traditional, conservative Catholic family. He does not recall his parents ever talking about sex or issues related to bodily changes during puberty:

> My parents didn't talk about this stuff, just about at all. The only thing I do remember is when the AIDS epidemic was kind of breaking on the scene and Dad had us come in and sit down and he said, "All this stuff on the news about this, they're talking about how anybody can get it. You need to know, behave yourself and, except in a very odd situation, you're not going to get it, if you do what you're supposed to do."

Scott said his father did not have to explain to him what "behave yourself" and "do what you're supposed to do" meant. Even though his parents never explicitly talked about sexuality, they imparted their values about it: "I knew what they thought. I got one sister who didn't follow too well because she's not as perceptive or maybe a little ditzy or maybe she just didn't pick up on it as well, but I knew what they thought." Scott absorbed his parents' reactions to television programs, for example: "I knew how they felt about things from having watched the news with them or whatever else. [They would say], 'that's ridiculous' or 'that's terrible.'"

Scott also knew his parents "were devout Catholics, right along the church's teachings. So I didn't have any questions about what they were teaching as being right and wrong." Scott knew, without being explicitly told, that sex outside marriage was wrong and that contraception was forbidden. He accepted, and still accepts, these doctrines of the Catholic faith. In fact, during the early part of our interview, I had the impression that Scott experiences his conservative beliefs in black and white. For example, he is concerned about school-based sex education because he believes it "probably teaches stuff that maybe I'd rather not have the kids be exposed to." When I asked what kind of information worries him, he replied, "Like contraception." Scott is also unwilling to talk about contraception to Jamie, his 14-year-old son, because "I told him that I support the Church's teaching that sex is for within marriage." In this respect, Scott said, he himself sets a good example: "Miranda is the only woman I've ever slept with."

But as Scott and Miranda continued to talk, I was reminded once again that, as with Sharon and other parents I interviewed, daily life is more complicated than it is made out to appear in debates over sex education. One might assume, for example, that sex would rarely be discussed in a conservative Catholic household, but both Scott and Miranda said that Jamie is very curious about sex and related stories of his frequent questions about sex and his body, as well as his predilection for pornography.

Jamie has come to Scott on numerous occasions to ask about sex and the bodily changes he is experiencing. This may be partly because Scott is not Jamie's biological father. As discussed earlier, parents may be better able to see other people's children as sexual beings; indeed, Scott suspects this dynamic: "[Jamie] chooses to come to me and won't talk to Miranda about a lot of it, being I'm his adoptive father." Even though his parents did not talk about sex and he turned out okay, Scott believes Jamie needs a lot of guidance. He and Miranda view Jamie as "a follower, [who] acts immature for his age." In addition, Scott said that "honesty or truthfulness is a very difficult thing for him." Miranda questioned whether Jamie's personality and problematic habits, such as lying, are based on "nature or nurture . . . because his biological father would lie through his teeth no matter what." Through these depictions, Scott and Miranda seemed to distance themselves somewhat from responsibility for Jamie's behavior, and this perhaps facilitates their willingness to see Jamie as a sexual subject, even though they do not necessarily view his sexual curiosity in a positive light.

When Jamie was in fifth grade, he asked Scott "a bunch of questions—he grilled me for thirty minutes." According to Scott, much of the conversation was about sex:

> He asked about some of the mechanics of sex and [then said], "Why would you do that?" And I explained that that's how babies are made and all. Then, as we were finishing up the conversation he said, "Well, have you ever?" Well, he has two little brothers, one at the time and one on the way, so I said yes. And then, of course, the next follow up question was, "Well, how many times?" And my answer was, "Well, I don't really keep track." I thought of saying, well, twice. You got two brothers [*laugh*]! But I didn't say that.

Scott was torn about how honest to be in this discussion with his son. If sex is for procreation, then a person should only have sex with that explicit intention. Yet despite wanting to follow Catholic doctrine, Scott and Miranda use condoms to limit the number of children they have. Scott wishes that his life more closely fit the Catholic model. He is conflicted about the example he is setting but believes that, ultimately, honesty is the key to effective parenting, and so he is honest with Jamie. At the same time Scott, as a heterosexual man, may be proud of his sexual competence and wish to convey to Jamie—as a future fellow man—a sense of sexual agency. According to gender scholar Raewyn Connell, an important part of hegemonic masculinity—the dominant form of masculinity at any given time—is bodily agency, or acting through one's body, and this includes heterosexual prowess.[29] Seen in this light, hegemonic masculinity may have trumped religious faith in the conversation between Scott and his son.

This is not to say that Scott wants to have an explicit conversation with Jamie about contraception. He has shied away from this largely because, despite using contraception himself, he expects Jamie to follow the church's teachings here. But both Scott and Miranda described Jamie as such an inquisitive child that it is difficult to keep information from him. On one occasion, Scott came home from a fishing trip and found Jamie in his bathroom trying on one of his condoms:

> I walked up and saw him there and looked at him for a second going, how do I respond to this? So I just turned around and walked out. So he notices that I'm walking out and he runs out [yelling] "Dad! Dad! What are you doing? What's wrong?" He was very concerned that I was going to go nuts or something. And I said, "I'm not going anywhere. I'm getting my wet clothes out of the car."

Scott confessed that he does not fully remember how he handled this situation:

> I know I didn't get mad about it, but we didn't talk in-depth. I guess I wasn't quite one hundred percent sure what to tell him about it. Some of it may be being self-conflicted myself. I was brought up Catholic and condoms aren't a part of the equation and so, I'm going to have this discussion with him and talk about condoms and, on the one hand, say it's okay? Well, then, that's kind of against how I'm bringing him up in the church and stuff. So I'm self-conflicted about it. Honesty is how I want to handle everything, so I'm not quite sure what to say. So I didn't say much of anything in reaction to that.

Scott is well aware that the prohibition on contraception does not fit easily into today's world where sex is deemed an integral part of marital life.[30] Even though he believes that contraception is wrong, he and his wife, as noted, use condoms to limit the number of children they have. He wants to be honest with Jamie: he and Miranda said that honesty propels all their parenting practices. Yet on the condom issue, Scott is torn. He does not want to be a hypocrite, but he also does not want to condone sex outside marriage. Ultimately he wants Jamie to follow the traditional Catholic decree on contraception.

Scott is not convinced that Jamie will wait to have sex until marriage, however: "I have that feeling of, what's the likelihood he's going to make it there without [having sex]. There's that certain level of cynicism." Yet despite Jamie's active sexual curiosity, Scott sees him as someone who is "not the type to initiate [sex]." But he does worry that Jamie might succumb to sexual advances: "There are girls out there these days that would [initiate sex]. And he's not a, oh no, I can't do that [type of person]. [The] willpower to say, 'Oh no, that's not good,' is probably not going to be there for him."

As we have seen, parents often have difficulty imagining that their children might have sex out of their own sexual desire. At the same time parents believe that their teens face powerful pressures to have sex and worry that their teens may have sex *not* because they want to but because they are forced or pressured into it. Although the belief that young people are pressured into sex before they are ready has been a common understanding of teen girls' sexuality,[31] the parents of both daughters *and* sons expressed fears that their children might be forced into doing something sexual before they are ready.

Given their concerns about Jamie's ability to abstain from sex until marriage, I asked Scott and Miranda if, hypothetically, Jamie did have sex as a teen, what might encourage him to use contraception. Scott replied, "Well, because of my conflicts, I guess we haven't addressed that. I've thought about it but I haven't said anything because I'm not sure what to say or which way to go." Despite their open discussions, Scott believes he may be incapable of talking to Jamie about contraception. In fact, even though he voiced annoyance that school-based sex education provides information about contraception, he later added: "It's hard to say but I guess it's a bit of a relief that Jamie gets that [information] someplace."

Scott is similarly conflicted about Jamie's interest in pornography. Over the past two years he and Miranda have often discovered that Jamie viewed pornography in one format or another. During the summer, between sixth and seventh grade, Jamie ordered "one hundred and twenty dollars worth of pay-per-view adult movies." The charges for these movies appeared on the family's cable bill at the end of the month. "We didn't know that there are ways to block it," Scott told me. "Didn't have it blocked. Of course [we] blocked it after that." More recently Jamie has "somehow managed to get through [the parental blocks] and he ordered a couple more," which also showed up on the bill. When Miranda confronted Jamie about these latest charges,

> He was like, "Well, after five minutes I turned them off. I didn't want to watch them anymore." But he did try to use psychology on me a little. When we were discussing this he goes, "Mom, you know, they have research studies out there that say once you watch it one time, it becomes almost an obsession that you need to continue to watch it." So, now that he's 14, he's started trying to play that logic.

Jamie tried to imply that he is not really interested in pornography but at the same time seemed to suggest that he is obsessed with it. Miranda prefers the former explanation, telling me: "I really, honestly don't think he's that interested." But in addition to ordering pay-per-view movies, Jamie has also accessed pornography online. According to Scott, "It's varied with time and, of course, he's gotten better with time in covering his tracks. In fact, the last time I found he was going to those sites was by reviewing what he was doing on his MySpace site."

The first time Scott and Miranda discovered Jamie was viewing pornography, they decided the best "deterrent of repeat offenses" (Scott) was to sit him down and make him tell them everything he saw. As Miranda put it, "We asked him, on the spot, 'What did you see? We want vivid descriptions. We want actuals.'" For Miranda this tactic was primarily intended to counter the messages about sex her son had seen. In particular, she worries about how women and female sexuality are portrayed in pornography. Scott said that his goal, however, was simply to embarrass Jamie into never watching pornography again.

Miranda described the conversation that unfolded: "[We asked him], 'How were they having sex? Who?' We explained to him, 'If you're old enough to watch this, we need to sit and discuss this so you know that this is not everyday, routine life.'" After an hour and a half of a very detailed and explicit discussion about the material Jamie had viewed, Miranda excused herself. "That's when Jamie really opened up," Miranda said. "That meeting opened up a floodgate, because they were in there another hour talking about his body and things that were happening and stuff like that."

I asked Scott and Miranda if, during these discussions or at any other time, Jamie has ever said that watching pornography excited him. Scott cleared his throat before replying:

> I don't think. . . .And one of the things that's interesting that I haven't fully gotten to the bottom of is that a lot of the sites that he goes to end up being the gay sites. And I've talked to him about that quite a bit. I don't—I think some of that may be his concern with size. He's wanting to see how he sizes up. He insists that he's not [gay] and I have not played upon, well you better not be or anything like that. I've expressed to him that he needs to let us know if he has feelings that way. "Let us know because you can't go through life hiding those feelings, it's too hard on you." But he's so ready to lie about little things, something big like that is going to be really hard for him to come clean on. So that's another issue that mixes in there and I'm not sure how that works out. There's not—besides that, I don't have any indications that he's attracted to guys.

As Miranda did earlier, Scott downplayed the extent to which Jamie watches pornography out of sexual interest or desire. Despite wanting to deter "repeat offenses," Scott views Jamie's interest in pornography primarily in terms of technical curiosity: "to see how he sizes up." Scott also revealed that, as a teenager, he learned about "the mechanics" of sex by watching pornography. He laughingly explained that because his parents were unwilling to talk about sex, when he was younger, "I didn't necessarily know a lot about the mechanics—although, I did have a friend who had a satellite dish!" Growing somber, he quickly added, "I don't try and operate from the [idea that] it's okay because I did it or whatever." Yet his own personal experiences with pornography clearly influence how he makes sense of Jamie's interest in it.

Here Scott also reveals concern about the possibility that Jamie is gay. He minimizes the extent to which Jamie might actually be gay, stating that Jamie seeks out gay pornography because of practical concerns—he wants to see how his penis sizes up relative to adult men—and not because he is gay. Penis size has been an ongoing worry of Jamie's, Scott explained: "[When he was younger], he was fixated on size for a while. Like he wasn't sure if he was normal or something." And although he professed acceptance if Jamie is gay, Scott indicated deep unease about this possibility, stressing that he doesn't have any other indication that Jamie is "attracted to guys" and that being gay is a big thing "to come clean on." Revealing a conservative stance on homosexuality, Scott also mentioned later in his interview that he is against gay marriage, unlike his liberal neighbor. All this suggests that Scott is uncomfortable with the idea that Jamie might be gay.

Connell argues that "compulsory heterosexuality," a term coined by Adrienne Rich to describe the enforcement of female heterosexuality, is an important component of masculine enactment—to be masculine is to be heterosexual.[32] Sociologist C. J. Pascoe, in her ethnographic study of a working-class high school, has more recently used the term "compulsive heterosexuality" to emphasize boys' ritualized and interactional accomplishment of heterosexuality.[33] Compulsory and compulsive heterosexuality seem to shape the sex talk between Scott and Jamie. Although Scott is highly conflicted about his own contraceptive use and has been unable to talk to Jamie about contraception, they have talked openly about a range of sexual and bodily issues. Through these talks, Scott implicitly introduces Jamie to a masculine world of sexual agency and privilege. His status as a heterosexual man and his desire that Jamie develop a similar sexual identity, demonstrated by his concern over his son's interest in gay pornography, facilitate their open discussions about sexuality. In this sense, despite identifying as very conservative and opposed to contraception, Scott may be well positioned to talk with his son about sexuality; it provides an opportunity for bonding and for Scott to establish his competence as a heterosexual man and help Jamie accomplish the same status.

Conclusion

When I began this project, based on what I knew about the polarized and polarizing debates over sex education, I expected a significant number of parents to talk about sex education and their children's sexuality as Melissa and Rosalia do below. When I asked Melissa her thoughts about schools teaching sex education, she replied:

No way José! Parents brought them into this world; they're the ones that need to introduce it to them. That is a private conversation depending on your faith and how you want to explain it to your children. Why would you leave something that is of ultimate importance up to someone else concerning your children?

And Rosalia had this to say:

I just remind [my daughters], I've heard that a lot of the girls in other families use methods of contraception, and [I tell them], "You're not going to do that, so if you're going to be promiscuous you're going to end up getting pregnant, and if you are promiscuous you're not going to know who the father is like these other girls."

It turned out, however, that these two mothers were the exceptions; among the other parents ambivalence reigned. Parents, for instance, are markedly uncertain about the role sexual information plays in young people's lives, partly because it is hard for many of them to see their children as sexual subjects, even though they remember their own teenage years. They are conflicted about when to talk, how much to say, and the manner in which they should speak.

Some parents focus exclusively on abstinence when they talk with their children about sexuality, even though they do not believe it is realistic or the best course of action. Parents are impressed that abstinence promises physical, emotional, and psychological health and well-being; but they are also deeply skeptical about that promise. Other parents encourage abstinence but still provide information about contraception, as they believe it is necessary and life-saving knowledge. Some of the more sexually conservative parents, such as Lorena and Denise, have talked explicitly about sex and contraception, whereas other, more liberal parents, such as Beth and Paula, have not. Their conflict and ambivalence derive, at least partly, from their own experiences and social-structural positions as parents who feel accountable for their teen children's safety and well-being.

The stories in this chapter also show how gender and sexual dynamics and inequalities shape parental uncertainty. Sharon, a self-identified liberal mother, wants her daughters to develop sexual subjectivity but simultaneously fears that her daughters may be sexually victimized; she is torn about how and when her daughters can exercise sexual agency. Sharon's story shows how hard it is for parents to navigate the topics of desire and coercion in discussing sex with their children—daughters in particular—as well as in thinking about their children's sexuality. It also underscores the contradictory role of relationships in young women's lives. Sharon would like her daughters to date and be monogamous and yet does not want them to be tied down, as she fears "the tyranny of coupling."[34] She believes her daughters will find it difficult to maintain independence in the context of a committed relationship but would like to see her daughters engage in such relationships. Her story highlights the contradictions embedded in gender and sexual discourses and identities.[35] Because contradictions often expose fissures—what Connell calls "crisis tendencies"[36]—identifying them can be troubling and can lead to new and different ways of thinking and acting—a point I return to in the concluding chapter.

Crisis tendencies are also evident in Scott's attempt to negotiate gender and sexuality. Scott, a self-avowed conservative father, engages in detailed and regular sex talks with his adopted son, ostensibly hoping to control his son's sexual behavior but also solidify his masculine identity. The tension embodied in Scott's gender and sexual work is palpable: he wants his son to be both asexual (chaste, virginal) and heteronormatively masculine (heterosexual, virile, a leader and not a follower). By stressing abstinence and religious faith, Scott strives for a masculinized version of his son as one who has leadership qualities and self-control. Male high school students who identify as religious also use sexual restraint to "cast themselves as more mature than other boys,"[37] and young Christian men who pledge abstinence "claim that they are not only *real* men but, in fact, *better* men" based on their ability to resist sexual temptation.[38] In doing so, these young men rely on longstanding discourses of masculinity centering on self-control and maturity.[39] Similarly Scott's gender and sexual practices, and hopes for his son, rest on the understanding that to be a man is to exercise authority over others and mastery over one's own bodily desires, despite nagging doubts that his "follower" son may not achieve this ideal.

These parents' stories underscore the importance of examining the larger social structures that shape parents' sexual lessons—what sexuality scholar Jeffrey Weeks calls "the forms of control, the patterns of domination, subordination, and resistance that shape the sexual."[40] Parents' ambivalence is informed not only by dominant discourses about teens and teen sexuality but also by sexist and heteronormative conditions and cultural logics in U.S. society that create a climate encouraging the perception that sexuality is dangerous for girls and women and an achievement for boys and men, and that homosexuality is a second-class identity. Parents want their children to follow a path of normative, legitimate, valued sexuality. Yet they are not sure that path is the only route to happiness—they want their children to be sexually safe but also to feel good about themselves sexually. Parents take their cues from their children, their understanding of society, and their own sexual experiences, all of which are often more complex than they appear to be in the polarized debates over sex education and, by association, teen sexuality.

8

Conclusion

Reconstructing Teen Sexuality

In the debates over sex education, both sides often use parents to support their position, even though neither side seriously considers their attitudes, beliefs, and strategies to intervene in their teens' sexual lives. The parents I interviewed do not believe that their own teenagers are sexually desiring subjects, whereas they described other teens as highly sexually motivated. Parents articulated this binary thinking across race and social class, regardless of their children's actual sexual behavior, underscoring the difficulty parents have in thinking of their children as sexual beings.

And yet, does it matter that parents do this, that they construct their own children as asexual but think of other teenagers as hypersexual? As I have argued, binaries are a critical component of social inequality, serving to reinforce difference. Through their binary thinking, parents contribute to the notion that because teen sexuality is bad, teens who have sex are bad and therefore solely responsible for any negative consequences that befall them—unless, of course, the teenagers in question are their own.

There are of course cultural, structural and psychological reasons why parents feel this way about teen sexuality, as I have tried to demonstrate throughout the book. To understand why parents have difficulty viewing their children as sexual beings, we must return then to the factors that influence their beliefs: the pervasive danger discourse of teen sexuality, dominant constructions of adolescence, social inequality, and the American ethos of personal responsibility and individualism which faults parents and children for any bad outcomes of teen sexual activity while overlooking the larger social structures that shape teenagers' and parents' life choices and opportunities.

I began this book with a description of the battle over sex education in Texas in 2004, in which one side was advocating teaching teenagers abstinence-only-until-marriage, and the other side supported offering contraceptive information alongside abstinence education. After three heated school board meetings, the abstinence-only position prevailed. The new student health textbook adopted in Texas contains no information about contraception, and the gender-neutral descriptors are now gender-specific— for example, marriage is defined as a lifelong union between a man and a woman. These changes were not made without controversy and resistance: the debates exposed a raw undercurrent of anger and dissent, and publishers ultimately rejected changes emphasizing the "negative aspects" of homosexuality, including language claiming that homosexuals are more likely to use illegal drugs and to commit suicide.

Rather than express firm support for either abstinence-only or comprehensive sex education, the parents I interviewed articulated a complex, sometimes contradictory mix of both: regardless of political views, parents want their children to delay sex until marriage or adulthood, and yet many also believe that this is unrealistic. These parents are conflicted over what they see as an ideal sexual trajectory (abstinence-until-marriage) versus a realistic path which recognizes that most people do not wait until marriage. At the same time they consistently depicted teen sexual activity as far more dangerous today than in the past. Parents' understandings are in line with the discourse of risk that dominates debates about teen sexuality in the United States.[1] Based on this dominant discourse, teen sex is equated with intercourse, which in turn is equated with heartache and emotional distress, economic hardship, danger, disease, even death. Indeed, despite their differences, both sides of the sex education debate in Texas framed teen sexuality in similar ways. During one of the meetings I wrote the following in my field notes:

Although people all around me are engaged in heated debate, what they are saying sounds remarkably similar. Today two speakers—one for [and] one against abstinence-only sex education—provided graphic and horrific descriptions of the damage sexual activity can wreak on young people's bodies. One described seeing herpes that looked like cigarette burns on young women's vulva. The other said that young people use plastic bags as condoms and douche with Coke in the hope that this will prevent pregnancy and STDs. These testimonies, although very similar in content, reached very different conclusions. In the first instance, the graphic descriptions of STDs were given as an example of what happens when young people have sex. In the second, the graphic examples were used to show what happens when young people are deprived of information about how to protect themselves and have sex.

In other words, framing the debate over sex education as a debate between whether to teach teens either to abstain or use contraception misses the similarities in how these two positions construct teen sexuality. Both abstinence-only and comprehensive sex education curricula rely on and reproduce the danger discourse of teen sexuality.

Although sex, like many activities, poses certain risks, the danger discourse of teen sexuality does not accurately reflect the realities of teen sexual health and behavior: teens can act responsibly, and the majority do, when it comes to sex.[2] Moreover, the risks of teen sexuality are not isolated from, but are deeply interwoven with, social inequalities based on race, class, gender, and sexuality. For instance, the beliefs that girls are sexually desirable but not desiring and that boys are sexually driven and insatiable may make it more difficult for girls to think of themselves as agentic, sexual beings and may encourage boys to think about sex as something they must do to prove their masculinity.[3] These discourses can profoundly shape young people's sexual experiences.

When boys believe they must compulsively have sex with girls, and girls think they should not have sex but feel pressured to do so, the result can be unsatisfying, unsafe, and coercive sexual encounters. Risk is not reduced but in fact is magnified when youth are disconnected from a sense of themselves as sexual subjects—when, for example, they do not feel entitled to sexual pleasure and safety. These discourses also shape public health policy, such as whether to make the HPV vaccine mandatory for all girls entering the sixth grade. They are also heteronormative; they marginalize same-sex desire by assuming that girls will have sex with and need protection from boys, and that boys are on the prowl for girls. Similarly when parents assume or prefer that their children are heterosexual—as did many of the interviewed parents—they may make it more difficult for gay, lesbian, bisexual, and questioning youth to believe that they are acceptable and appropriate, sexually, and therefore deserving of positive, safe sexual experiences. The danger discourse reifies teen sexuality as risky without addressing the underlying factors that make sex more or less risky for teenagers.

Yet even as American social policy and discourse frame teen sexuality in risk-based terms, sex is regularly depicted as a drive that teenagers cannot control as a result of hormones and teenagers' lack of impulse control.[4] At the same time, dominant ways of thinking deem teenagers too irresponsible and immature to handle the responsibilities associated with sexual activity. Even parents who believe that their children might have sex in adolescence have a difficult time viewing this positively. They decide that their teenagers need contraceptive information in case they are pressured by their more sexually aggressive peers to have sex or are overwhelmed by sexual "urges" and "do something crazy." And partly owing to a pervasive culture of sexual shame, parents who provide this information often feel uncomfortable and embarrassed, and prefer to distance themselves from sexuality, sensing that their children are appalled by the idea that their parents are sexual subjects. Most parents, instead, focus their discussions on the risks and negative consequences of heterosexual intercourse, including pregnancy, disease, and victimization. Talking about their sex lives is out of the question. Any discussion of pleasure is unthinkable.

Thus parents' difficulty viewing and describing their own children as sexual subjects is based partly on the danger discourse of teen sexuality and the dominant ways of thinking about teenagers. These understandings are neither preordained nor set in stone: it is precisely when sexuality is fiercely contested that "the domain of the erotic life . . . is renegotiated."[5] Sexuality is not a fixed entity but a fluid, changing, and contested site of social control and resistance. The Dutch, for example, currently view teen sexuality as normal, not problematic, but they did not always see it this way. A vigorous public health campaign initiated more than two decades ago in the Netherlands supported this belief through

> the emphasis on the self-regulatory capacities and responsibilities of adolescents; the norm that sex should take place in intimate relationships of mutual respect; and, finally, the desire to have sex be a normal topic of discussion between parents and teenagers, and not a cause for anxiety and deception.[6]

Based on the Dutch model, avenues for transforming the culture of sexual fear and shame in America include widely available public health campaigns that normalize teen sexuality and widely available, low-cost contraception. An expanded understanding of sexual activity may also help parents view their children as sexual subjects. Instead of defining sexual activity as (hetero)sexual intercourse, sexual activity should be defined as sexual behaviors that range from sexual intercourse to just talking and thinking about sexuality. This would encourage a new discourse of teen sexuality that does not dichotomize youth as asexual or hypersexual but defines all young people as sexually active, because they "live in a world filled with sexual images, opportunities, narratives, and possibilities."[7]

In challenging current understandings of teen sexuality, however, it is important to recognize that Dutch society is significantly different from U.S. society; the Netherlands, for example, has a national health care system, and its population is far more ethno-racially and economically homogeneous compared to the U.S. population. As I have argued throughout this book, social inequality plays an important role in parents' understandings of their children's sexuality. Parents do not simply struggle to see their children as sexual subjects because sexual activity implies danger and adulthood; they also struggle to view teen sexuality in positive terms. They equate teen sexual activity not just with heartache, disease, and pregnancy, but promiscuity and deviance, a lack of focus or drive—all characteristics they do not associate with their own children. In doing so, they rely on dominant discourses of teen sexuality laced with inequalities of race, class, gender, and sexuality.

The problem of teen sexual activity in America is habitually constructed in terms of race, class, and gender,[8] and homosexuality is stigmatized, marginalized, and all too often described as a problem.[9] Because parents' understandings reflect these dominant discourses, along with challenging the danger discourse, we need also to confront and resist understandings of sexuality that evoke and rely on racialized, classed, gendered, and heteronormative cultural logics. Not only do these understandings establish the belief that some of us are inferior to others, but they also generate distrust and a sense of differentness, all of which serve to perpetuate and justify social hierarchies and inequalities.[10]

Many parents, however, base their concerns about teen sexuality not simply upon the beliefs and stereotypes that focus on the race, class, and gender of sexual Others but also upon their experiences of inequality. Many mothers shared stories of their own struggles to achieve sexual autonomy and pleasure as teenagers and adults in a society that denigrates female sexuality. Given their experiences, they worry that if their children, especially daughters, have sex as teenagers, they will be hurt socially, physically, and emotionally.

Mothers also said that they felt discredited by their children, especially sons, when they tried to talk with them about sexuality. Thus, although parents often reproduce social inequality in their lessons about sexuality, they may also grapple with inequality in their own lives. The tensions emanating from these crosscurrents of inequality expose "crisis tendencies"[11]—schisms in the dominant social order—that may lead parents to question and challenge hegemonic understandings of teen sexuality. By examining how inequality has shaped their own experiences, parents can begin to critically confront their reliance on and reproduction of these very inequalities in discussing sexuality with their children.

Parents also feel morally accountable for protecting their teen children and ushering them safely to adulthood, and they also spoke of the enormous pressures and financial hardships of raising children, fearing their own and their children's economic futures. Even burdened by these pressures, they still demanded much of themselves and other parents. Consistent with a dominant American cultural ideal, they placed the responsibility for children's actions and well-being on their own and other parents' shoulders. Children's behavior and outcomes, I was frequently told, reflect how well they have been parented. Corina expressed the prevailing opinion: despite her belief that the American government "sucks," that then President Bush "is screwing all of us over," and that "it takes a village to raise a child," when I asked, "How do you think we can make it better?" she replied:

> Well I guess one is we start with your own family first—your own family first. Start with your family. Can they help out with the kids? Can they help out with the picking up and the dropping off? Spending time, going to do activities together as a family. I'm a true believer in families—closeness, bonding, stuff like that . . . I think it starts with the family. I think if you have a close-knit family that can rectify the problems.

Although parenting practices may vary based on social class, parents across the class spectrum believe that parents are accountable for "passing on social values to children."[12] Most of the parents with whom I spoke think, as Corina does, that it is ultimately the parents' responsibility to direct and control teen sexuality; they feel responsible for their children's sexual behavior and consider the outcomes of teen sex to be largely negative.

In contrast, this book points out the need to employ the "sociological imagination"[13]—to see that the problems and challenges around teen sexuality that parents and their children face are not rooted in parental failure or teen behavior but rather originate in the larger cultural ideologies and institutional arrangements that structure parents' and children's lives. Federal policy around sex education ever since the 1990s, for example, explicitly states that abstinence is key for youth to achieve happy, well-adjusted lives and promising futures.[14] These policies inform parents' sense that their own children are asexual.

The beliefs parents hold about teen sexuality also reflect the myriad sexual inequalities and hierarchies in American society. In a society where teen sexuality is equated with deviance as well as imperilment, the asexual teen is lauded as the good teenaged citizen. For these reasons, among others, parents have difficulty imagining their children expressing a full range of sexual feelings and behaviors. Parents also find that their teenagers are highly resistant to family sex talk, with teens actively rebuffing their attempts to talk about sexuality, telling their parents they neither need nor want this information. Parents do not simply conjure an image of their teenagers as asexual; their children may actively encourage this notion.

Based on their ideas about teen sexuality and their own sense of accountability, parents practice protection and surveillance to keep their children safe, yet draw on different resources to do so. Parental protection and surveillance, therefore, is an individual, privatized solution to the "problem" of teen sexuality, with different consequences for young people depending on social class. If, as a nation, we continue to depict teen sexuality solely in terms of risk and danger, then we need to establish a national social safety net that better protects all young people. Youth deserve access to a good education, safe neighborhoods, promising futures, and quality health care—including a full range of contraceptive and reproductive services and diverse information about sexuality.

Also essential, however, is that we begin to radically alter current understandings of teenagers that inform and perpetuate the danger discourse of teen sexuality. When teens are constructed as irresponsible or irredeemable, as sexually voracious but incapable of handling the responsibilities of sexual activity, the tendency is to deny their agency and power and to treat them as problems in need of solutions.

Theoretical Implications

What are the implications of this book? Generally, when one examines family life, the assessment often assumes a hierarchical and authoritative quality, with parents holding all the power and children largely powerless. These assumptions frame understandings of family sexual communication. Parents are typically pictured as the active agents in "the talk" who provide or do not provide their children with sexual knowledge.

Although teenage voices are not included here, this book demonstrates that parents perceive their children as active participants in family sex talks. Parental power may be considerable, but it is not absolute: it is contested and negotiated in the context of family life. Rather than conceptualize power as hierarchical and repressive, this book points to the importance of viewing power as relational and productive. A new conception of family sex talk is needed, one that values negotiation and collaboration rather than hierarchy and authority, and recognizes that children are not just passive audiences but play active roles in these conversations.

In addition to parent-teen sex talk being an interactive endeavor, these talks are shaped by social inequalities. Although scholars of inequality are often loath to grant sexuality the same weight as race, class, and gender,[15] this book illustrates that sexuality is central to organizing and sustaining boundaries and status hierarchies. Parents construct the "hypersexual teen" based on notions of raging hormones and hypersexualized teen culture, and these understandings are deeply inflected with racialized, gendered, and classed sexual meanings. This book, therefore, contributes to a growing call to examine gender, race, class, and sexuality as mutually reinforcing forms of inequality.

As scientific studies and public discourse increasingly divide adults from adolescents, the material presented here also underscores the importance of age and developmental narratives as axes of social inequality. Americans generally construct teenagers as impulsive, irrational, and immature, in contrast to cautious, rational, and mature adults. Parents' ideas about what it means to be a sexual subject and teenagers' capabilities in this regard are profoundly shaped by this binary understanding of adolescence versus adulthood. *Not My Kid* calls on scholars to examine these age and developmental discourses as mechanisms of social inequality.

Finally, this book underscores parents' uncertainty and ambivalence over their lessons to their teen children about sexuality. Theorists contend that ambivalence is a significant feature of modern life, and yet it is often overlooked in sociological research.[16] Given the parent-child relationship, some degree of ambivalence is inevitable, but this book demonstrates that gender and sexual inequalities magnify parents' ambivalent feelings about what is best for their teen children regarding sexuality. Parents cannot easily be divided into sexual liberals and sexual conservatives; even those with very liberal views on sexuality fear for their children's sexual safety and well-being, and are unsure about their teens' ability to attain sexual subjectivity in a sexist and heteronormative context. The abstinence-until-marriage discourse, coupled with the discourse of sex as an uncontrollable drive, also shape parents' uncertainty about their sexual lessons. In line with abstinence only, parents want their children to abstain from sex until adulthood, ideally until marriage, but many also suspect that this is unrealistic and feel accountable for preparing their children to navigate sexuality safely, responsibly, and agentically. In negotiating these conflicted feelings, many parents promote abstinence in their conversations with their teens about sexuality but also infuse these lessons with information about contraception. The parents' stories thus reveal the conditions that give rise to ambivalence as well as how individuals experience and negotiate this structurally created ambivalence.

Practical Implications

Over the past three decades governmental policies and decisions around sex education have been based on the understanding that parents have the right and the obligation to teach their own children about sexuality. This book, in contrast, underscores the difficulties parents encounter in seeing their children as sexual subjects and talking to their teenagers about sexuality. In this era of panic over sexual behavior, parents lack ways to think about their children's sexuality that do not involve deviance, ruin, and parental failure. As we have seen, parents' ability to view their children as sexual subjects is also hindered by dominant understandings of adolescents as irresponsible vessels of raging hormones. Rather than simply encouraging parents to talk more openly and frequently with their children about sex, the fraught and complex dynamics underpinning these conversations need to be taken seriously. Parents may not be their children's best sex educators and certainly should not be their *only* sex educators; this book, at the very least, signals the need for resources that would enable parents and children to explore these topics in myriad ways, for example, books, magazines, videos, and websites, as well as third parties such as Planned Parenthood and school-based sex education.

Because parents' advice to their children is shaped by larger social policies and discourses around teen sexuality, these policies and discourses deserve critical examination. As I have argued, the debate between abstinence-only and comprehensive sex education is predicated on a false binary. Although the curricula differ on the importance of marriage for sexual activity, they are markedly similar in many other ways. Specifically both abstinence-only and comprehensive sex education rely on and reproduce the danger discourse of teen sexuality. Although sexual activity is risky, obviously it can also be pleasurable and fulfilling. Moreover, current discourses and policies draw a false dichotomy between risky, disappointing teen sexuality and safe, satisfying adult sexuality. Both adults and teenagers can experience sex as positive and affirming as well as negative and painful.[17] Social policy and discourse need to embrace this more complicated reality: adults are not, just because of their age, immune to the negative consequences of sex, just as teenagers are not immune to the positive effects.

Not My Kid calls for new discourses that facilitate communication about both the pleasures and dangers of sexual activity without dichotomizing youth from adults. By constructing teen sexuality in wholly negative, fear-based terms, existing policies and discourses fail to address the skills that might help youth (and adults) discern good sex from bad and facilitate positive sexual experiences. Teens are sexual beings, broadly defined; and, more specifically, they are engaging in sexual intercourse.[18] We need policies that recognize this reality, and we also need affirming ways to talk about teen sexuality that do not divide young people into neat categories of good or bad, asexual or hypersexual. These binaries, as noted, rest upon and reinforce race, class, gender, and sexual inequalities.

Regarding sex education, we should move beyond abstinence-only versus comprehensive models and think about new models of sex education that actively resist social injustice and acknowledge youth as sexual subjects. This type of sex education would, for example, emphasize the ongoing and interactive accomplishment of sexual health and happiness; recognize and promote the active role youth take in constructing their own sex education lessons, thereby emphasizing agency as an important component of sexual learning; and include social justice as an integral component and aim. A model of sex education that includes these goals potentially can support parents as they understand their teens' active participation in family sex talks, and can also encourage parents (as well as youth) to question and challenge how current sexual discourses and lessons are organized around and serve to sustain social inequalities.[19]

Beyond these larger policies and discourses, the present work also has practical implications for the sex education classroom. Because parents experience their children as active in family sexual communication, it matters how sex educators talk to their students about parents. The sex educators I observed commonly referred to parents as highly conservative and out of touch concerning issues of sexuality. Although, to be sure, some parents *are* conservative[20] and some may be uninformed, these kinds of blanket statements potentially shape how young people think about their parents as sex educators. Instead, school-based sex education can support and listen to students. Rather than tell youth what their parents are like, these classes afford opportunities to ask students about their experiences talking to their parents and to support youth as they come to understand their parents' lessons, including the parents' silences, binary thinking, and contradictions. These classes also offer a chance to challenge the inequalities that shape and are often reproduced through parent-teen sex talk. School-based lessons about gender inequality, for example, can provide a space for boys to critically examine male privilege and to resist using and reproducing male dominance in interactions with their mothers.

Not My Kid reveals the enormous amount of work and worry that goes into parenting teenagers. Parents largely take responsibility for keeping their children safe but have varying access to resources that may help them buffer their children from harm. All the parents I spoke with told me that the best way to keep teenagers safe was to occupy their time in extracurricular activities, but not all families have access to the resources necessary to implement this strategy. Middle-class parents casually spoke of the numerous activities in which their children participate, including academic tutoring, dance and voice lessons, athletics, band, and karate. Although Annette Lareau, in her study of families of fourth graders, finds that working-class and poor parents feel sorry for tightly scheduled middle-class kids,[21] the working-class and poor parents I interviewed want their teenage children to participate in extracurricular activities. Because of financial constraints, however, these parents typically rely on activities linked to their children's schools and find it difficult to transport their children to events and practices, and purchase the equipment needed for their children's participation. If institutional discourses continue to emphasize extracurricular activities as the only way to cultivate young people's talents and keep them occupied, focused, and safe, then social policy should be directed at providing tangible resources to help all young people participate in extracurricular activities, such as transportation services and scholarships for membership fees and equipment.

Final Thoughts

At the time of this writing, I had a 17-year-old son and 14-year-old daughter, and we talk, frequently, about sex. I do a lot of talking but also a good deal of listening, and treat intercourse as just one part of sex and one way among many to be sexual. I also try to make pleasure a frequent topic of conversation, telling my children that sex is about feeling good in your body. Sexual intimacy, in whatever form it takes, is about sharing those good feelings.

Pleasure is important to discuss, because it is a reminder that we are supposed to enjoy our bodies and that an ethic of care, for ourselves and for others, is a fundamental part of this. Using the language of care and pleasure also helps me address practical matters. For example, I tell my children that we should ask others if they have been tested for sexually transmitted infections, because we care about their bodies and about our own. We should use condoms and other forms of contraception for the same reason. I'm not always sure that I say the right things, but I am honest and straightforward. As with other aspects of raising children, I suspect that being open and real when talking about sex goes a long way.

Not too long ago, I was made jarringly aware of the consequences that this talk potentially poses for my children in the current social environment. My daughter was labeled a slut in eighth grade, because she vocally opposed her sex education teacher's singular focus on abstinence. In the view of some of her classmates, if she was opposed to abstinence, she must be having sex. I told my daughter that, in a more perfect world, young women would be able to advocate for sexual information without being negatively labeled or feeling ashamed. We also talked about how difficult and confusing the topic of sex can be for adults and youth alike, and how people may resolve some of their discomfort by denigrating other people. And we talked about the word "slut." I told her that there is no such thing as a slut: the term was created and is designed to control girls' and women's sexuality. This seemed to make sense to her and has inflamed her feminist consciousness. So although this was a difficult experience, it also created a productive space for us to talk and for her to continue developing a critical sense of social justice.

As attested by my own experiences and those of the parents in this book, parents need an affirming language to talk and think about teen sexuality, but they should also be able to do so without fearing societal condemnation. Parents need permission to see their children as sexual beings and to present themselves as sexual subjects. We and our children need mutually respectful, safe, fulfilling relationships, whether or not the relationships conform to normative standards. Parents and children also need and deserve safe neighborhoods, good schools and extracurricular activities, quality health care, and optimistic economic futures. We need new ways to think about teenagers, as well as diverse policies designed to address the pervasive culture of sexual fear and the conditions of inequality that structure our own and our children's lives. These changes, I believe, will go a long way toward helping parents recognize their children as fully sexual subjects. Meanwhile, we can help our children to identify and criticize sexual stereotypes and inequalities, and build positive, agentic sexual lives for themselves and others.

Methods Appendix

The aim of this book is to provide a detailed look at parents' inner worlds—the "processes of interpretation that give meaning to everyday lives"[1]—and to examine parents' understandings sociologically, as shaped by and in conversation with larger discourses around teen sexuality. Thus, in addition to conducting in-depth interviews with parents of teenagers, I also focused on what was being said and done publicly about teenagers and teen sexuality, and observed school-based sex education classes. Here I describe in more detail the methodological decisions I made regarding the interviews and observations that ultimately shaped the contours of this book.

Because activist parents dominate the public discourse on sex education, I intentionally chose to interview non-activist parents. The challenge was to find parents who, for whatever reason, are not visibly or vocally apparent in this debate. I resolved this dilemma by recruiting parents through their children's health classes in three high schools and one middle school, and, in so doing, accomplished a second goal: to nestle parents' responses within institutional discourses of teen sexuality.

Upon gaining permission from my university's and the school district's research ethics Review Boards, I was able to recruit forty parents of teens in the health classes of these four schools. Of the remaining seven parents interviewed, three responded to advertisements I placed in community newspapers in school neighborhoods and four were referrals. To protect the identities of the schools, parents, teenagers, and teachers who allowed me to recruit participants through their classrooms, pseudonyms are used throughout.

All four schools are located in large cities with histories of racial segregation. Taylor and Eastside High Schools are located in low-income, predominantly black and Latino neighborhoods, which is reflected in the schools' student bodies: black and Latino/a students comprise more than 75 percent of the student body at Taylor and 88 percent at Eastside. Also suggesting the legacy and persistence of racial discrimination,[2] well over half the student body at each school is classified as economically disadvantaged. In contrast, Hayden Middle School and Medlin High School are located in high-income, predominantly white neighborhoods, with student bodies that are mostly white and significantly better off economically. Less than one-quarter of the students at these schools are classified as economically disadvantaged.

Parents responded to letters I sent home through their children inviting them to participate in a study about their "experiences raising teenagers," including issues related to "puberty, dating, and sex." The voluntary nature of the sample helped me find parents who were highly reflective about their experiences talking or not talking with their children about sex and sexuality.

Of the forty-seven parents interviewed, forty were mothers, six were fathers, and one was a grandmother with custody of her stepgrandson. Just over half the parents identified as white, about one-third as Latino/a, one-eighth as black, and one as multiracial; about one-fifth were upper-middle class, half were lower-middle class, and almost one-third were working class or poor (for the parents' demographics, see Table.Appendix 1). To determine parents' social class and capture the social and cultural aspects of class,[3] I relied on the parents' own reports of their household income, the types of job they held (and, if applicable, their partner's occupation), and their level of education. I also asked parents about their own parents' educational attainment and class background. Even taking these various strands of class status into account, the resulting class designations cannot adequately capture the myriad factors shaping one's social class. Consistent with recent studies stressing the social construction of race, ethnicity, and social class,[4] these categories are not monolithic or representative of all people who identify as a particular race, ethnicity, or social class. My interest in these factors was on how they mattered to the study participants.

Forty parents indicated a religious affiliation, with Catholic the most common (n = 16), followed by Christian (n = 11) and Baptist (n = 5). Most parents who identified a religion said that they attended religious services regularly. Perhaps reflecting Americans' sense that political discussion is best avoided because of its divisiveness,[5] over one-third of parents identified as politically moderate (n = 11) or said they were undecided or apolitical (n = 8). The remaining parents identified as "somewhat conservative" (n = 13), "somewhat liberal" (n = 8), "very liberal" (n = 5), "very conservative" (n = 1), and "libertarian" (n = 1). Regarding the parents' relationship status, two-thirds identified as married (n = 31), eight as divorced, four as separated, two as widowed, and two as single. All study participants identified as heterosexual.

Interviews lasted from one to two and a half hours and were generally conducted in parents' homes although occasionally at the parent's workplace or in a public setting. I began with open-ended questions, such as "How would you describe your children?" or prompts, such as "Describe your child's typical day." In-depth interviews, emphasizing meanings, dynamics, and processes,[6] enabled me to explore why parents say what they say, how they feel about it, and how they perceive the dynamics of family sex talk. My effort throughout was to elicit parents' stories about their teens.[7] All interviews were tape-recorded and transcribed.

To situate parents' narratives in the larger social context, I paid close attention to how teen sexuality was being talked and written about over the two-and-a-half-year period of my research. In addition to the Texas school board debate, which provided a rich arena to explore public conversations about teenagers, sexuality, and family life, I followed sex education debates in the local and national media, as well as reports pertaining to teenagers, adolescence, or sexuality. I also observed sex-education classes and presentations at Taylor and Eastside High Schools in the fall of 2006.

In the state where I conducted my fieldwork, sex education was offered in health class, which, at the time, was a required subject, although students could take it at any time between seventh and twelfth grades. Even though sex education is included in the health class curriculum, health teachers, in collaboration with their school principals, have a fair amount of discretion about the actual content of the sex-education unit. Ms. Fox, the health teacher at Taylor High, spends two weeks on the topic, covering abstinence, sexually transmitted infections, and contraception. I observed two classes daily during Ms. Fox's sex-education unit and attended one of the

Appendix Table 1. Parents' Demographic Characteristics

Pseudonym	Age	Race/Ethnicity	Social Class	Occupation	Education
Angie	42	Latina	working class	warehouse manager	high school
Barb	55	white	lower middle	midwife	some college
Beatrice	52	white	lower middle	social services	post college degree
Beth	39	white	upper middle	accountant	college degree
Charlene	37	black	poor	temp office worker	1 yr vocational degree
Charles	50	white	lower middle	engineer	college degree
Corina	39	black	working class	social services	high school
Delores	33	Latina	lower middle	patient services rep	college degree
Denise	52	black	lower middle	nurse	college degree
Elena	41	Latina	working class	medical biller	some college
Fern	55	white	lower middle	teacher's aide	college degree
Gabriela	44	Latina	upper middle	substitute teacher	college degree
Gail	58	multiracial	lower middle	homemaker	some college
Gina	51	white	upper middle	lawyer	post college degree
Greg	43	white	lower middle	teacher	college degree
Hector	35	Latino	working class	shipping/receiving	less than high school
Josefina	31	Latina	lower middle	graduate student	college degree
Juanita	34	Latina	working class	homemaker	less than high school
Kate	43	white	lower middle	accountant	some college
Kelly	37	white	working class	office assistant	some college
Kim	45	black	lower middle	social services	college degree
Kirk	45	white	lower middle	internal auditor	college degree
Lorena	32	Latina	working class	social services	some college
Melissa	43	white	upper middle	massage therapist	college degree
Miranda	37	white	lower middle	accountant	college degree
Nicole	32	white	working class	office assistant	college degree
Norma	36	Latina	lower middle	financial analyst	college degree
Olivia	32	Latina	working class	office assistant	some college
Pamela	47	white	lower middle	retired	college degree
Paula	43	Latina	upper middle	homemaker	college degree
Penny	52	white	lower middle	homemaker	college degree
Portia	46	Latina	upper middle	homemaker	post college degree
Rebecca	49	white	lower middle	customer care	some college
Renae	43	black	working class	teacher's aide	college degree
Robin	46	white	lower middle	homemaker/artist	college degree
Ron	50	white	working class	mechanic	high school
Rosalia	43	Latina	poor	dry cleaner	less than high school
Rose	43	white	upper middle	homemaker	college degree
Ruth	45	white	upper middle	investor	college degree
Sandra	45	white	upper middle	homemaker	college degree
Scott	34	white	lower middle	engineer	college degree
Sharon	51	white	upper middle	consumer education	post college degree
Shawna	45	black	lower middle	teacher/coach	college degree
Shelia	48	white	lower middle	teacher	college degree
Sylvia	44	Latina	lower middle	auditor	college degree
Teresa	43	Latina	working class	homemaker	less than high school
Yolanda	30	Latina	lower middle	social services	some college

Relationship Status	Teenage Children	Religion	Political Affiliation
separated	daughter (19) son (16)	Catholic	moderate
separated	daughters (16, 18) son (14)	non-denominational	don't know/not political
married	daughter (16)	Methodist	somewhat liberal
married	son (16)	Episcopalian	moderate
divorced	daughters (15, 17) son (19)	Christian	don't know/not political
married	daughter (14)	Unitarian	somewhat liberal
single	daughter (14)	Baptist	don't know/not political
married	daughter (13)	Christian	moderate
separated	daughters (13, 16) son (14)	Baptist	somewhat conservative
single	daughter (16)	none	somewhat liberal
married	daughter (14)	Jewish/Unitarian	don't know/not political
married	daughters (13, 16)	Methodist	somewhat conservative
married	grandson (15)	Scientology	don't know/not political
married	sons (14, 19)	none	moderate
married	daughters (15, 17, 18)	Christian	moderate
married	daughter (14)	Catholic	don't know/not political
married	son (14)	none	very liberal
married	daughter (14)	Catholic	don't know/not political
divorced	son (14)	none	very liberal
widowed	sons (14, 16)	Christian	somewhat conservative
divorced	son (17)	Christian	moderate
married	son (15)	Christian	somewhat conservative
separated	son (16)	Christian	somewhat conservative
divorced	daughters (13, 14) son (16)	Christian	somewhat conservative
married	son (14)	Catholic	somewhat conservative
divorced	daughter (14) son (16)	Penecostal	somewhat conservative
divorced	daughter (17) son (15)	Catholic	moderate
married	daughter (14)	Catholic	somewhat liberal
married	daughter (15)	Catholic	somewhat conservative
married	son (14)	Catholic	very liberal
married	sons (16, 17)	none	somewhat liberal
married	daughter (14) son (16)	Catholic	somewhat conservative
married	son (19)	none	very liberal
married	sons (13, 19)	Baptist	moderate
married	sons (14, 16)	Christian	somewhat liberal
divorced	daughter (17) son (15)	Catholic	moderate
married	daughters (14, 17, 19)	Catholic	don't know/not political
married	son (14)	Catholic	libertarian
divorced	daughter (14) son (16)	Jewish	somewhat to very liberal
married	sons (15, 17)	Catholic	somewhat conservative
married	son (14)	Catholic	very conservative
married	daughters (14, 16)	Christian	very liberal
widowed	son (15)	Baptist	moderate
married	daughter (16)	Baptist	somewhat conservative
married	daughters (14, 15)	none	somewhat liberal
married	son (14)	Catholic	somewhat conservative
married	daughter (13)	Catholic	moderate

presentations on sexually transmitted infections that she gives annually to all incoming Taylor ninth graders in the school auditorium. This presentation spans two consecutive days.

Unlike Ms. Fox, Coach Jones, the health teacher at Eastside High, allocates one week for sex education, with guest speakers occupying four of the five weekdays. For three days I observed lectures led by an abstinence-only sex educator. On the fourth day three peer mentors, each of whom had their first child between their teenage years and early twenties, and unmarried, spoke to the class about sexual responsibility and, especially, about male responsibility. During these presentations Coach Jones did not interact with the students or with those presenting the lectures.[8] On the fifth day of the week, she discussed contraception with her students but did not invite me to observe this lesson. The classroom observations provided opportunities to hear what some of the interviewed parents' teenage children were learning in school about sexuality and how teachers and other sex educators were talking about parents. In addition, as a way to take "the pulse" of the school's Parent-Teacher Association and the school in general, I attended PTA meetings at Hayden Middle School as well as five meetings that were broadly advertised (with the lure of guest speakers) to Hayden parents between the spring of 2006 and the fall of 2007. I also attended parent information night at Hayden in the fall of 2006.

Throughout this project I tried to remain reflexive about my role as a researcher.[9] True for any study, the material reported reflects the researcher's background, interests, and experiences. "All knowledge," as Kristin Esterberg points out, "is created within human interaction."[10] Acknowledging this fact of social research helped me remain aware of my own blind spots, values, and preoccupations, regularly considering parents' motivations for their actions and thoughts, as well as how I was filtering these through my own life experiences and academic training. Although parents are obviously a heterogeneous group, as a parent I was an insider in this group.[11] I, like other parents, think and hear a lot about teenagers and teen sexuality, and I too am immersed in family life. Thus, as a researcher studying a familiar topic, I had to "make the familiar strange" and question the shared understandings parents often articulated in their interviews.

Despite being a parent, I did not identify as such during the interviews unless directly asked, which rarely happened. It is unusual, perhaps, not to use one's insider status to gain trust and rapport with study participants, so I should explain my rationale. I did not deliberately decide at the beginning of the project to withhold my parental status, but nor did I directly identify as a parent. Parents generally assumed I was a young graduate student, not a parent, probably because I look younger than I am. I came to realize that this assumption might be methodologically important, as some parents, in effect, took me under their wing as though genuinely wanting to introduce me to the myriad intricacies of raising children and parenting teenagers. Others showed a great deal of vulnerability and confusion about parenting during their interviews, which they may not have been as willing to do had they known I was a parent. From my own experience, as well as talking with many parents, I have found that parents are often sensitive and highly attuned to the judgmental attitudes of other parents. Had they known that I was a parent, parents might have worried that I was judging them or edited their stories based on their ideas about *my* parenting beliefs and practices. Or they might have assumed that I knew all about parenting and would not have been as descriptive in their interviews.

I remain conflicted about my nondisclosure, however. It allowed me to position myself strategically as uninformed and inexperienced with respect to parenting, and it also helped me avoid feeling as though I were in collusion with some parents about other parents not doing their job. Whenever a parent expressed anger, disgust, or frustration about other parents, I was relieved not to be seen as aligning myself with this position as a parent. Perhaps, however, by not identifying as a parent, I missed an opportunity to develop greater rapport with the participants.

Although I did not tell parents that I too was a parent, raising children reminds me daily of the challenges of parenting, and I hope that my own anxieties and foibles have given me a deeper appreciation for the beliefs, experiences, and actions of the parents in this book, as well as a better understanding of the complex processes by which parents make sense of teen sexuality.

INTRODUCTION

1. To protect privacy, all names of parents, children, sex educators, and schools have been changed.

2. Generally parents are more likely to engage in conversations about puberty and sexual issues with children who share their biological sex, as they feel better equipped to answer these children's questions (DiIorio, Kelley, and Hockenberry-Eaton 1999; Kirkman, Rosenthal, and Feldman 2002; McHale, Crouter, and Whiteman 2003; Nolin and Petersen 1992; Omar, McElderry, and Zakharia 2003; Rosenthal and Feldman 1999; Walker 2001). Nevertheless, the responsibility of providing sex education falls on mothers most often, regardless of the child's gender (DiIorio, Kelley, and Hockenberry-Eaton 1999; Lefkowitz et al. 2003; Kim and Ward 2007; Raffaelli and Green 2003; Romo et al. 2004; Walker 2001) and mothers report being the primary providers of sex education in the home (Jaccard, Dittus, and Gordon 2000; Miller et al. 1998; Regnerus 2005, 2007).

3. Martin 2009; Martin and Luke 2010.

4. Books that provide generalizable findings about Americans' sexual values and behaviors include Cahn and Carbone 2010; Laumann et al. 1994; and D'Emilio and Freedman 1988.

5. Cahn and Carbone 2010.

CHAPTER 1

1. Excerpts from President's speech to National Association of Evangelicals 1983.

2. Levine 2002, 105.

3. Jewell 1998; Luker 1996; Moran 2000.

4. Irvine 2002; Kendall 2008.

5. Moran 2000.

6. The Adolescent Family Life Act, as quoted in Moran 2000, 204.

7. Irvine 2002, 90. See also di Mauro and Joffe 2009; Irvine 2002; and Luker 2006.

8. Moran 2000, 213.

9. Personal Responsibility Act 1996.

10. Hays 2003.

11. National Public Radio, Kaiser, Kennedy Poll 2004.

12. Abstinence-only sex education is more likely to be taught in public schools in the south than in other parts of the country. During the time I conducted my research, however, more than three-quarters of the public school districts nationwide that had a sex-education policy required the promotion of abstinence (Guttmacher Institute 2006).

13. For national polls showing parental support for sex education, see National Public Radio 2004; and Rose and Gallup 1998. For debates over sex education see Fields 2008; Irvine 2002; and Luker 2006. See also Herdt 2009; Irvine 2007; and Vance 1984.

14. Boonstra 2009; Trenholm et al. 2007. Criticism of abstinence-only sex education mounted throughout the 2000s, and many states chose not to receive federal funds for abstinence-only sex education (twenty-five states by October 2009). The Obama administration has also distanced itself from abstinence-only sex education. President Obama's 2010 budget eliminated funding for abstinence-only programs and instead stated support for "medically accurate and age appropriate programs" that have been shown to reduce teen pregnancy (http://www.whitehouse.gov/omb/budget/fy2010/assets/hhs.pdf).

15. Fine and McClelland 2006, 299.

16. Chapkis 1997; Stein 1989.

17. The terms "heterosexual" and "homosexual," for example, and all that they imply today, have not always existed and have not always structured sexual identities, behaviors, and desires (Katz 1995; Valocchi 2005). See Katz (1995) for an examination of the historical, medical, and legal invention of the term "heterosexuality" in Western culture during the nineteenth and twentieth centuries.

18. My theoretical approach blends Simon and Gagnon's (1986) sexual scripting theory with poststructuralist queer theory insights into power and inequality (Foucault 1990; Gamson and Moon 2004; Plummer 2003b). In scripting theory, Simon and Gagnon (1986) use the term "cultural scenarios" rather than "discourses." For continuity and clarity, as well as to emphasize power relations, I prefer to use the term "discourse." As Plummer (2003b) notes, sexual scripting theory attends well to agency, context, interaction, and meaning making, but lacks a direct analysis of power and inequality, something that is foremost in poststructuralist queer theory accounts of sexuality. Plummer

also takes queer theory to task for a lack of attention to "the ordinary everyday lived experiences of sexuality" (2003b, 521), a strength of scripting theory. Combining these approaches can therefore balance their strengths and weaknesses (see also Williams, Giuffre, and Dellinger 2009). Discourses encapsulate what is dominantly understood as "the Truth" but are often too broad or abstract to fit the nuances and complexities of everyday life. Thus individuals craft their own "interpersonal scripts" to fit the context of their particular situation and experiences (Simon and Gagnon 1986). These interpersonal scripts play out on the interactional arena. On the level of the psyche, individuals engage in what Simon and Gagnon term "intrapsychic scripting." This concept captures internal motivations, desires, and anxieties in the construction of sexual subjectivities, what Simon and Gagnon (1986, 99) refer to as an individual's "many-layered and sometimes multi-voiced wishes." Simon and Gagnon's sexual scripting theory has primarily been used to explain how individuals develop a sense of themselves as sexual beings. I use this framework in the book to attend to the multilayered process by which parents make sense of teenagers as sexual subjects. My focus is on "sexual ascription . . . the assignment of sexual meanings, evaluations, and categories to others" (Nagel 2001, 124). Parents may be deeply invested in and concerned about their children's sexual behaviors and attitudes. Not only are parents charged with being their children's sex educators (and hence implicated in any negative outcomes of teen sexual activity), the dominant discourse of teen sexual activity emphasizes that it is fraught with devastating consequences. As such, parents may feel responsible for their children's sexual behavior and, when it comes to sex, consider the outcomes to be largely negative. The goal of this book is to offer insight into parents' understandings of teen sexuality in the making, understandings that are dynamic, processual, and linked to, but not determined by, broader sociocultural conditions and discourses.

19. Irvine 2002; Stein 2006.
20. Rofes 2000, 442. See also Altman 2001; and Irvine 1994.
21. D'Emilio and Freedman 1988.
22. See Godbeer (2002) for sexual regulation during the fifteenth and sixteenth centuries. See D'Emilio and Freedman (1988) and Smith and Hindus (1975) for historical rates of premarital pregnancy.
23. For a comprehensive examination of the demographic, sociocultural, political, and economic forces behind the shift in sexual culture and

regulation during the Victorian era, see D'Emilio and Freedman 1988, 53–167; Foucault 1990; and Seidman 1991.

24. Seidman 1991, 39.

25. Foucault 1990.

26. Carpenter 2005; D'Emilio and Freedman 1988.

27. Luker 1996, 28. See also Irvine 2002.

28. Glosser, Gardiner, and Fishman 2004.

29. Levine 2002; Luker 1996.

30. Moran 2000.

31. Palladino 1996; Warner 1994; Zelizer 1985.

32. Stearns 2003.

33. The discourse of parental blame is especially virulent when it comes to marginalized families (Glassner 1999). Poor, black, single-mother households, in particular, are often the target of blame from those outside as well as within the black community (Cohen 2009; Kaplan 1996). To be sure, parents matter in their children's lives; some research, for example, suggests that parents' involvement in their teenage children's lives influences the probability that they will form delinquent friendships (Warr 2005)—but parents are not the only influences on youth, especially in adolescence. Schools, peers, and neighborhoods also shape, in complicated and not always predictable ways, young people's attitudes and behaviors (Duncan, Boisjoly, and Harris 2001; Ferguson 2000; Furstenberg et al. 1999; Harding 2007, 2009). For example, Harding (2007) finds that in disadvantaged neighborhoods, those characterized by high unemployment, poverty, and violence, youth encounter a number of different, sometimes competing models of behavior, some in line with their parents' socialization messages and some not. More advantaged neighborhoods, on the other hand, tend to have fewer behavioral models and those that exist tend to support, rather than undermine, parents' socialization efforts.

34. Altheide 2002; Glassner 1999; Stearns 2003.

35. Irvine 2002, 135.

36. Whittier 2009.

37. As stressed in the Convention on the Rights of the Child, ratified by nearly all governments save the United States and Somalia, treating children with dignity is not about treating children as adults, but rather treating children with respect "as persons" (Melton 2005, 648).

38. Angelides 2004. Casper and Moore (2009) observe an additional consequence of the construction of children as innocent and asexual: it is currently virtually impossible to gain Institutional Review Board

approval to conduct research with children about sex and sexuality. The dearth of research on children and sexuality in turn reifies their asexuality.

39. On the prevalence of discourses of child sexual abuse in the late twentieth century, see Irvine 2002. On media's role in disseminating these discourses, see Altheide 2002; and Glassner 1999.

40. Casper and Moore 2009, 47.

41. Finkelhor et al. 2010.

42. Fields 2008, 48.

43. Fields 2005, 562; see also Fields 2008.

44. Lesko 2001; Schalet 2000.

45. Bettie 2003; Collins 2000; Fields 2005, 2008; Garcia 2009; Ortner 1996, 1998; Wilkins 2008.

46. Fields 2005, 2008; Irvine 2002; Luker 2006.

47. Fields 2008, 56.

48. Fields 2008; Irvine 2002.

49. Valocchi 2005, 756.

50. D'Emilio and Freedman 1988, 52.

51. Luker 1996.

52. Palladino 1996.

53. In chronicling the proliferation of sexual speech by the Christian Right in the 1980s and 1990s, Irvine (2002, 195) observes: "More sexual speech does not inevitably bring more sexual freedom." Sex is regulated not by silence but by endless attention to and talk about it—by the "deployment of sexuality" (Foucault 1990, 107). See also Fields 2008; Garcia 2009; Katz 1995; and Moon 2004.

CHAPTER 2

1. Rosalia is not fluent in English and I am not fluent in Spanish, so this interview was conducted with the help of a bilingual translator.

2. For research that takes a positive view of parents' role in their children's sex education see, e.g., Baumeister et al. 1995; Dittus and Jaccard 1998; Fasula and Miller 2006; Hutchinson 2002; and Resnick et al. 1997.

3. Studies more critical of parents' sexuality lessons, especially for how these lessons may reproduce gender inequality, include De Gaston et al. 1996; Martin 1996; Martin and Luke 2010; Moore and Rosenthal 1991; Nolin and Petersen 1992; and Phillips 2000.

4. Some research has examined parents' understandings of their younger children's sexuality. For mothers' perceptions of their 3- to 6-year-old children's sexuality, see Martin 2009; and Martin and Luke 2010.

5. Much expert advice encourages parents to talk with their children about sex-related issues only after a child broaches the subject and many of the parents I interviewed followed this pattern (see also Frankham 2006; Martin, Luke, and Verduzco-Baker 2007).

6. American teen girls are also adamant that even if their parents know they are having sex, sex should be furtive "out of respect" (Schalet 2010).

7. Many parents, particularly middle-class parents, envisioned their children remaining dependent on them well into their twenties, informing their sense of their teen children as young and immature. A study of contemporary parenting strategies also finds that parents, especially highly educated and affluent parents, anticipate, and some even relish, a prolonged adolescence for their children (Nelson 2010).

8. Middle-class female college students also embrace a "self-development imperative" and see relationships as a hindrance in college—something that ties them down and may prevent them from pursuing their goals and aspirations or succeeding academically (Hamilton and Armstrong 2009, 593).

9. Fisher, Cullen, and Turner 2000.

10. Bogle 2008; England, Shafer, and Fogarty 2010; Hamilton and Armstrong 2009; Ronen 2010.

11. Martin 1996; Phillips 2000; Thompson 1995.

12. Brown 1986; Peiser and Peter 2000; Taylor and Brown 1988.

13. Taylor and Brown 1988.

14. Personal Responsibility Act 1996, 2354.

15. Bettie 2003; Fields 2005; Kaplan 1996; Luttrell 2003.

16. Using nationally representative data, Regnerus (2005) finds that parents who identify as highly religious (based on frequency of formal attendance at their religious institution) are less likely to talk with their children about sex and birth control and, when they do talk, are more likely to focus on sexual values. Regnerus (2005, 102), however, also cautions against inferring that religion plays a major role on parent-child sex talk, concluding that "parental religion still appears to be less influential on communication habits than several demographic characteristics of parent and child (e.g., age, race/ethnicity, gender)." My research bears out this conclusion. Religion alone does not explain the complex reasons and ways parents talk with their children about sexuality (see, for example, Denise's story in chapter 4 and Scott's story in chapter 7; see also Gonzalez-Lopez 2003, 2004).

17. I also asked parents like Pamela, who seemed somewhat more willing than other parents to acknowledge their children as potentially sexual

subjects, whether they would help their children get birth control or condoms at the age of 14 or 15. At that age, these parents said, they would strongly discourage, if not outright forbid, this. Some think 16 is still too young and prefer their children do not come to them with that request until they have graduated from high school, if at all.

18. Irvine 2002; Luker 2006.

19. Irvine 2002.

20. Stearns 2003; Wyness 2006.

21. In their analysis of recent media coverage of HIV/AIDS, Casper and Moore (2009, 104) conclude that it tends to focus on "dramatic bodies that evoke an imagined seedy, underground community of deviants reminiscent of the early days of AIDS."

22. Centers for Disease Control and Prevention 2010a.

23. Mr. Marks, the abstinence-only sex educator I observed during the course of my field research, spent much of the first day of his three-day presentation establishing a heightened climate of risk around teen sexual activity since the 1950s (much of which he attributed to the sexual revolution of the 1960s). See also Fields 2008; and Irvine 2002.

24. Centers for Disease Control and Prevention 2009.

25. Centers for Disease Control and Prevention 2009; Saslow et al. 2002.

26. In addition to cervical cancer and genital warts, HPV has been linked to cases of anal, vulvar, vaginal, and penile cancer (Centers for Disease Control and Prevention 2009).

27. Most states forego mandatory Gardasil 2009.

28. Casper and Carpenter 2008.

29. Centers for Disease Control and Prevention 2010c.

30. Ibid.

31. For information on teen contraception use at first sexual intercourse, see Abma, Martinez, and Copen 2010. For statistics on teen contraception use at most recent intercourse, see Centers for Disease Control and Prevention 2010c; and Santelli et al. 2009. According to the 2010 National Survey of Sexual Health and Behavior, teens are engaging in sex in a more responsible manner than singles in their 50s. Teenagers are more likely to report using a condom during sexual intercourse than are single adults in their 50s, for example (Reece et al. 2010).

32. Centers for Disease Control and Prevention 2010a, 2010c; Fields 2008; Rangel et al. 2006.

33. Centers for Disease Control and Prevention 2008.

34. Ibid., 2010b.

35. The birthrate for U.S. teenagers (15 to 19 years old) was 41.5 per 1,000 in 2008; 18 to 19 year olds account for two-thirds of all teen pregnancies (Guttmacher 2010); and births among 15 to 17 year olds (i.e., legally minors) declined by nearly half (45 percent) between 1991 and 2005, rose by 4 percent between 2005 and 2007, and declined by 2 percent in 2008 (see Hamilton, Martin, and Ventura 2010). For a discussion of the sensational reporting around teen pregnancy, see Males 2010.

36. Mamo, Nelson, and Clark 2010, 127; emphasis in original. See also Casper and Carpenter 2008; and Males 2010.

37. Casper and Carpenter 2008, 892.

38. Mamo, Nelson, and Clark 2010, 121.

39. Fields 2008; Irvine 1994; Luker 2006.

40. Centers for Disease Control and Prevention 2010b, 2010c; Finkelhor et al. 2010; Guttmacher Institute 2010; Santelli et al. 2009.

41. Ferguson 2000; Rose 2003; Ross 1998.

42. The definitions in the middle school health class glossary overwhelmingly assume heterosexuality and assign more sexual agency to male than female bodies. Sexual intercourse, for example, is defined as "the erect penis of the male entering the vagina of the female." Ejaculation is defined as "forceful sending out of seminal fluid from the penis." Orgasm is not defined. The definition of a virgin is: "a person who has not had sexual intercourse"—defining all those who have not had heterosexual intercourse as virgins. This, of course, obscures and marginalizes the sexual experiences of many youth, including gays and lesbians. Ms. Blanton's glossary is not unusual. As those who study school-based sex education have observed, sexist and heteronormative lessons about sexuality are all too common in the sex education classroom (e.g., Fields 2008; Fine 1988; Trudell 1992).

43. Fields 2008.

44. Bettie 2003; Jewell 1998; Luker 1996.

CHAPTER 3

1. Best 2006, 58.

2. Best 2006; Corsaro 2004; Kurz 2002; Pugh 2009. Longitudinal research on the interactional nature of family life, for example, finds that children who intercede when their parents argue help defuse marital conflict. How this happens is complex and may depend on parents' efforts to reduce discord after recognizing the children's distress (Schermerhorn et al. 2007).

3. Foucault 1977.

4. West and Zimmerman 1987.

5. Martin and Luke 2010.

6. Twenty-four of the mothers have at least one teenage son.

7. For popular discourses of masculinity see Connell 1995; and Messner 2007. Here and elsewhere in her interview, Kate referred to her 14-year-old son as a "man." A few other mothers did so as well, especially single mothers (like Kate), who described their sons' attempts to fill the role of "man of the house." Some mothers also referred to their teen daughters as "women" but typically when referring to a daughter's menarche (or in one instance, use of birth control), implicitly linking the adult status of a girl to her reproductive ability.

8. Connell 1987; Osmond and Thorne 1993; West and Zimmerman 1987.

9. Du Plessis 1993; Robinson and Spivey 2007.

10. Glassner 1999. For examples of books that blame single mother families for the "problems of masculinity," see Blankenhorn 1995; and Popenoe 1996.

11. For research on differences between boys' versus girls' reports of family sex talks, see DiIorio, Kelley, and Hockenberry-Eaton 1999; Feldman and Rosenthal 2000; Lefkowitz et al. 2002; and Raffaelli, Bogenschneider, and Flood 1998.

12. Nicole must have decided that her suspicions were correct, for, as we saw in chapter 2, she bought her son a box of condoms.

13. Fields 2008, 164. For studies on embarrassment surrounding family sex talk, see Jaccard, Dittus, and Gordon 2000; and Walker 2001.

14. Blau 1964.

15. Stein 2001, 100, quoting Scheff 1990.

16. Irvine 2002; Stein 2006.

17. Stein 2006, 18.

18. Ibid., 3.

19. Irvine 2002, 195. See also Irvine 2009.

20. Rohter 2008.

21. Irvine 2002.

22. Stein 2001.

23. An interview is more than just an occasion for relaying information. It is a social encounter in its own right, the contours of which are shaped by both interviewer and interviewee. The interview setting is "a dynamic, meaning-making occasion" (Holstein and Gubrium 2002, 116).

24. Hochschild 1983, 56.

25. Schwalbe et al. 2000.

26. Schwalbe et al. 2000, 435.

27. Just as teens play a role in whether and how parents talk with them about sex, parents may also shape teens' willingness to talk. For example, Fasula and Miller (2006, 198) argue that youth "who perceive that they have established open and comfortable rapport with their mothers regarding sex topics will be more likely to discuss questions and concerns with their mothers."

28. Jaccard, Dittus, and Gordon 1998; Lefkowitz et al. 2002.

29. Ibid.

30. Lefkowitz et al. 2002, 235.

31. For a discussion of social roles, see Garfinkel 1967. For an examination of the links between social roles and individual identities, see Fein 1990.

32. Flavin 2009; Luker 1996; Luttrell 2003.

33. Connell 1995.

34. Taylor and Eastside High School are two of the schools from which I recruited parents for the interviews discussed in this book.

35. Irvine 2002; Levine 2002; Stein 2006.

CHAPTER 4

1. Bourdieu 1984; Collins 2000; Schwalbe et al. 2000; Schwalbe 2008; Valocchi 2005.

2. Collins 2000. See also Valocchi 2005.

3. Rubin 1984, 276.

4. Levine 2002, 27. See also Kincaid 1998.

5. Levine 2002, 27.

6. Casper and Moore 2009.

7. If the controversy and hyperbole generated by *Harmful to Minors* is any indication, then Levine may be on to something. Conservative media commentators and activists, including radio talk-show host Laura Schlessinger, lambasted Levine for supposedly condoning child sexual abuse and promoting pedophilia (see Benfer 2002).

8. Pascoe 2007; Schalet 2000, 2004.

9. For a thorough treatment of the child anti-sexual abuse movement and heightened concerns about sex predators, see Angelides 2004; Casper and Moore 2009; Irvine 2002; Kincaid 1998; and Levine 2002.

10. Collins 2000, 2004.

11. Collins 2004, 159.

12. Fields 2008; Fine 1988; Fine and McClelland 2006. For example, studying sex education in two public schools and one private school,

Fields (2008) finds that sex educators in both the public school class-rooms were reluctant to discuss topics deemed controversial, including homosexuality and bisexuality, sexism, and sexual pleasure. In contrast, although Fields is also critical of some of the sexual lessons taught at the private school, the predominantly affluent, white students at this school "were more likely to hear that sexuality offered them a site of personal fulfillment and expression" (2008, 167).

13. Teens in the United States, Germany, and the Netherlands start having sex at about the same age (between 16 and 17 years old, on average), yet rates of teen pregnancy and STIs are much lower in Germany and the Netherlands than in the United States, and German and Dutch teens are more likely to describe their early sexual experiences positively com-pared to American teens (Carpenter 2001; Schalet 2000, 2010).

14. Carpenter 2001.

15. For the "evaded lessons" of school-based sex education, see Fields 2008.

16. In her study of teenage girls' sexuality, Tolman (1994a, 1994b) observes that many girls resist their own sexual feelings and desires out of a fear of being abused, taken advantage of, or labeled "bad" girls (see also Martin 1996; and Phillips 2000).

17. Irvine 2002; Levine 2002; Luker 1996; Palladino 1996.

18. For the historical and cultural construction of adolescence in the United States, see Lesko 2001; Luker 1996; and Palladino 1996.

19. Schalet 2000, 2004.

20. Brody 2007, D7.

21. Angelides 2004; Cavanagh 2007; Irvine 2002.

22. Casper and Moore 2009; Finkelhor et al. 2010; Glassner 1999.

23. Angelides 2004, 141.

24. Irvine 2002, 135.

25. Elliott and Umberson 2008; Gonzalez-Lopez 2005; Rubin 1990.

26. Of course, Denise and her children are not unique in avoiding talk about positive bodily and sexual feelings. Almost all the parents I spoke with said that they do not discuss positive aspects of sexuality with their children.

27. Collins 2004; Kaplan 1996.

28. Collins 2004, 282.

29. Bearman and Bruckner 2001; Kaplan 1996; Philips 2000.

30. Bearman and Bruckner (2001) find that teenagers who pledge to remain abstinent are less likely to have sex compared to their peers who have not made similar pledges. Those who make a pledge but break that pledge and have sex, however, are 35 percent more likely to forego

contraception than their peers who make no such pledge. According to Bearman, "It makes sense if you think about it . . . If you've made this pledge to remain pure, you wouldn't go around carrying condoms. The cognitive dissonance would be too much" (quoted in Dicker 2004).

31. Lesko 2001, 12; emphasis in original.
32. Nathanson 1991, 176.
33. Although teen sex in the United States may be risky, it is not inherently so. Gender, race, class, and sexual hierarchies and inequalities shape teens' sexual experiences; including how safe, positive, and fulfilling they are (Fields 2008; Gonzalez-Lopez 2004; Luker 1996; Nathanson 1991).
34. Stearns 2003.

CHAPTER 5

1. Palladino 1996, xi.
2. Glassner 1999.
3. Ferguson 2000.
4. Glassner 1999, 68; emphasis in original.
5. Ferguson 2000.
6. Fields 2005, 560. See also Bettie 2003; Collins 2000, 2004; Jewell 1998; Kaplan 1996; and Rose 2003.
7. Bonilla-Silva 2002, 2003; Collins 2004.
8. Bonilla-Silva 2002; Bonilla-Silva and Forman 2000.
9. Bettie 2003, 48, quoting Ortner 1991.
10. Bettie 2003, 49.
11. Ferguson 2000; Fields 2008.
12. Collins (2000, 70) argues that "the 'Others' of society . . . threaten the moral and social order. But they are simultaneously essential for its survival because those individuals who stand at the margins of society clarify its boundaries" (see also Douglas 1966; and Durkheim 2001 [1912]).
13. Luker 1996.
14. See Collins 2000, 2004; Kaplan 1996; Luker 1996; and Solinger 2000. On race and welfare reform see Hays 2003.
15. Bonilla-Silva 2003; Collins 2000, 2004; Wilkins 2008.
16. Martin 2009, 190.
17. See also Solebello and Elliott 2011.
18. That the parents I spoke with warn both sons and daughters about the "opposite sex" is in contrast to research showing that parents stress sexual vulnerability to their daughters but give their sons more leeway

to explore sexuality (e.g., Martin 1996). A study comparing middle-class white parents and their children in the United States and the Netherlands, however, also finds that American parents stress sexual danger to both their sons and daughters, and that American teenage girls *and* boys believe sex is risky regardless of how careful one is, that no amount of planning and contraceptives can save one from the dangers of sex (Schalet 2000, 2004).

19. One in ten high school students have experienced dating violence. Seven percent say they have been physically forced to have sex (Centers for Disease Control and Prevention 2010c).

20. Martin 1996; Phillips 2000; Thompson 1995.

21. Eleven percent of high school girls report being physically forced to have sex compared to 5 percent of high school boys (Centers for Disease Control and Prevention 2010c).

22. Hamilton and Armstrong 2009; Tolman 1994b; Wilkins 2008.

23. For research on the sexual epithet "slut" and how it is used to police and constrain young women's gender and sexual identities and performances, see Hamilton and Armstrong 2009; Martin 1996; Phillips 2000; Tanenbaum 1999; and Thompson 1995.

24. Wilkins 2004.

25. Tanenbaum 1999.

26. Collins 2004; Luker 1996.

27. Pattillo-McCoy 2003.

28. Collins 2004.

29. White parents I interviewed may have felt more comfortable sharing their racial prejudices with me, a fellow white person. Some of the Latino/a parents also articulated racist beliefs mainly directed at African Americans. The few black mothers I interviewed expressed the least racist sentiments of all the parents. These parents may not have felt comfortable disclosing to me any racist beliefs they may hold (Waters 1999); also, however, black parents likely have the least to gain and the most to lose from racism.

30. D'Emilio and Freedman 1988; Palladino 1996.

31. Collins 2004; Nagel 2001.

32. Collins 2004; Pascoe 2007; Ross 1998.

33. Haug 1987; Phillips 2000; Thompson 1995.

34. Collins 2004; Ross 1998.

35. Ehrenreich 1989.

36. Weeks 1981, 92.

37. Plummer 2003a; Rubin 1984.

CHAPTER 6

1. Foucault 1990; Irvine 2002.
2. Lareau 2003.
3. Edin and Kefalas 2005; McCormack 2005.
4. Duncan, Boisjoly, and Harris 2001; Harding 2009; Warr and Stafford 1991.
5. Pugh 2009, 6.
6. Collins 2004; Ross 1998.
7. Affluent and highly educated parents who can afford to use technology such as GPS devices to monitor their teen children are apparently loathe to do so, preferring instead to use technology that helps them keep tabs on their children through more intimate forms of communication such as cell phones and email (Nelson 2010).
8. One advertisement for Mobile Teen GPS, for example, states: "Monitor and track your teen driver with MobileTEEN GPS™ real-time feedback." With Mobile Teen, parents can track their children's location online, monitor their speed, receive instant notification if their children's vehicles enter "unapproved locations," and be notified if their children exceed the speed limit (http://www.mobileteengps.com/).
9. See, for example, Furstenberg et al. 1999; Harding 2009; and Lareau 2003. Neighborhoods were especially salient for black parents I interviewed. In their study of five hundred Philadelphia families, Furstenberg and his colleagues (1999, 218) also found that black parents, regardless of the characteristics of their neighborhoods, worry about their children's safety.
10. As Charlene put it, her daughters "can dress like, the way you are [referring to my gray slacks and blue, button-up shirt], and I'll have to tell some guys off." That is, even dressed in drab, conservative clothing (as presumably I was), her teen daughters attract men's attention.
11. This dominant ideology perpetuates a strict code of women's behavior that includes dressing conservatively and avoiding dangerous or inappropriate places and persons. This code of behavior may be especially burdensome for women of color who are more likely to be hypersexualized by dominant culture and more likely than white women to be victims of sexual assault (Collins 2000; Madriz 1997).
12. Ehrenreich 2001; Hays 2003.
13. See, e.g., Britt 2005; Marvel and Churnin 2006; Saillant 2006; and Dateline NBC 2006.
14. Nelson 2010, 156.

15. This is consistent with a Pew survey of young people and their parents conducted in the mid-2000s, around the time I interviewed parents. Seventy-three percent of online teenagers said their home computer was located in a public area in the house, and 64 percent of parents said they set rules about how long their children can spend online. Although the study finds that parents in 2005 were more likely to use filters—such as Net Nanny or Cyberpatrol—than parents in 2000, the number of parents who reported that the Internet is good for their children rose from 55 percent in 2000 to 67 percent in 2005 (Lenhart 2005).

16. Cyberbullying was in the media over the course of my writing this book in the late 2000s, with headlines such as "Schoolyard Bullies Get Nastier Online." Coverage of cyberbullying increased once a teen girl committed suicide after being bullied online by a parent masquerading as a teenage boy and with studies documenting high rates of cyberbullying among teens (e.g., Juvonen and Gross 2008).

17. Hoffman 2010.

CHAPTER 7

1. Luker 2006.

2. Smelser 1998, 11. The tendency to reduce complex issues to polarized views is not unique to studies on sex education. Ambivalence is often overlooked in the social sciences, particularly over the latter half of the twentieth century as scientific rationality, with a concomitant focus on instrumental efficiency and rational choice, gained prominence across disciplines (Smelser 1998).

3. Smelser 1998, 5.

4. Connidis and McMullin 2002; Smelser 1998; Willson et al. 2006.

5. Willson et al. 2006, 236.

6. Elliott 2010.

7. My analysis is in line with research highlighting Americans' ambivalence about sexuality (e.g., Fine 1988; Gonzalez-Lopez 2004; Regnerus 2007; Schalet 2004).

8. Benjamin 1988; Chodorow 1999; Simmel 1971.

9. Connell and Elliott 2009; Fields 2008.

10. Fields 2008; Fine 1988; Fine and McClelland 2006.

11. Connidis and McMullin 2002; Willson et al. 2006.

12. Plummer 2004, 190. Plummer's use of "deep stories" is akin to Clifford Geertz's notion of "thick description" (Geertz 2001).

13. See also Solebello and Elliott 2011.

14. Although Sharon did not opt out of the workforce (Stone 2007), she purposely reduced her stress and workload (along with her salary) to be more available to her family. This tactic is common among professional middle-class parents, particularly mothers, in their efforts to balance careers and intensively raise their children (Nelson 2010; Webber and Williams 2008). Professional working mothers perceive few options—and numerous obstacles—to their ability to balance both a family and a career.

15. Benjamin 1988; Martin 1996; Schalet 2010.

16. Bettie 2003; Bourdieu 1984; Ortner 1991.

17. Valocchi 2005, 765.

18. Martin 1996, 2.

19. Gonzalez-Lopez 2003; Phillips 2000; Vance 1984.

20. Hamilton and Armstrong 2009; Phillips 2000; Tanenbaum 1999.

21. Issues of privacy and autonomy are endemic in households with teens. Some parents said they simply have to give their teen children their own privacy in order to maintain a good working relationship (mothers were more likely to say this about sons than daughters). Others said their teens can have privacy when they are financially independent, but not a minute before. Until that time, parents are responsible for knowing, I was told—should, and indeed must, know—what their teenagers are doing. Some parents were more blasé. As Ruth put it, "I probably only hear about 30 percent of what goes on in their lives, you know . . . But until he takes the road of irresponsibility, I probably don't need to be in that 70 percent." Parents such as Ruth said that as long as their teen children aren't "cross[ing] a line that's unhealthy for them" (Ruth), they merit a degree of privacy and autonomy.

22. Nelson (2010, 161) finds that although professional middle-class parents such as Sharon said that they trust their children, they still engage in "a wide range of 'sneaky' behaviors to ensure that their children are doing what they want them to do (and not doing what they don't want them to do)." Elite parents, however, do not want their children to know that they do not necessarily trust them, so they tend to avoid talking with their children about the information that they have gleaned, for example, from furtively reading a diary.

23. Rubin 1984.

24. Fields 2008; Luker 2006.

25. Hamilton and Armstrong 2009, 593.

26. Ingraham 1999.

27. Hamilton and Armstrong 2009, 593.

28. Research suggests that religion plays a less influential role in parent-child communication about sexuality than other demographic characteristics, such as age, race/ethnicity, gender, immigration status, and social class (Gonzalez-Lopez 2003, 2004; Regnerus 2005, 2007). My findings are consistent with these other studies.
29. Connell 1995.
30. Elliott and Umberson 2008; Giddens 1992; Rubin 1990.
31. Martin 1996; Phillips 2000.
32. Connell 1995; Rich 1986.
33. Pascoe 2007.
34. Ingraham 1999, 167.
35. Halley 1993.
36. Connell 1995, 84.
37. Pascoe 2007, 112.
38. Wilkins 2008, 131; emphasis in original.
39. Kimmel 1996.
40. Weeks 1992, 394.

CHAPTER 8

1. Connell and Elliott 2009; Fields 2008; Irvine 1994, 2002; Luker 2006.
2. Reece et al. 2010.
3. Martin 1996; Pascoe 2007; Phillips 2000; Tolman, Striepe, and Harmon 2003.
4. Schalet 2000, 2004.
5. Rubin 1984, 267.
6. Schalet 2004, 13.
7. Fields 2008, 169; see also Russell 2005.
8. Bettie 2003; Fields 2008; Kaplan 1996; Luttrell 2003.
9. Irvine 2002; Pascoe 2007; Rubin 1984; Solebello and Elliott 2011; Stein 2006.
10. Collins 2000; Schwalbe et al. 2000; Schwalbe 2008.
11. Connell 1995, 84.
12. Kaplan 1996, 82. For research on social class variations in parenting practices see Lareau 2003; Nelson 2010; and Pugh 2009.
13. Mills 1959.
14. Personal Responsibility Act 1996.
15. Schilt 2008.
16. Smelser 1998.
17. Carpenter 2005.
18. Abma, Martinez, and Copen 2010.

19. See, for example, the National Sexuality Resource Center's (2008) work on "sexual literacy" as a model of sex education. Following a social justice perspective, some scholars argue that sexuality should not simply be relegated to sex education but should be integrated into the public-school curriculum because "addressing sexuality serves not only (or even primarily) public health goals but...academic and democratic goals as well" (Ashcraft 2008, 632).

20. Most parents, however, support comprehensive sex education (e.g., Boonstra 2004; National Public Radio 2004).

21. Lareau 2003.

METHODS APPENDIX

1. DeVault 1991, 11.
2. Conley 1999; Shapiro 2004.
3. Bourdieu 1984; Weber 1947.
4. See, for example, Bettie 2003; Bonnet 1996; Bourdieu 1984; and Winant 2000.
5. Eliasoph and Lichterman 2003.
6. Esterberg 2002; Weiss 1994.
7. Plummer 2001.
8. Fields (2008) notes that a similar dynamic occurred during presentations in the sex education classes she observed.
9. On the role of reflexivity in research see Collins 1986; Davies 1999; Holstein and Gubrium 2002; and Merton 1972.
10. Esterberg 2002, 12.
11. Collins 1986; Kaplan 1996; Merton 1972.

REFERENCES

Abma, Joyce C., Gladys Martinez, and Casey E. Copen. 2010. Teenagers in the United States: Sexual activity, contraceptive use, and childbearing, National Survey of Family Growth 2006–2008. National Center for Health Statistics. *Vital Health Stat* 23, 30: 1–86. http://www.cdc.gov/nchs/data/series/sr_23/sr23_030.pdf.

Altheide, David L. 2002. *Creating fear: News and the construction of crisis.* New York: Aldine De Gruyter.

Altman, Dennis. 2001. *Global sex.* Chicago: University of Chicago Press.

Angelides, Steven. 2004. Feminism, child sexual abuse, and the erasure of child sexuality. *GLQ: A Journal of Lesbian and Gay Studies* 10, 2: 141–177.

Ashcraft, Catherine. 2008. So much more than "sex ed": Teen sexuality as a vehicle for improving academic success and democratic education for diverse youth. *American Educational Research Journal* 45, 3: 631–667.

Baumeister, L. M., E. Flores, and B. V. Marin. 1995. Sex information given to Latina adolescents by parents. *Health Education Research* 10: 233–239.

Bearman, Peter S., and Hannah Bruckner. 2001. Promising the future: Abstinence pledges and the transition to first intercourse. *American Journal of Sociology* 106: 859–912.

Benfer, Amy. 2002. What's so bad about good sex? salon.com. http://dir.salon.com/mwt/feature/2002/04/19/levine_talks/.

Benjamin, Jessica. 1988. *The bonds of love: Psychoanalysis, feminism, and the problem of domination.* New York: Pantheon Books.

Best, Amy L. 2006. Freedom, constraint, and family responsibility: Teens and parents collaboratively negotiate around the car, class, gender, and culture. *Journal of Family Issues* 27: 55–84.

Bettie, Julie. 2003. *Women without class: Girls, race, and identity.* Berkeley: University of California Press.

Blankenhorn, David. 1995. *Fatherless America: Confronting our most urgent social problem.* New York: Basic Books.

Blau, Peter M. 1964. *Exchange and power in social life.* New York: Wiley.

Bogle, Kathleen A. 2008. *Hooking up: Sex, dating, and relationships on campus.* New York: New York University Press.

Bonilla-Silva, Eduardo. 2002. The linguistics of color blind racism: How to talk nasty about Blacks without sounding "racist." *Critical Sociology* 28: 41–64.

———. 2003. *Racism without racists: Color-blind racism and the persistence of racial inequality in the United States*. New York: Rowman and Littlefield.

Bonilla-Silva, Eduardo, and Tyrone Forman. 2000. "I am not a racist but . . .": Mapping White college students' racial ideology in the USA. *Discourse Society* 11: 50–85.

Bonnett, Alistair. 1996. Antiracism and the critique of "white" identities. *New Community* 22, 1: 97–110.

Boonstra, Heather. 2004. Comprehensive approach needed to combat sexually-transmitted infections among youth. *Guttmacher Report on Public Policy* 7, 3: 3–4, 13.

———. 2009. Advocates call for a new approach after the era of "abstinence-only" sex education. *Guttmacher Policy Review* 12, 1. http://www.guttmacher.org/pubs/gpr/12/1/gpr120106.html.

Bourdieu, Pierre. 1984. *Distinction: A social critique of the judgment of taste*. London: Routledge.

Britt, Robert Roy. 2005. Report: Teens routinely exposed to pornography and sexual advances on Internet. *LiveScience*, March 2. http://www.livescience.com/strangenews/050302_teen_sex.html.

Brody, Jane E. 2007. Teenage risks, and how to avoid them. *New York Times*, Science section, December 18.

Brown, Jonathan D. 1986. Evaluations of self and others: Self-enhancement biases in social judgments. *Social Cognition* 4, 4: 353–376.

Cahn, Naomi, and June Carbone. 2010. *Red families v. blue families: Legal polarization and the creation of culture*. New York: Oxford University Press.

Carpenter, Laura M. 2001. The first time/Das erstes mal: Approaches to virginity loss in U.S. and German teen magazines. *Youth & Society* 33, 1: 31–61.

———. 2005. *Virginity lost: An intimate portrait of first sexual experiences*. New York: New York University Press.

Casper, Monica J., and Laura M. Carpenter. 2008. Sex, drugs, and politics: The HPV vaccine for cervical cancer. *Sociology of Health & Illness* 30, 6: 886–899.

Casper, Monica J., and Lisa Jean Moore. 2009. *Missing bodies: The politics of visibility*. New York: New York University Press.

Cavanagh, Sheila Lynn. 2007. *Sexing the teacher: School sex scandals and queer pedagogies*. Vancouver, British Columbia: University of British Columbia Press.

Centers for Disease Control and Prevention. 2008. HIV prevalence estimates—United States, 2006. *Morbidity and Mortality Weekly Report*
57, 39: 1073–1076, October 3. http://www.cdc.gov/mmwr/preview/
mmwrhtml/mm5739a2.htm.

———. 2009. Genital HPV infection—CDC fact sheet. Department of
Health and Human Services, November 24.
http://www.cdc.gov/std/hpv/stdfact-hpv.htm.

———. 2010a. HIV and AIDs in the United States—CDC fact sheet. Department of Health and Human Services, July 20.
http://www.cdc.gov/hiv/resources/factsheets/us.htm.

———. 2010b. Trends in sexually transmitted diseases in the United States:
2009 data for gonorrhea, chlamydia, and syphilis. Department of Health
and Human Services, November 22. http://www.cdc.gov/std/stats09/
trends.htm.

———. 2010c. Youth risk behavior surveillance—United States, 2009. Surveillance Summaries, June 4. *Morbidity and Mortality Weekly Report* 59,
SS-5. http://www.cdc.gov/mmwr/pdf/ss/ss5905.pdf.

Chapkis, Wendy. 1997. *Live sex acts: Women performing erotic labor.* New
York: Routledge.

Chodorow, Nancy J. 1999. *The reproduction of mothering: Psychoanalysis and
the sociology of gender.* 2nd ed. Berkeley: University of California Press.

Cohen, Cathy J. 2009. Black sexuality, indigenous moral panics, and
respectability: From Bill Cosby to the down low. In *Moral panics, sex panics: Fear and the fight over sexual rights,* edited by Gilbert Herdt, 104–129.
New York: New York University Press.

Collins, Patricia Hill. 1986. Learning from the outsider within: The sociological significance of Black feminist thought. *Social Problems* 33: 14–32.

———. 1991. The meaning of motherhood in Black culture and Black
mother-daughter relationships. In *Double stitch: Black women write about
mothers and daughters,* edited by Patricia Bell-Scott, 42–60. Boston:
Beacon Press.

———. 2000. *Black feminist thought: Knowledge, consciousness, and the politics of empowerment.* 2nd ed. New York: Routledge.

———. 2004. *Black sexual politics: African Americans, gender, and the new
racism.* New York: Routledge.

Conley, Dalton. 1999. *Being black, living in the red: Race, wealth, and social
policy in America.* Berkeley: University of California Press.

Connell, Catherine, and Sinikka Elliott. 2009. Beyond the birds and the
bees: Learning inequality through sexuality education. *American Journal
of Sexuality Education* 4, 2: 83–102.

Connell, R. W. 1987. *Gender and power.* Stanford: Stanford University Press.

———. 1995. *Masculinities.* Berkeley: University of California Press.

Connidis, Ingrid Arnet, and Julie Ann McMullin. 2002. Sociological ambivalence and family ties: A critical perspective. *Journal of Marriage and Family* 64: 558–567.

Corsaro, William. 2004. *The sociology of childhood.* 2nd ed. Thousand Oaks, CA: Pine Forge.

Crawford, Mary, and Danielle Popp. 2003. Sexual double standards: A review and methodological critique of two decades of research. *Journal of Sex Research* 40, 1: 13–26.

Dateline NBC. 2006. Most teens say they've met strangers online. MSNBC. com, April 26. http://www.msnbc.msn.com/id/12502825/.

Davies, Charlotte Aull. 1999. *Reflexive ethnography: A guide to researching selves and others.* London: Routledge.

Davis, Angela. 1998. *Blues legacies and black feminism: Gertrude "Ma" Rainey, Bessie Smith and Billie Holiday.* New York: Vintage.

De Gaston, Jacqueline F., Stan Weed, and Larry Jensen. 1996. Understanding gender differences in adolescent sexuality. *Adolescence* 31: 217–231.

D'Emilio, John, and Estelle B. Freedman. 1988. *Intimate matters: A history of sexuality in America.* New York: Harper & Row.

DeVault, Marjorie L. 1991. *Feeding the family: The social organization of caring as gendered work.* Chicago: University of Chicago Press.

Dicker, John. 2004. The young and the sexless: The abstinence-only movement is flush with funds, but where's the evidence that it works? Colorado Springs Independent, March 18. http://www.csindy.com/colorado/the-young-and-the-sexless/Content?oid=1122937.

DiIorio, Colleen, Maureen Kelley, and Marilyn Hockenberry-Eaton. 1999. Communication about sexual issues: Mothers, fathers, and friends. *Journal of Adolescent Health* 24: 181–189.

di Mauro, Diane, and Carole Joffe. 2009. The Religious Right and the reshaping of sexual policy: Reproductive rights and sexuality education during the Bush years. In *Moral panics, sex panics: Fear and the fight over sexual rights,* edited by Gilbert Herdt, 47–103. New York: New York University Press.

Dittus, Patricia J., and James Jaccard. 1998. Adolescent perceptions of maternal disapproval of sex and the mother-adolescent relationship: The impact on sexual outcomes. University of Albany, State University of New York. Manuscript.

Douglas, Mary. 1966. *Purity and danger: An analysis of the concepts of pollution and taboo.* New York: Praeger.

Duncan, Greg J., Johanne Boisjoly, and Katherine Mullan Harris. 2001. Sibling, peer, neighbor, and schoolmate correlations as indicators of the importance of context for adolescent development. *Demography* 38: 437–447.

du Plessis, Michael. 1993. Mother's boys: Maternity, "homosexuality," and melancholia. *Discourse* 16: 145–173.

Durkheim, Émile. 2001 [1912]. *The elementary forms of religious life.* Translated by C. Cosman. New York: Oxford University Press.

Edin, Kathryn, and Maria Kefalas. 2005. *Promises I can keep: Why poor women put motherhood before marriage.* Berkeley: University of California Press.

Ehrenreich, Barbara. 1989. *Fear of falling.* New York: Pantheon Books.

———. 2001. *Nickel and dimed: On (not) getting by in America.* New York: Metropolitan Books.

Eliasoph, Nina, and Paul Lichterman. 2003. Culture in interaction. *American Journal of Sociology* 108, 4: 735–794.

Elliott, Sinikka. 2010. Parents' constructions of teen sexuality: Sex panics, contradictory discourses, and social inequality. *Symbolic Interaction* 33, 2: 191–212.

Elliott, Sinikka, and Debra Umberson. 2008. The performance of desire: Gender and sexual negotiation in long-term marriages. *Journal of Marriage and Family* 70: 391–406.

England, Paula, Emily Fitzgibbons Shafer, and Alison C. K. Fogarty. 2010. Hooking up and forming romantic relationships on today's college campuses. In *The gendered society reader,* 4th ed., edited by Michael Kimmel and Amy Aronson, 531–547. New York: Oxford University Press.

Espiritu, Yen Lee. 2000. "We don't sleep around like white girls do": Family, culture, and gender in Filipina lives. *Signs: A Journal of Women in Culture and Society* 26, 2: 415–440.

Esterberg, Kristin G. 2002. *Qualitative methods in social research.* Boston: McGraw-Hill.

Excerpts from President's speech to National Association of Evangelicals. 1983. *New York Times,* March 9. http://www.nytimes.com/1983/03/09/us/excerpts-from-president-s-speech-to-national-association-of-evangelicals.html.

Fasula, Amy M., and Kim S. Miller. 2006. African-American and Hispanic adolescents' intentions to delay first intercourse: Parental communication as a buffer for sexually active peers. *Journal of Adolescent Health* 38: 193–200.

Fein, Melvyn L. 1990. *Role change: A resocialization perspective.* Westport, CT: Praeger.

Feldman, S. Shirley, and Doreen A. Rosenthal. 2000. The effect of communication characteristics on family members' perceptions of parents as sex
educators. *Journal of Research on Adolescence* 10: 119–150.

Ferguson, Ann Arnett. 2000. *Bad boys: Public schools in the making of black
masculinity.* Ann Arbor: University of Michigan Press.

Fields, Jessica. 2001. Normal queers: Straight parents respond to their children's "coming out." *Symbolic Interaction* 24: 165–187.

———. 2005. "Children having children": Race, innocence, and sexuality
education. *Social Problems* 52, 4: 549–571.

———. 2008. *Risky Lessons: Sex education and social inequality.* New Bruns-
wick, NJ: Rutgers University Press.

Fine, Gary Alan. 1993. Ten lies of ethnography: Moral dilemmas of field
research. *Journal of Contemporary Ethnography* 22, 3: 258–263.

Fine, Michelle. 1988. Sexuality, schooling, and adolescent females: The missing discourse of desire. *Harvard Educational Review* 58, 1: 29–53.

Fine, Michelle, and Sara I. McClelland. 2006. Sexuality education and
desire: Still missing after all these years. *Harvard Educational Review* 76,
3: 297–337.

Finkelhor, David, Heather Turner, Richard Ormrod, and Sherry L. Hamby.
2010. Trends in childhood violence and abuse exposure: Evidence from
2 national surveys. *Archives of Pediatric and Adolescent Medicine* 164, 3:
238–242.

Fisher, Bonnie, Francis Cullen, and Michael Turner. 2000. The sexual
victimization of college women. Washington, DC: National Institute of
Justice and the Bureau of Justice Statistics.

Flavin, Jeanne. 2009. *Our bodies, our crimes: The policing of women's reproduction in America.* New York: New York University Press.

Foucault, Michel. 1977. *Discipline and punish: The birth of the prison.* New
York: Pantheon.

———. 1990. *The history of sexuality.* Vol. 1, *An Introduction.* Translated by
R. Hurley. New York: Vintage Books.

Frankenberg, Ruth. 1992. *White women, race matters: The social construction
of whiteness.* Minneapolis: University of Minnesota Press.

Frankham, Jo. 2006. Sexual antimonies and parent/child sex education:
Learning from foreclosure. *Sexualities* 9: 236–254.

Furstenberg, Frank F., Jr. 2003. Teenage childbearing as a public issue and
private concern. *Annual Review of Sociology* 29: 23–39.

Furstenberg, Frank F., Jr., Thomas D. Cook, Jacquelynne Eccles, Glen H.
Elder Jr., and Arnold Sameroff. 1999. *Managing to make it: Urban families
and adolescent success.* Chicago: University of Chicago Press.

Gamson, Joshua, and Dawne Moon. 2004. The sociology of sexualities: Queer and beyond. *Annual Review of Sociology* 30: 47–64.

Garcia, Lorena. 2009. "Now why do you want to know about that?": Heteronormativity, sexism, and racism in the sexual (mis)education of Latina youth. *Gender & Society* 23, 4: 520–541.

Garfinkel, Harold. 1967. *Studies in ethnomethodology.* Englewood Cliffs, NJ: Prentice Hall.

Geertz, Clifford. 2001. Thick description: Toward an interpretive theory of culture. In *Contemporary field research: Perspectives and formulations,* 2nd ed., edited by Robert M. Emerson. Long Grove, IL: Waveland.

Giddens, Anthony. 1991. *Modernity and self-identity.* Stanford: Stanford University Press.

———. 1992. *The transformation of intimacy: Sexuality, love and eroticism in modern societies.* Stanford, CA: Stanford University Press.

Glassner, Barry. 1999. *The culture of fear: Why Americans are afraid of the wrong things.* New York: Basic Books.

Glosser, Asaph, Karen Gardiner, and Mike Fishman. 2004. Statutory rape: A guide to state laws and reporting requirements. U.S. Department of Health and Human Services, December 15. http://www.lewin.com/Lewin_Publications/Human_Services/StateLawsReport.htm.

Gonzalez-Lopez, Gloria. 2003. De madres a hijas: Gendered lessons on virginity across generations of Mexican immigrant women. In *Gender and U.S. immigration: Contemporary trends,* edited by Pierrette Hondagneu-Sotelo, 217–240. Berkeley: University of California Press.

———. 2004. Fathering Latina sexualities: Mexican men and the virginity of their daughters. *Journal of Marriage and Family* 66: 1118–1130.

———. 2005. *Erotic journeys: Mexican immigrants and their sex lives.* Berkeley: University of California Press.

Godbeer, Richard. 2002. *Sexual revolution in early America.* Baltimore, MD: Johns Hopkins University Press.

Guttmacher Institute. 1999. *Facts in brief: Teen sex and pregnancy.* New York: Alan Guttmacher Institute.

———. 2006. Facts on sex education in the United States. http://www.guttmacher.org/pubs/fb_sexEd2006.html.

———. 2010. U.S. teenage pregnancies, births and abortions: National and state trends and trends by race and ethnicity. New York: Alan Guttmacher Institute. http://www.guttmacher.org/pubs/USTPtrends.pdf.

Halley, Janet E. 1993. The construction of heterosexuality. In *Fear of a queer planet: Queer politics and social theory,* edited by Michael Warner, 82–102. Minneapolis: University of Minnesota Press.

Hamilton Brady E., Joyce A. Martin, and Stephanie J. Ventura. 2010. Births: Preliminary data for 2008. National vital statistics reports Web release, vol. 58, no 16. Hyattsville, MD: National Center for Health Statistics. http://www.cdc.gov/nchs/data/nvsr/nvsr58/nvsr58_16.pdf.

Hamilton, Laura, and Elizabeth A. Armstrong. 2009. Gendered sexuality in young adulthood: Double binds and flawed options. *Gender & Society* 23, 5: 589–616.

Harding, David J. 2007. Cultural context, sexual behavior, and romantic relationships in disadvantaged neighborhoods. *American Sociological Review* 72: 341–364.

———. 2009. Violence, older peers, and the socialization of adolescent boys in disadvantaged neighborhoods. *American Sociological Review* 74: 445–464.

Haug, Frigga. 1987. *Female sexualization: A collective work of memory.* Translated by E. Carter. London: Verso.

Hays, Sharon. 2003. *Flat broke with children: Women in the age of welfare reform.* New York: Oxford University Press.

Herdt, Gilbert. 2009. Moral panics, sexual rights, and cultural anger. In *Moral panics, sex panics: Fear and the fight over sexual rights,* edited by Gilbert Herdt, 1–46. New York: New York University Press.

Hochschild, Arlie Russell. 1983. *The managed heart: Commercialization of human feeling.* Berkeley: University of California Press.

Hofer, Barbara, Constance Souder, Elena K. Kennedy, Nancy Fullman, and Kathryn Hurd. 2009. The "electronic tether": Communication and parental monitoring during the college years. In *Who's watching? Daily practices of surveillance among contemporary families,* edited by Margaret K. Nelson and Anita Ilta Garey, 277–294. Nashville, TN: Vanderbilt University Press.

Hoffman, Jan. 2010. Online bullies pull schools into the fray. *New York Times,* Style section, June 27.

Holstein, James A., and Jaber F. Gubrium. 2002. Active interviewing. In *Qualitative research methods,* edited by Darin Weinberg, 112–126. Oxford: Blackwell.

Hutchinson, M. Katherine. 2002. The influence of sexual risk communications between parents and daughters on sexual risk behaviors. *Family Relations* 51: 238–247.

Ingraham, Chrys. 1999. *White weddings: Romancing heterosexuality in popular culture.* New York: Routledge.

Irvine, Janice., ed. 1994. *Sexual cultures and the construction of adolescent identities.* Philadelphia: Temple University Press.

———. 2002. *Talk about sex: The battles over sex education in the United States*. Berkeley: University of California Press.

———. 2007. Transient feelings: Sex panics and the politics of emotions. *GLQ: A Journal of Lesbian and Gay Studies* 14, 1: 1–40.

———. 2009. Shame comes out of the closet. *Sexuality Research & Social Policy* 6: 70–79.

Jaccard, James, Patricia J. Dittus, and Vivian V. Gordon. 1996. Maternal correlates of adolescent sexual and contraceptive behavior. *Family Planning Perspectives* 28: 159–165.

———. 1998. Parent-adolescent congruency in reports of adolescent sexual behavior and in communications about sexual behavior. *Child Development* 69: 247–261.

———. 2000. Parent-teen communication about premarital sex: Factors associated with the extent of communication. *Journal of Adolescent Research* 15: 187–208.

Jewell, K. Sue. 1998. *From Mammy to Miss America and beyond: Cultural images and the shaping of U.S. social policy*. London: Routledge.

Jones, Elise. F., Jacqueline Darroch Forrest, Noreen Goldman, Stanley Henshaw, Richard Lincoln, Jeannie I. Rosoff, Charles F. Westoff, and Deirdre Wulf. 1986. *Teenage pregnancy in industrialized countries. A study sponsored by the Alan Guttmacher Institute*. New Haven, CT: Yale University Press.

Juvonen, Jaana, and Elisheva F. Gross. 2008. Extending the school grounds?—Bullying experiences in cyberspace. *Journal of School Health* 78, 9: 496–505.

Kaplan, Elaine Bell. 1996. *Not our kind of girl: Unraveling the myths of black teenage motherhood*. Berkeley: University of California Press.

Katz, Jonathan Ned. 1995. *The invention of heterosexuality*. New York: Penguin Books.

Kelly, Gary F. 2005. Re-visioning sexuality education: A challenge for the future. *American Journal of Sexuality Education* 1, 1: 5–21.

Kendall, Nancy. 2008. Sexuality education in an abstinence-only era: A comparative case study of two U.S. states. *Sexuality Research & Social Policy* 5, 2: 23–44.

Kim, Janna L., and L. Monique Ward. 2007. Silence speaks volumes: Parental sexual communication among Asian American emerging adults. *Journal of Adolescent Research* 22: 3–31.

Kimmel, Michael. 1996. *Manhood in America: A cultural history*. New York: Free Press.

Kincaid, James R. 1998. *Erotic innocence: The culture of child molesting*. Durham, NC: Duke University Press.

Kirby, Douglas. 2002. Do abstinence-only programs delay the initiation of sex among young people and reduce teen pregnancy? Washington, DC: National Campaign to Prevent Teen Pregnancy. http://www.teenpregnancy.org/resources/data/pdf/abstinence_eval.pdf.

Kirkman, Maggie, Doreen A. Rosenthal, and S. Shirley Feldman. 2002. Talking to a tiger: Fathers reveal their difficulties in communicating about sexuality with adolescents. *New Directions for Child and Adolescent Development* 97: 57–74.

Kurz, Demie. 2002. Caring for teenage children. *Journal of Family Issues* 23: 748–767.

Lareau, Annette. 2003. *Unequal childhoods: Class, race, and family life.* Berkeley: University of California Press.

Laumann, Edward O., John H. Gagnon, Robert T. Michael, and Stuart Michaels. 1994. *The social organization of sexuality: Sexual practices in the United States.* Chicago: University of Chicago Press.

Lefkowitz, Eva S., Tanya L. Boone, Terry K. Au, and Marian Sigman. 2003. No sex or safe sex? Mothers' and adolescents' discussions about sexuality and AIDS/HIV. *Health Education Research* 18: 341–351.

Lefkowitz, Eva S., Tanya L. Boone, Marian Sigman, and Terry K. Au. 2002. He said, she said: Gender differences in mother-adolescent conversations about sexuality. *Journal of Research on Adolescence* 12, 2: 217–242.

Lenhart, Amanda. 2005. Protecting teens online. Pew Internet & American Life Project, March 17. http://www.pewinternet.org/Reports/2005/Protecting-Teens-Online.aspx.

Lesko, Nancy. 2001. *Act your age! A cultural construction of adolescence.* New York: Routledge Falmer.

Levine, Judith. 2002. *Harmful to minors: The perils of protecting children from sex.* Minneapolis: University of Minnesota Press.

Luker, Kristin. 1996. *Dubious conceptions: The politics of teenage pregnancy.* Cambridge, MA: Harvard University Press.

———. 2006. *When sex goes to school: Warring views on sex— and sex education—since the sixties.* New York: Norton.

Luttrell, Wendy. 2003. *Pregnant bodies, fertile minds: Gender, race, and the schooling of pregnant teens.* New York: Routledge.

Madriz, Esther. 1997. *Nothing bad happens to good girls: Fear of crime in women's lives.* Berkeley: University of California Press.

Males, Mike A. 2010. *Teenage sex and pregnancy: Modern myths, unsexy realities.* Santa Barbara, CA: Praeger.

Mamo, Laura, Amber Nelson, and Aleia Clark. 2010. Producing and protecting risky girlhoods. In *Three shots at prevention: The HPV vaccine and the politics of medicine's simple solutions*, edited by K. Wailoo, J. Livingston, S. Epstein, and R. Aronowitz, 121–145. Baltimore, MD: Johns Hopkins University Press.

Martin, Karin A. 1996. *Puberty, sexuality, and the self: Boys and girls at adolescence.* New York: Routledge.

———. 2009. Normalizing heterosexuality: Mothers' assumptions, talk, and strategies with young children. *American Sociological Review* 74: 190–207.

Martin, Karin A., and Katherine Luke. 2010. Gender differences in the ABC's of the birds and the bees: What mothers teach young children about sexuality and reproduction. *Sex Roles* 62: 278–291.

Martin, Karin A., Katherine Luke, and Lynn Verduzco-Baker. 2007. The sexual socialization of young children: Setting the research agenda. In *Advances in group processes: Social psychology of gender*, edited by S. Correll, 231–259. Oxford: Elsevier.

Marvel, Bill, and Nancy Churnin. 2006. Parents fear MySpace is playground for pedophiles. *Dallas Morning News*, March 5. http://www.dallasnews.com/sharedcontent/dws/dn/latestnews/stories/030506dnlivmyspace.2976283.html.

McCormack, Karen. 2005. Stratified reproduction and poor women's resistance. *Gender & Society* 19, 5: 660–679.

McHale, Susan M., Ann C. Crouter, and Shawn Whiteman. 2003. The family contexts of gender development in childhood adolescence. *Social Development* 12: 125–148.

Melody, Michael E., and Linda M. Peterson. 1999. *Teaching America about sex: Marriage guides and sex manuals from the late Victorians to Dr. Ruth.* New York: New York University Press.

Melton, Gary B. 2005. Treating children like people: A framework for research and advocacy. *Journal of Clinical Child and Adolescent Psychology* 34, 4: 646–657.

Merton, Robert K. 1972. Insiders and outsiders: A chapter in the sociology of knowledge. *American Journal of Sociology* 77, 1: 9–47.

Messner, Michael A. 2000. Barbie girls versus sea monsters: Children constructing gender. *Gender & Society* 14: 765–784.

———. 2007. The masculinity of the governator: Muscle and compassion in American politics. *Gender & Society* 21, 4: 461–480.

Miller, Kim, Beth Kotchick, Shannon Dorsey, Rex Forehand, and Anissa Ham. 1998. Family communication about sex: What are parents saying and are their adolescents listening? *Family Planning Perspectives* 30, 5: 218–222.

Mills, C. Wright. 1959. *The sociological imagination.* New York: Oxford University Press.

Moon, Dawne. 2004. *God, sex and politics: Homosexuality and everyday theologies.* Chicago: University of Chicago Press.

Moore, Susan, and Doreen Rosenthal. 1991. Adolescents' perceptions of friends' and parents' attitudes to sex and sexual risk-taking. *Journal of Community and Applied Social Psychology* 1: 189–200.

Moran, Jeffrey P. 2000. *Teaching sex: The shaping of adolescence in the 20th century.* Cambridge, MA: Harvard University Press.

Morris, Ronald. 1997. Myths of sexuality education. *Journal of Moral Education* 26: 353–361.

Most states forego mandatory Gardasil. 2009. *24-7 News,* September 2. http://www.24-7-news.com/archives/4021.

Nagel, Joane. 2001. Racial, ethnic, and national boundaries: Sexual intersections and symbolic interactions. *Symbolic Interaction* 24, 2: 123–139.

Nathanson, Constance A. 1991. *Dangerous passage: The social control of sexuality in women's adolescence.* Philadelphia: Temple University Press.

National Communication Association. 1998. How Americans communicate. Roper Starch. http://www.natcom.org/research/Roper/how_americans_communicate.htm.

National Public Radio, Kaiser Family Foundation, Harvard Kennedy School of Government Poll. 2004. *Sex education in America.* Publication no. 7015, January 29. http://www.kff.org/newsmedia/7015.cfm.

National Sexuality Resource Center. 2008. About sexual literacy. San Francisco State University. http://nsrc.sfsu.edu/what_sexual_literacy.

Nelson, Margaret. 2010. *Parenting out of control: Anxious parents in uncertain times.* New York: New York University Press.

Newcomer, Susan F., and J. Richard Udry. 1985. Parent-child communication and adolescent sexual behavior. *Family Planning Perspectives* 17, 4: 169–174.

Nolin, Mary J., and Karen K. Petersen. 1992. Gender differences in parent-child communication about sexuality: An exploratory study. *Journal of Adolescent Research* 7: 59–79.

Omar, Hatim, Darby McElderry, and Rana Zakharia. 2003. Educating adolescents about puberty: What are we missing? *International Journal of Adolescent Medicine and Health* 15: 79–83.

Ortner, Sherry B. 1991. Reading America: Preliminary notes on class and culture. In *Recapturing anthropology: Working in the present,* edited by Richard G. Fox, 73–92. Santa Fe, NM: School of American Research Press.

———. 1996. *Making gender: The politics and erotics of culture.* Boston: Beacon.

———. 1998. Identities: The hidden life of class. *Journal of Anthropological Research* 54, 1: 1–17.

Osmond, Marie Withers, and Barrie Thorne. 1993. Feminist theories: The social construction of gender in families and society. In *Sourcebook of family theories and methods: A contextual approach,* edited by P. G. Boss, W. J. Doherty, R. LaRossa, W. R. Schumm, and S. K. Steinmetz, 591–625. New York: Plenum.

Palladino, Grace. 1996. *Teenagers: An American history.* New York: Basic Books.

Pascoe, C. J. 2007. *Dude, you're a fag: Masculinity and sexuality in high school.* Berkeley: University of California Press.

Pattillo-McCoy, Mary. 2003. Black picket fences: Privilege and peril among the black middle class. In *Wealth and poverty in America: A reader,* edited by D. Conley, 96–114. Malden, MA: Blackwell.

Peiser, Wolfram, and Jochen Peter. 2000. Third-person perception of television viewing behavior. *Journal of Communication* 50, 1:25–45.

Personal Responsibility and Work Opportunity Reconciliation Act. 1996. Pub. L. No. 104–193, §912, 110 Stat. 2105–2355.

Phillips, Lynn M. 2000. *Flirting with danger: Young women's reflections on sexuality and dominance.* New York: New York University Press.

Plummer, Ken. 2001. The call of life stories in ethnographic research. In *Handbook of ethnography,* edited by P. Atkinson, A. J. Coffey, S. Delamont, J. Lofland, and L. H. Lofland, 395–406. Thousand Oaks, CA: Sage.

———. 2003a. *Intimate citizenship: Private decisions and public dialogues.* Seattle: University of Washington Press.

———. 2003b. Queers, bodies, and postmodern sexualities: A note on revisiting the "sexual" in symbolic interactionism. *Qualitative Sociology* 26, 4: 515–530.

———. 2004. Male sexualities. In *Handbook of studies on men and masculinities,* edited by M. Kimmel, J. Hearn, and R. W. Connell, 178–195. Thousand Oaks, CA: Sage.

Popenoe, David. 1996. *Life without father.* New York: Free Press.

Pugh, Allison J. 2009. *Longing and belonging: Parents, children, and consumer culture.* Berkeley: University of California Press.

Raffaelli, Marcela, Karen Bogenschneider, and Mary F. Flood. 1998. Parent-teen communication about sexual topics. *Journal of Family Issues* 19: 315–333.

Raffaelli, Marcela, and Stephanie Green. 2003. Parent-adolescent communication about sex: Retrospective reports by Latino college students. *Journal of Marriage and Family* 65: 474–481.

Rangel, Maria C., Loretta Gavin, Christie Reed, Mary G. Fowler, and Lisa M. Lee. 2006. Epidemiology of HIV and AIDS among adolescents and young adults in the United States. *Journal of Adolescent Health* 39, 2: 156–163.

Reece, Michael, Debbie Herbenick, Vanessa Schick, Stephanie A. Sanders, Brian Dodge, and J. Dennis Fortenberry. 2010. Condom use rates in a national probability sample of males and female ages 14 to 94 in the United States. *Journal of Sexual Medicine* 7 (suppl 5): 266–276.

Regnerus, Mark D. 2005. Talking about sex: Religion and patterns of parent-child communication about sex and contraception. *Sociological Quarterly* 46: 79–105.

———. 2007. *Forbidden fruit: Sex and religion in the lives of American teenagers*. New York: Oxford University Press.

Resnick, Michael D., Peter S. Bearman, Robert W. Blum, Karl E. Bauman, Kathleen M. Harris, Jo Jones, Joyce Tabor, et al. 1997. Protecting adolescents from harm: Findings from the National Longitudinal Study on Adolescent Health. *Journal of the American Medical Association* 278, 10: 823–832.

Rich, Adrienne. 1986. Compulsory heterosexuality and lesbian existence. In *Feminist frontiers II: Rethinking sex, gender, and society*, edited by Laurel Richardson and Verta Taylor, 120–141. New York: Random House.

Robinson, Christine M., and Sue E. Spivey. 2007. The politics of masculinity and the ex-gay movement. *Gender & Society* 21: 650–675.

Rofes, Eric. 2000. Bound and gagged: Sexual silences, gender conformity and the gay male teacher. *Sexualities* 3, 4: 439–462.

Rohter, Larry. 2008. Ad on sex education distorts Obama policy. *New York Times*, September 10. http://www.nytimes.com/2008/09/11/us/politics/11checkpoint.html?fta=y.

Romo, Laura, Erum Nadeem, Terry K. Au, and Marian Sigman. 2004. Mexican American adolescents' responsiveness to their mother's questions about dating and sexuality. *Applied Developmental Psychology* 25: 501–522.

Ronen, Shelly. 2010. Grinding on the dance floor: Gendered scripts and sexualized dancing at college parties. *Gender & Society* 24: 355–377.

Rose, Lowell C., and Alec M. Gallup. 1998. The thirtieth annual Phi Delta Kappa Gallup Poll of the public's attitudes toward the public schools. *Phi Delta Kappan* 80, 1: 41–58.

Rose, Tricia. 2003. *Longing to tell: Black women's stories of sexuality and intimacy.* New York: Farrar Straus & Giroux.

Rosenthal, Doreen A., and S. Shirley Feldman. 1999. The importance of importance: Adolescents' perceptions of parental communication about sexuality. *Journal of Adolescence* 22: 835–851.

Ross, Marlon B. 1998. In search of Black men's masculinities. *Feminist Studies* 24, 3: 599–626.

Rubin, Gayle. 1975. The traffic in women: Notes on the "political economy" of sex. In *Toward an anthropology of women*, edited by R. R. Reiter, 157–210. New York: Monthly Review Press.

———. 1984. Thinking sex: Notes for a radical theory of the politics of sexuality. In *Pleasure and danger: Exploring female sexuality*, edited by Carole S. Vance, 267–319. Boston: Routledge & Kegan Paul.

Rubin, Lillian B. 1990. *Erotic wars: What happened to the sexual revolution?* New York: Farrar, Straus & Giroux.

Russell, Stephen T. 2005. Conceptualizing positive adolescent sexuality development. *Sexuality Research & Social Policy* 2, 3: 3–12.

Saillant, Catherine. 2006. Testing the bounds of MySpace. *Los Angeles Times*, April 8. http://articles.latimes.com/2006/apr/08/local/me-myspace8.

Santelli, John, Marion Carter, Mark Orr, and Patricia Dittus. 2009. Trends in sexual risk behaviors, by nonsexual risk behavior involvement, U.S. high school students, 1991–2007. *Journal of Adolescent Health* 44, 4: 372–379.

Saslow, Debbie, Carolyn D. Runowicz, Diane Solomon, Anna-Barbara Moscicki, Robert A. Smith, Harmon J. Eyre, and Carmel Cohen. 2002. American Cancer Society guideline for the early detection of cervical neoplasia and cancer. *CA: A Cancer Journal for Clinicians* 52: 342–362.

Schalet, Amy. 2000. Raging hormones, regulated love: Adolescent sexuality and the constitution of the modern individual in the United States and the Netherlands. *Body & Society* 6, 1: 75–105.

———. 2004. Must we fear adolescent sexuality? *Medscape General Medicine* 6, 4: 1–16.

———. 2010. Sexual subjectivity revisited: The significance of relationships in Dutch and American girls' experiences of sexuality. *Gender & Society* 24, 3: 304–329.

Schermerhorn, Alice C., E. Mark Cummings, Catherine A. DeCarlo, and Patrick T. Davies. 2007. Children's influence on the marital relationship. *Journal of Family Psychology* 21, 2: 259–269.

Schilt, Kristen. 2008. The unfinished business of sexuality: Comment on Andersen. *Gender & Society* 22, 1:109–114.

Schwalbe, Michael. 2008. *Rigging the game: How inequality is reproduced in everyday life*. New York: Oxford University Press.

Schwalbe, Michael, Sandra Godwin, Daphne Holden, Douglas Schrock, Shealy Thompson, and Michelle Wolkomir. 2000. Generic processes in the reproduction of inequality: An interactionist analysis. *Social Forces* 79: 419–452.

Seidman, Steven. 1991. *Romantic longings: Love in America, 1830–1980*. New York: Routledge.

Shapiro, Thomas M. 2004. *The hidden cost of being African American: How wealth perpetuates inequality*. New York: Oxford University Press.

Simmel, Georg. 1971. *Georg Simmel on individuality and social forms: Selected writings*. Edited and translated by Donald N. Levine. Chicago: University of Chicago Press.

Simon, William, and John Gagnon. 1986. "Sexual scripts: Permanence and change." *Archives of Sexual Behavior* 15(2): 97–120.

Smelser, Neil J. 1998. The rational and the ambivalent in the social sciences: 1997 presidential address. *American Sociological Review* 63: 1–16.

Smith, Daniel Scott, and Michael S. Hindus. 1975. Premarital pregnancy in America 1640–1971: An overview and interpretation. *Journal of Interdisciplinary History* 5, 4: 537–570.

Solebello, Nicholas and Sinikka Elliott. 2011. "We want them to be as heterosexual as possible": Fathers talk about their teen children's sexuality. *Gender & Society* 25, 3: 293–315.

Solinger, Rickie. 2000. *Wake up little Susie: Single pregnancy before Roe v. Wade*. New York: Routledge.

Stanton, B. F., M. Black, L. Kalijee, and I. Ricardo. 1993. Perceptions of sexual behavior among urban early adolescents: Translating theory through focus groups. *Journal of Early Adolescence* 13: 44–66.

Stearns, Peter N. 2003. *Anxious parents: A history of modern childrearing in America*. New York: New York University Press.

Stein, Arlene. 1989. Three models of sexuality: Drives, identities, and practices. *Sociological Theory* 7, 1: 1–13.

———. 2001. *The stranger next door: The story of a small community's battle over sex, faith, and civil rights*. Boston: Beacon.

———. 2006. *Shameless: Sexual dissidence in American culture*. New York: New York University Press.

Stone, Pamela. 2007. *Opting out? Why women really quit careers and head home*. Berkeley: University of California Press.

Strauss, Anselm L. 1987. *Qualitative analysis for social scientists*. Cambridge: Cambridge University Press.

Tanenbaum, Leora. 1999. *Slut! Growing up female with a bad reputation.* New York: Seven Stories.

Taylor, Shelley E., and Jonathan D. Brown. 1988. Illusion and well-being: A social psychological perspective on mental health. *Psychological Bulletin* 103, 2: 193–210.

Thompson, Sharon. 1990. Putting a big thing into a little hole: Teenage girls' accounts of sexual initiation. *Journal of Sex Research* 27: 341–361.

———. 1992. Search for tomorrow: On feminism and the reconstruction of teen romance. In *Pleasure and danger: Exploring female sexuality*, edited by Carole S. Vance, 350–384. London: Pandora.

———. 1995. *Going all the way: Teenage girls' tales of sex, romance, and pregnancy.* New York: Hill and Wang.

Thorne, Barrie, and Zella Luria. 1986. Sexuality and gender in children's daily worlds. *Social Problems* 33: 176–190.

Tolman, Deborah L. 1994a. Daring to desire: Culture and the bodies of adolescent girls. In *Sexual cultures and the construction of adolescent identities*, edited by Janice M. Irvine, 250–284. Philadelphia: Temple University Press.

———. 1994b. Doing desire: Adolescent girls' struggles for/with sexuality. *Gender & Society* 8, 3: 324–342.

Tolman, Deborah L., Meg L. Striepe, and Tricia Harmon. 2003. Gender matters: Constructing a model of adolescent sexual health. *Journal of Sex Research* 40, 1: 4–12.

Trenholm, Christopher, Barbara Devaney, Ken Fortson, Lisa Quay, Justin Wheeler, and Melissa Clark. 2007. *Impacts of four Title V, Section 510 abstinence education programs: Final report.* Congressional Report by Mathematica Policy Research. http://www.mathematica-mpr.com/welfare/abstinence.asp.

Trudell, Bonnie Nelson. 1992. Inside a ninth-grade sexuality classroom: The process of knowledge construction. In *Sexuality and the curriculum: The politics and practices of sexuality education*, edited by James T. Sears, 203–225. New York: Teachers College Press.

U.S. Census Bureau. 2003. American community survey. http://factfinder.census.gov/servlet/ADPTable?geo_id=16000US4805000&qr_name=ACS_2003_EST_G00_DP1&ds_name=ACS_2003_EST_G00_.

Valocchi, Stephen. 2005. Not yet queer enough: The lessons of queer theory for the sociology of gender and sexuality. *Gender & Society* 19, 6: 750–770.

Vance, Carole S., ed. 1984. *Pleasure and danger: Exploring female sexuality.* Boston: Routledge and Kegan Paul.

Walker, Joy L. 2001. A qualitative study of parents' experiences of providing sex education for their children: The implications for health education. *Health Education Journal* 60: 132–146.

Warner, Marina. 1994. *Six myths of our time: Little angels, little monsters, beautiful beasts, and more.* New York: Vintage Books.

Warner, Michael. 1999. *The trouble with normal.* New York: Free Press.

Warr, Mark. 2005. Making delinquent friends: Adult supervision and children's affiliations. *Criminology* 43, 1: 77–105.

Warr, Mark, and Mark Stafford. 1991. The influence of delinquent peers: What they think or what they do? *Criminology* 29: 851–866.

Waters, Mary C. 1999. *Black identities: West Indian immigrant dreams and realities.* Cambridge, MA: Harvard University Press.

Webber, Gretchen, and Christine Williams. 2008. Mothers in "good" and "bad" part-time jobs: Different problems, same results. *Gender & Society* 22, 6: 752–777.

Weber, Max. 1947. *The theory of social and economic organization.* New York: Free Press.

Weeks, Jeffrey. 1981. *Sex, politics and society: The regulation of sexuality since 1800.* New York: Longman.

———. 1992. Values in an age of uncertainty. In *Discourses of sexuality: From Aristotle to AIDS,* edited by Domna C. Stanton, 389–411. Ann Arbor: University of Michigan Press.

Weiss, Robert S. 1994. *Learning from strangers: The art and method of qualitative interview studies.* New York: Free Press.

West, Candace, and Don H. Zimmerman. 1987. Doing gender. *Gender & Society* 1: 125–151.

Whittier, Nancy. 2009. *The politics of child sexual abuse: Emotion, social movements, and the state.* New York: Oxford University Press.

Wilkins, Amy. 2004. "So full of myself as a chick": Goth women, sexual independence, and gender egalitarianism. *Gender & Society* 18, 3: 328–349.

———. 2008. *Wannabes, Goths, and Christians: The boundaries of sex, style, and status.* Chicago: University of Chicago Press.

Williams, Christine, Patti A. Giuffre, and Kirsten Dellinger. 2009. The gay-friendly closet. *Sexuality Research and Social Policy* 6, 1: 29–45.

Willson, Andrea E., Kim M. Shuey, Glen H. Elder Jr., and K. A. S. Wickrama. 2006. Ambivalence in mother-adult child relations: A dyadic analysis. *Social Psychology Quarterly* 69, 3: 235–252.

Winant, Howard. 2000. Race and race theory. *Annual Review of Sociology* 26: 169–185.

Wyness, Michael. 2006. *Childhood and society: An introduction to the sociology of childhood.* New York: Palgrave Macmillan.

Zelizer, Viviana A. 1985. *Pricing the priceless child: The changing social value of children.* New York: Basic Books.

Abortion, 5, 11

Abstinence: Christian masculinity and, 142; cognitive dissonance, contraception, and, 81, 175–176n30; as dominant discourse around teen sexuality, 12–13, 122, 152; in parent–teen conversations about sex, 2–3, 26, 30, 119–120, 123–124, 137, 141, 152. *See also* Abstinence–only sex education; Family sexual communication

Abstinence–only sex education: criticism of, 166n14; danger discourse of teen sexuality and, 123, 146, 152; debates over, 9–10, 145–146, 152; federal policy and, 11–12, 150; parents' ambivalence about, 120, 122–123, 141; parents' rights and, 62; parents' support for, 145; proponents of, 17, 32; sex educators and, 12, 61, 155; state policies of, 166n12. *See also* Adolescent Family Life Act; Community Based Abstinence Education; Personal Responsibility and Work Opportunity Reconciliation Act

Adolescence, adolescents: adultification of, 84; as asexual and innocent, 16–17, 24, 29–30, 65, 97; binary thinking and, 63, 66,

81–82, 151; as coined in early twentieth century, 15, 175n18; cultural understandings of, 71; as developmental narrative, 50–51, 64, 70–72, 151; hormones and, 17, 51, 65–66; as immature and irresponsible, 2, 66, 85, 147; as sexualized, 67, 85; as sexually driven, 17, 64–65, 147. *See also* Teen sexual activity; Teen sexuality, discourses of

Adolescent Family Life Act (AFLA), 11. *See also* "Chastity Act"

African Americans. *See* Race/ethnicity

Age of sexual consent, 14–15

AIDS. *See* HIV/AIDS

Ambivalence: as defined sociologically, 121; in parents' sexual lessons, 120, 122–126, 141, 151; social science research and, 120–122, 179n2. *See also* Family sexual communication

Angelides, Steven, 16, 174n9

Anti-sexual abuse movement, 16, 174n9

Are You There God? It's Me, Margaret (book), 25

Armstrong, Elizabeth, 177n23

Asexual, asexuality: age, immaturity, and, 24; anti-sexual abuse movement, children, and, 16;

Asexual, asexuality (*continued*)
  as good teenaged citizen, 98,
  150; parents' perceptions of
  children as, 24–28, 39, 42, 113;
  parents' psychological investment in seeing children as, 44;
  social policy and, 150; women
  in Victorian era and, 14. *See also*
  Binary thinking
Autonomy. *See* Privacy and
  autonomy

Bearman, Peter, 175n30
Bettie, Julie, 86
Binary thinking, 63–64, 87: ado-
  lescent/adult binary, 63, 81–82,
  151, 153; ambivalence and, 122;
  asexual/sexual binary, 83–84;
  90, 97–98, 144, 151, 153; homo-
  sexual/heterosexual binary, 89
Birth control. *See* Contraception
Birthrate. *See* Teen birthrate
Bisexuals, bisexuality: parents'
  beliefs about, 89. *See also* Gay,
  lesbian, bisexual, and questioning youth; Homosexuality
"Blue" state. *See* Liberals
Blume, Judy, 25
Bodies and physical presence:
  parents' use as way to safeguard
  teen children, 109–111
Bonilla–Silva, Eduardo, 86
Boys, men: agentic sexuality and,
  49, 136, 142–143, 176–177n18;
  dominance and, 52, 64, 173n7;
  heterosexuality and, 136, 140,
  142; repudiation of femininity
  and, 49, 54; as sexual aggressors, 93–96, 116, 146; as sexually
  vulnerable, 91–92; as stoical and

independent, 52–53. *See also*
  Family sexual communication;
  Fathers, fathering; Hegemonic
  masculinity; Male sexuality;
  Mothers, mothering
Brody, Jane (*New York Times* health
  columnist), 71–72
Brokeback Mountain (movie), 89
Bruckner, Hannah, 175n30
Bush, George W. (administration):
  Community Based Abstinence
  Education program, 12

Casper, Monica, 17, 168n38, 171n21
Centers for Disease Control and
  Prevention, 36, 38
Cervical cancer. *See* Human papilloma virus
"Chastity Act," 10, 11. *See also* Adolescent Family Life Act
Child Protective Services (CPS), 7,
  43–44
Children and teens. *See* Adolescence, adolescents; Childhood
  sexuality; Teen sexual activity;
  Teen sexuality, discourses of
Child sexual abuse: anti–sexual
  abuse movement, 16; media
  and, 17; parents' accused of,
  43–44; parents' lessons about,
  73–75; protecting children from,
  15–17. *See also* Sex offender
  registry; Sex predators
Childhood sexuality, discourses
  of: age of sexual consent laws
  and, 14–15; child sexual abuse
  and, 16–17, 43–44, 73–75; as
  innocent and vulnerable, 15,
  17, 65, 168–169n38; as natural
  component of childhood, 16; in

Victorian era, 14

Citizenship. *See* Sexual citizen, citizenship

Class–blind discourse, 86, 92–93. *See also* Social class

Clinton, Bill (administration): Joycelyn Elders as Surgeon General, 56; Personal Responsibility and Work Opportunity Reconciliation Act (Personal Responsibility Act), 11, 29, 98

Coach Jones (pseud., Eastside health teacher), 162

Cognitive dissonance: abstinence pledge, contraceptive use and, 81, 175–176n30

College: dating and, 27–28, 64, 87, 92, 94; self–reliance and, 26; sexual assault and, 27

Collins, Patricia Hill, 64, 86–87, 176n12

Colorblind racism, 86

Community Based Abstinence Education, 12

Comprehensive sex education: in 1970s and 1980s, 11; danger discourse of teen sexuality and, 123, 146, 152; debates over, 9–10, 145–146, 152; opposition to, 32, 57; parents' support for, 145, 182n20

Compulsive heterosexuality, 56, 140. *See also* Heterosexuality

Compulsory heterosexuality, 140. *See also* Heterosexuality

Computers. *See* Internet

Condoms. *See* Contraception

Connell, Raewyn, 136, 140, 142

Conservatives: anti–sexual abuse movement and, 16; in debates over sex education, 120–121, 132; in debates over the HPV vaccine, 37; mystery of sexuality and, 132; parents described by sex educators as, 61, 153; sex education curricula of, 11; shame and, 56–57; "red" state and, 5

Contraception: parent–teen conversations about, 3, 26, 28, 30–34, 80, 119, 123, 125, 135–138, 141 152, 170–171n17; religion and, 31, 134–138; social class and, 31; statistics on teen use of, 38. *See also* Family sexual communication

"Controlling images," 66

Convention on the Rights of the Child, 168n37

"Crisis tendencies," 142, 149

Culture of sexual fear, 7, 44, 62, 147, 155

Cyberbullying, 179n16

Danger discourse of teen sexuality, 3, 34–39, 42, 69, 73–74, 100, 123, 145–147, 150, 176–177n18. *See also* Teen sexuality, discourses of

Dating relationships: girls and, 94, 132–133, 142; interracial, 88, 94–96; parents' lessons about, 90–97; parents' rules around, 27, 28, 87, 88, 92; violence in, 177n19. *See also* College; Heterosexuality

Debates over sex education. *See* School–based sex education

D'Emilio, John, 14,

Desire. *See* Pleasure and desire

"Doing gender," 49. *See also* Boys, men; Fathers, fathering; Femininity; Gender; Girls, women; Hegemonic masculinity; Masculinity; Mothers, mothering

Eastside High School (pseud.), 61, 69, 86–87, 158, 159, 162, 174n34
Economy: competitive college and labor markets, 34; deindustrialization and, 12; parents' concerns about teens' uncertain financial futures, 26, 149; urbanization, industrialization, and, 14
Elders, Joycelyn, 56
Esterberg, Kristin, 162
Extracurricular activities: as parental strategy to keep teens safe and occupied, 100–103, 154
Eugenics movement: sterilization laws and, 18

Family sexual communication: abstinence and, 3, 26, 30, 33, 119–120, 123–124, 137, 141, 152; ambivalence and, 120, 122–126, 141, 151–152; contraception and, 3, 26, 28, 30–34, 80, 119, 123, 125, 135–138, 141 152, 170–171n17; emotions of, 54–58, 127; expert advice about, 170n5; gaps in family members' reports of, 57–59, 173n11; gender and, 49, 51–54, 59–60, 136, 140, 165n2; parents as sexual beings and, 55–56, 62, 147; positive aspects of sexuality and, 69, 129, 175n26; power dynamics of, 48–49, 150–151, 174n27; religion and,

134–136, 142; shame and, 56–58; specter of sexual intimacy in, 55–56, 60; teen resistance to, 49–51. *See also* Fathers, fathering; Mothers, mothering
Fathers, fathering: as daughters' sexual protector, 93–94, 96; depicted as overly sexual, 44; family sexual communication and, 4, 48–49, 50, 53, 126; masculinity, heterosexuality, and, 136, 142; pornography and, 114, 139; talk about contraception and, 31, 136
Fear. *See* Culture of sexual fear
Female sexuality: autonomy and agency, 130; cultural anxiety over, 42, 91; denigration of, 148; good girl/bad girl dichotomy, 91–92; reputation and, 130, 155; sexism and, 129, 148; in Victorian era, 14, 15; vulnerability and victimization, 96. *See also* Girls, women; Sexual double standard; Sexual subjectivity; Slut
Femininity: binary thinking and, 64; contradictory discourses of, 133; repudiation and devaluation of, 49, 53–54. *See also* Gender; Girls, women; Mothers, mothering
Feminist, feminism: anti–sexual abuse movement and, 16, 73; consciousness and, 155
Ferguson, Ann Arnett, 85
Fields, Jessica, 17, 44, 174–175n12
Foucault, Michel, 13
Freedman, Estelle, 14
Freud, Sigmund, 16
Friends, friendships: autonomy to

choose, 103–104; as bad influences, 23, 103–106; "friends with benefits," 91; parental monitoring of, 86–87, 104–105, 106; racialized notions of, 85, 105. *See also* Peer pressure

Furstenberg, Frank, 178n9

Gagnon, John, 166–167n18
Gardasil. *See* Human papilloma virus
Gay, lesbian, bisexual, and questioning youth, 17, 147, 172n42. *See also* Bisexuals, bisexuality; Homosexuality
Gays. *See* Gay, lesbian, bisexual, and questioning youth; Homosexuality
Geertz, Clifford, 179n12
Gender: as axis of inequality, 64; distrust in heterosexual relationships and, 120; in family sexual communication, 49, 51–54, 59–60, 136, 140, 165n2. *See also* Boys, men; "Doing gender;" Fathers, fathering; Femininity; Girls, women; Hegemonic masculinity; Masculinity; Mothers, mothering; Sexual double standard
Genital warts. *See* Human papilloma virus
Germany: discourse of pleasure to encourage teen contraceptive use in, 69; teen sexual health in, 175n13
Girls, women: as asexual, 14; being "ready," 91; dating and, 133; as infantilized, 51; "at risk," 39; menarche and womanhood,

173n7; "self–development imperative" of, 133, 170n8; sex as something that "just happens," 27–28; as sexual aggressors, 2, 91–93, 137, 176n18; sexual competence and, 15, 129; sexual desire, agency, and, 28, 129, 175n16; as sexually desirable but not desiring, 146; sexual reputation of, 130; sexual victimization and, 96, 116, 129–130, 141, 142, 178n11. *See also* Female sexuality; Sexual double standard; Slut
Glassner, Barry, 84
Glossary of sexual and reproductive terms, 45–46, 172n42

Hall, G. Stanley, 71
Harding, David, 168n33
Harmful to Minors (book), 65, 174n7
Hamilton, Laura, 177n23
Hayden Middle School (pseud.), 70, 112, 158, 162
Hegemonic masculinity, 136. *See also* Boys, men; Masculinity
Heteronormativity: in debates over sex education, 17–18, 145; in discourses of teen sexuality, 72, 142–143, 146; in parents' sexual lessons, 34, 89–90, 146–147; in school–based sex education, 172n42. *See also* Heterosexuality; Homosexuality
Heterosexual intercourse. *See* Heterosexuality
Heterosexuality: as compulsive, 140; as compulsory, 56, 140; historical, medical, and legal invention of, 166n17; intercourse as sexual activity, 24–25, 42, 148;

Heterosexuality (*continued*)
parents' assumption of, 24, 34,
89, 146–147; parents' preference
for, 89–90, 140, 146–147; in sex
education debates, 17–18. *See
also* Heteronomativity
HIV/AIDS, 11, 35–36, 38; annual
number of new infections,
36; media coverage of, 171n21;
parents' knowledge, fears about,
35–36, 67; rates of infection by
race and income, 38; sex education and, 11
Homophobia. *See* Homosexuality
Homosexuality: affirming messages
about, 128; binary thinking
and, 87; discrimination, prejudice and, 90, 142–143, 145, 148;
as innate, not a choice, 88–89;
parents' responses to, 89–90,
128, 140, 142; in sex education debates, 17–18, 145. *See
also* Gay, lesbian, bisexual and
questioning youth; Heteronormativity; Lesbian, Gay, Bisexual, and Transgender (LGBT)
movement
Hooking up: anxiety about female
sexuality and, 91
Human immunodeficiency virus.
See HIV/AIDS
Human papilloma virus (HPV):
cancers and, 171n26; cervical
cancer and, 36–37; Gardasil vaccine for, 37–39, 42; genital warts
and, 37; mandatory vaccination
for, 37, 146; Merck's marketing
campaign for Gardasil vaccine,
38–39; parents' knowledge, fears
about, 36–37; rates of infection,

36; Rick Perry and Gardasil
vaccine, 37

Institutional Review Board: conducting research with children
about sexuality and, 168–169n38
Intercourse: as sexual activity, 24–25,
42, 148. *See also* Heterosexuality
Internet: danger and, 114–115; as
means of communication, 115;
MySpace and, 99, 112, 114–115;
parental monitoring and, 112–
115, 179n15; pornography and,
113–114, 138–139; as tool and
resource, 109–110, 112, 115. *See
also* Cyberbullying; Technology
Interracial relationships: anti–miscegenation laws and, 96; parents' acceptance of, 88; parents'
concerns about, 88, 95–96; as
used to resist school integration
in 1950s, 18
Interviews, interviewing: active
meaning–making in, 173n23;
racial dynamics of, 177n29;
recruiting non–activist parents
for, 157–159
Irvine, Janice, 57, 169n53

Katz, Jonathan, 166n17

Lareau, Annette, 100, 154
Latino/a. *See* Race/ethnicity
Lefkowitz, Eva, 59
Lesbian, Gay, Bisexual, and Trans-
gender (LGBT) movement, 18
Lesbians. *See* Gay, lesbian, bisex-
ual, and questioning youth;
Homosexuality
Levine, Judith, 65, 174n7

Liberals: "blue" state and, 5; in debates over sex education, 120–121, 132; demystifying sexuality and, 132; sex–positive perspective and, 130; Western nations and, 69

Luker, Kristin, 120

Male sexuality: agency and, 49, 136, 142–143, 176–177n18; sexism and, 129, 146; as sexually driven, 119. *See also* Boys, men; Fathers, fathering; Masculinity

Mamo, Laura, 38

Martin, Karin, 129, 176–177n18

Masculinity: binary thinking and, 64; boys, family sexual communication and, 60; repudiation of femininity and, 54; self–control, maturity and, 142; stoicism, independence and, 52–53. *See also* Boys, men; Gender; Fathers, fathering; Hegemonic masculinity; Male sexuality

Masturbation: parents' discussions of, 34–35, 41, 129; Surgeon General Joycelyn Elders and, 56

McCain, John (presidential campaign), 57

Media: "controlling images" in, 66; role in shaping parents' understandings of sexuality, 2, 36, 65, 93; role in spreading belief in children's sexual innocence and imperilment, 17, 38, 65

Medlin High School (pseud.), 158

Menarche, 173n7

Menstruation, 21, 26, 78–79. *See also* Menarche

Moore, Lisa Jean, 17, 168n38, 171n21

Moral entrepreneurs, 13

Moral panic, 98

Mothers, mothering: devaluation of, 53–54; as deviant and virtuous, 59–60; as main providers of sex education at home, 4, 165n2; moral accountability and, 114; "over–mothering," 52–53; professional careers and, 180n14; sexual communication with sons, 48–49, 51–54, 59–60, 149, 173n7

Mr. Marks (pseud., abstinence–only sex educator), 61, 69, 171n23

Ms. Blanton (pseud., middle school health teacher), 44: Glossary of Sexual and Reproductive Terms, 45–46, 172n42

Ms. Fox (pseud., Taylor health teacher), 61, 67, 159, 162

Nagel, Joane, 167n18

National Institute of Justice, 27

National Sexuality Resource Center, 182n19

National Survey of Sexual Health and Behavior, 171n31

Nelson, Margaret, 113, 170n7, 180n22

Netherlands: Dutch parents' beliefs about adolescence, 71; public health campaign to normalize teen sexuality, 147–148; teen sexual health in, 175n13

New York Times: coverage of research on teenagers' perceptions of risk, 71–72; reporting on American parents' reactions to sexting, 116

Obama, Barack, 57: administration policies on sex education, 166n14

Oral sex: parents' conversations with children about, 92, 130; in school-based sex education, 42

"Othering:" parents' use of, 3, 87, 97, 122; in social policy, discourse, and imagery, 17; as way to clarify moral and social boundaries, 176n12

Parental rights, 11, 37, 62

Parents, parenting: accountability and, 125, 141, 149–150; anxiety and, 23, 26; blame and, 15, 107, 168n33; as children's protectors, 15, 33, 72, 75, 100, 108–111, 117, 154; as critical of their own parents' discussions of sex, 56; demographics of, 158–159; "expert" advice on, 15, 52–53, 70; moral accountability and, 15, 32–33, 114; power and, 48–49, 56; religious and political affiliations of, 159; role in children's sexual attitudes and behaviors, 22, 169n2, 169n3; as sexual beings, 55–56, 62, 147; social class differences in resources, 100–103, 106–111, 154; understandings of children's sexuality, 22, 29, 33, 36, 66, 148, 169n4; views of school-based sex education, 61, 138, 140–141. See also Family sexual communication; Fathers, fathering; Mothers, mothering; Parental rights

Parent–Teacher Association meetings, Hayden Middle School

(pseud.), 5, 33–34, 162

Pascoe, C. J., 140

Peer pressure: parents' concerns about teens as susceptible to, 21–22, 104, 124

Period. See Menarche; Menstruation

Perry, Rick: mandatory HPV vaccination order, 37

Personal Responsibility and Work Opportunity Reconciliation Act (Personal Responsibility Act), 11–12, 29, 98

Phillips, Lynn, 177n23

Pill, the. See Contraception

Planned Parenthood, 3, 62, 119–120, 152

Pleasure and desire: as "evaded lesson" of family and school-based sex education, 68–70, 123, 147, 175n15; parents' discomfort talking with teens about, 34–35, 55, 175n26; in parents' sexual lessons, 129–131, 154–155; sexual activity in adulthood and, 80–81

Plummer, Ken, 126, 166–167n18, 179n12

Politics of respectability, 79

Pornography: parents' attitudes toward children viewing, 29–30, 113–114, 138–139

Power: denial of teenagers', in debates over sex education, 150; discourses of sexuality and, 13; in parent–child relationship, 48–49; sexual disclosure and, 56. See also Family sexual communication

Premarital sexual intercourse: in colonial and Victorian eras, 14.

See also Teen pregnancy and parenting

Privacy and autonomy: in parent–teen relationship, 180n21, 180n22

Puberty: parents' discussions of, 1, 21, 61, 165n2; in school–based sex education programs, 26, 44, 46. *See also* Adolescence, adolescents

Pugh, Allison, 106

Queer theory, 166–167n18

Race/ethnicity: anti–miscegenation laws and, 96; as axis of inequality, 64; coded language and, 17, 86, 95; colorblind racism and, 86; "controlling images" and, 66; eugenics movement, sterilization laws, and, 18; HIV infection rates and, 38; interracial relationships and, 88, 95–96; of interviewed parents, 158, 160; interviewing and, 177n29; lynching as institutionalized mechanism of segregation and, 96; neighborhoods and, 107–108, 109, 178n9; in parents' perceptions of teen sexuality, 84–87, 95–97, 148, 151; politics of respectability and, 79; rates of sexual assault and, 178n11; in sex education debates, 17; sexual stereotypes and, 17, 43–44, 59, 87, 94, 116; stereotypes, parental monitoring, and, 105, 107–108; "welfare queen," 87

Rape. *See* Sexual assault

Reagan, Ronald: "Chastity Act," 10;

parental rights, 11

"Red" state. *See* Conservatives

Reflexivity: in research, 162, 182n9

Regnerus, Mark, 170n16

Religion: family talk about contraception and, 31, 134–137, 170n16, 181n28; of interviewed parents, 4, 159; sexual shame and, 56

Rich, Adrienne, 140

Schalet, Amy, 71, 176–177n18

Schlessinger, Laura, 174n7

School–based sex education, 11, 153–154, 174–175n12; Americans' support of, 12; debates over, 9–10, 12, 120–121, 123, 125, 145–156; family sexual communication and, 60–61, 124, 138; glossary of sexual and reproductive terms used in, 45–46, 172n42; heteronormativity and, 17–18, 172n42; history of, 15; "naturalist perspective" in, 44; parents' views of, 60–61, 69–70, 77, 124, 138, 140–141, 145; sex educators' characterizations of parents in, 61; social policy and, 150, 152. *See also* Abstinence–only sex education; Comprehensive sex education; School board meetings

School board meetings: debates over sex education and, 9–10, 65, 145–146, 159

Sex education. *See* Abstinence–only sex education; Comprehensive sex education; Family sexual communication; Parents, parenting; School–based sex education

Sex offender registry, 109–110. *See also* Child sexual abuse; Sex predators

Sex panics, 12: over girls' participation in "casual" sex, 91; over teen sexuality, 98, 152

Sex predators: adults framed as, 16, 18; boys framed as, 72, 93–94, 97; children's peers framed as, 90, 97–98; family members as, 74–76; media and, 17; parents' fears about, 21, 72–76; sex educators and comprehensive sex education proponents framed as, 32. *See also* Anti–sexual abuse movement; Child sexual abuse; Sex offender registry

Sex talk, the. *See* Family sexual communication

Sexting, 2, 115–116. *See also* Internet; Technology

Sexual abstinence. *See* Abstinence; Abstinence–only sex education

Sexual assault: of children, 17; in college, rates of, 27; high school girls and boys, rates of, 177n21; in high school, rates of, 177n19; myth of "stranger danger" and, 73; race and, 178n11

Sexual citizen, citizenship: asexual teenagers constructed as, 98, 150; teenagers denied, 66, 117. *See also* Asexual, asexuality

Sexual conservatives. *See* Conservatives

Sexual double standard, 27–28, 130, 142–143. *See also* Girls, women; Female sexuality; Male sexuality

Sexual fluidity: as marginalized by homosexual/heterosexual binary, 89

Sexual harassment, 115

Sexuality, discourses of: childhood and, 14–15; contradictions in, 13, 18, 122, 142; as innate, 89; queer theory and, 166–167n18; self–regulation and, 14; as uncontrollable drive, 17, 131, 152. *See also* Childhood sexuality, discourses of; Female sexuality; Male sexuality; Teen sexual activity; Teen sexuality, discourses of

Sexual liberals. *See* Liberals

Sexual literacy: as a model of sex education, 182n19

Sexual politics. *See* Anti–sexual abuse movement; School–based sex education; School board meetings; Sexuality, discourses of; Teen sexuality, discourses of

Sexual scripting theory, 166–167n18

Sexually transmitted infections (STIs): 2, 155. *See also* HIV/AIDS; Human papilloma virus (HPV)

Sexual stereotypes. *See* Female sexuality; Male sexuality; Race/ethnicity; Social class; Teen sexuality, discourses of

Sexual subjectivity, 16, 62, 127, 129–130, 141

Sexual values: by state, 5. *See also* Conservatives; Liberals

Shame, 56: Christianity and, 56; culture of, 62, 147; as "feeling rule" of family sexual communication, 57–58; in interviews about sex, 57; public officials and, 56–57

Simon, William, 166–167n18

Slut: as sexual epithet, 130, 155, 177n23. *See also* Female sexuality; Girls, women; Sexual double standard

Smelser, Neil, 179n2

Social class: as axis of inequality, 64; class–blind discourse of, 85–86, 92–93; coded language and, 17, 85–87, 92–93; "controlling images" and, 66; HIV infection rates and, 38; of interviewed parents, 4, 158, 160; Merck's marketing campaign for the HPV vaccine Gardasil and, 39; parental monitoring of teens and, 100, 101–103, 106–111, 117, 154; in parents' perceptions of teen sexuality, 95–97, 148, 151; politics of sexual respectability and, 79; in sex education debates, 17; sexual stereotypes and, 31, 59, 116; stereotypes and, 128–129; variations in parenting practices by, 113, 181n12; "white trash," 128

Social roles, 59, 174n31

Sociological imagination, 149

Splitting: ambivalence and, 122

Stein, Arlene, 56, 57

"The talk." *See* Family sexual communication

Tanenbaum, Leora, 177n23

Taylor High School (pseud.), 61, 67, 158, 159, 174n34

Technology: parental monitoring and, 107–109, 112–115, 178n7–8. *See also* Cyberbullying; Internet; Sexting

Teen birthrate, 11, 37, 38, 172n35

Teen pregnancy and parenting: parents' experiences with, 21–22, 27–28, 30, 67, 92, 118–119, 124; in sex education debates, 9, 11; social class, race, and, 17, 31

Teen sexual activity: contraceptive use and, 38, 171n31; cultural differences in experiences of, 175n13; cultural differences in perceptions of, 71, 147; "danger discourse" of, 3, 9, 13, 42, 123, 147; panic over, 91; pleasure and, 64, 68–69, 153; politics of, 37; risk and, 38, 153, 176n33; risky behavior, rates of, 37–38, 43; sexual intercourse, rates of, 37, 53; social policy and, 37, 153

Teen sexuality, discourses of, 13–18, 117: absence of pleasure in, 69; abstinence–only–until–marriage and, 12–13, 122, 152; "at–risk," 9, 17, 38–39; binaries in, 63, 81–82, 83–85, 90, 97–98, 144, 151, 153; "children having children," 17; contradictions in, 121; danger and, 3, 34–39, 42, 69, 73–74, 82, 100, 123, 145–147, 150, 176–177n18; as heteronormative, 18, 34, 146; raging hormones and, 67, 82; as asexual and innocent, 17, 65; as sexually driven, 17, 64–65, 83–84, 122; "sexually unsalvageable, "17, 18; social inequality and, 17–18, 85, 93, 96, 148, 153

Thompson, Sharon, 177n23

Tolman, Deborah, 175n16

Valocchi, Stephen, 18

Virgin, virginity: definition of, in glossary of sexual and reproductive terms, 46, 172n42; parents' perceptions of teens as, 30, 64; parent–teen conversations about, 2, 30

Weeks, Jeffrey, 142
"Welfare queen," 87. *See also* Race/ethnicity

Welfare reform, 11, 12: consequences of, 111
"White trash," 128. *See also* Social class
World Wide Web. *See* Internet

Youth Risk Behavior Survey, 37–38
Youth, young people. *See* Adolescence, adolescents

ABOUT THE AUTHOR

Sinikka Elliott is Assistant Professor of Sociology at North Carolina State University.